I FOUGHT

WITH CUSTER

THE STORY OF SERGEANT WINDOLPH
Last Survivor of The Battle Of The Little Big Horn

As Told To
FRAZIER *and* ROBERT HUNT

With Explanatory Material
And Contemporary Sidelights On
The Custer Fight

Foreword by Neil Mangum

University of Nebraska Press
Lincoln and London

First Bison Book printing: 1987
Most recent printing indicated by the first digit below:
    5 6 7 8 9 10

Library of Congress Cataloging in Publication Data
Windolph, Charles, 1851–1950.
 I fought with Custer.
 Reprint. Originally published: New York: Scribner, 1954,
c1947.
 Bibliography: p.
 Includes index.
 1. Little Big Horn, Battle of the, 1876.
2. Windolph, Charles, 1851–1950. 3. Custer, George
Armstrong, 1839–1876. 4. United States. Army.
Cavalry, 7th. 5. Soldiers—United States—Biography.
I. Hunt, Frazier, b. 1885. II. Hunt, Robert.
III. Title.
E83.876.W5 1987   973.8'2'0924   87-5905
ISBN 0-8032-4746-X
ISBN 0-8032-9720-3 (pbk.)

Reprinted by arrangement with John Frazier Hunt

To the men and officers of the Seventh Cavalry Regiment, and to their other comrades in the First Cavalry Division, who in this latest war fought so magnificently from the Admiralty Islands, through Leyte and Luzon, and who were the first troops to enter Manila and Tokyo, this book is affectionately dedicated.

Contents

	Page
Preface	xi

Part One

Chapter	1.	I Join the Seventh Cavalry	1
""	2.	The Yellowstone Expedition	18
""	3.	To the Black Hills	32
""	4.	The March from Fort Lincoln	49
""	5.	March Up the Rosebud	63
""	6.	Into the Jaws of Death	78
""	7.	Where Was Custer?	96
""	8.	Where Custer Died	108

| Epilogue | 114 |

Part Two

Contemporary Narratives Bearing on the Custer Fight

| Chapter | 1. | Did Custer's Black Hills Expedition Bring on the Sioux War of 1876? | 116 |
| "" | 2. | Was Grant's Harsh Rebuke Responsible for Custer's Death? | 121 |

Contents

			Page
Chapter	*3.*	Did Custer Disobey Terry's Last Orders?	136
"	*4.*	Did Custer Refuse Advice from His Scouts?	151
"	*5.*	Was Reno's Retreat Responsible for Custer's Defeat?	162
"	*6.*	Did Benteen Disregard Custer's Order "Come On! Bring Packs"?	183
"	*7.*	Bitter Controversies that Lived Long After the Battle	194
"	*8.*	They Fought Against Custer: The Indians' Side	208
"	*9.*	The Death of Custer on the Lonely Ridge	220
Acknowledgments			225
Bibliography			226
Index			231

Illustrations

Facing Page

Former First Sergeant Charles Windolph, last survivor
of the Battle of the Little Big Horn   xvi

General Custer, Captain Tom Custer, and the General's wife   I

Officers and guests on the Yellowstone Expedition in
the summer of 1873   22

General Custer, officers and ladies at Fort Abraham
Lincoln, not long before the Battle   23

First Sergeant Windolph, taken about 1880   23

Captain Benteen   23

Custer Expeditions of 1873, 1874 and 1876   *Page*   37

Front page account of the discovery of gold in the
Black Hills   *Page*   41

March of the Custer column to the Black Hills in the
summer of 1874   44

"Lonesome Charley" Reynolds, Custer's Chief of Scouts   45

Rain-in-the-Face   45

Captain Grant Marsh   58

Steamer *Far West*   58

Captain Keogh's mount, "Comanche"   59

Curley, the Crow scout   59

Illustrations

Facing Page

The route of Custer's forces from June 22 to June 25
Page 69

Frederic Remington's drawing, showing each fourth trooper leading horses to safety when his comrades dismounted
92

Indian squaws hurriedly breaking camp. Drawn by Frederic Remington
93

The route of Custer's five troops and of Reno's defeat
Page 100

First account published in New York of the battle of the Little Big Horn
Page 111

Picnic shortly before Custer left on his fatal campaign
142

Brigadier General Alfred H. Terry
143

Major Reno
143

Famous picture of "Custer's Last Battle" that was hung in thousands of taverns over America for two generations
168

Last moments of Custer's Stand, painted by Colonel John W. Thomason, Jr.
169

Frank Weasel Bear, Cheyenne warrior, in front of his cabin
214

Chief Eagle Bear, last of the Ogallala Sioux who fought in the battle
214

Sitting Bull, chief medicine man of the Sioux
215

Sitting Bull's cabin on the Standing Rock Reservation in South Dakota
215

Foreword

By Neil C. Mangum

Bullets fired from the firearms of angry Sioux and Cheyenne warriors kicked up clods of dirt, leaving a thin veil of choking dust in their wake. The day was stifling hot. Private Charles Windolph, Company H, Seventh U.S. Cavalry, gave the incoming rounds scant notice, that is until one errant shot tore into his cavalry carbine, shattering his Springfield in two. Windolph considered himself lucky. The leaden missile of death had missed its intended target. Fortunately, the force of the projectile had been spent by the collision with the carbine stock. The bullet had only grazed the private, producing a superficial wound. Five miles away on a lonely hilltop, Windolph's fellow Seventh cavalrymen were not so lucky. Lieutenant Colonel George A. Custer and approximately 210 men under his immediate command had perished. There were no survivors. Neither Windolph nor any of the men under Major Marcus Reno were cognizant of Custer's fate. They did not know these same warriors, now converging on them, were hoping to repeat their earlier success against Custer.

It never occurred to Private Windolph as he huddled against the hillside towering over the meandering Little Bighorn that he and every other man there were making history. They could not possibly envision the fate that had selected them to become actors in a drama that would span epic proportions and create endless controversy.

Charles Windolph served just three days short of twelve years in the Seventh Cavalry, from 1872 to 1883, all of it in Company H. The German immigrant was a "gallant soldier," wrote Captain Frederick W. Benteen on Windolph's discharge certificate. Windolph was proud to be an American, and prouder still to have served under her colors during the height of the Indian wars. He was equally proud of his association with the Seventh Cavalry. Next to his family, he considered the regiment the finest thing in the world. He was a simple man, not prone to self-aggrandizing. His major ambition, he remarked, was to be a devoted, loving husband and father. He did not seek out publicity or fanfare. He kept his feelings about the Battle of the Little Bighorn largely to himself.

Yet, it is plainly evident from his narratives that Windolph possessed a burning pride toward his relationship with the cavalry and, in particular, a growing admiration for his former commanding officer, Captain Benteen. He saved his highest accolades for Benteen. Windolph considered him "just about the finest soldier and the greatest gentleman I ever knew." It was Benteen, Windolph relates, who had given him a field promotion on June 26 to the rank of sergeant. This fact is not borne out in the Monthly Returns for Company H. The records show Windolph remaining a private until October, when he is listed among the corporals in the company. In November Windolph appears on the returns as sergeant.

Windolph's account of the Battle of the Little Bighorn might never have surfaced if battle buffs had not searched out the quiet, unpretentious soldier and gleaned from him his personal experiences. Windolph's reminiscences have appeared in print twice. His first narrative of the battle was published in 1930 in *Sunshine Magazine*, volume 11, number 1. Then in 1946 the father-and-son team of Frazier and Robert Hunt extracted from the old top sergeant a more comprehensive manuscript and history. The Hunts produced a thorough accounting of Windolph's life and military experiences. It was published in 1947 under the title *I Fought with Custer: The Story of Sergeant Windolph, Last Survivor of the Battle of the Little Big Horn.*

Military engagements, like most events of singular historical significance, are dominated by individuals in positions of authority. History seldom accords anything more than a passing footnote to the ordinary. The Little Bighorn fight is remarkable for the unusually large number of accounts left by enlisted personnel. *I Fought with Custer* is significant for its straightforward approach. Windolph has no axes to grind. He prefers to tell his story without placing responsibility for the disastrous outcome on any one person. Toward Custer, Windolph is sympathetic, stating that Custer had his faults and made mistakes but that "there were just too many Indians for him that June afternoon."

Windolph does not dwell on the battle's "what ifs." His assessments are a compilation of simple, concise statements. His earthy remarks and conversational tone make *I Fought with Custer* a pleasure to read. He viewed the Black Hills expedition of 1874 for what it was to the enlisted man, "a prolonged picnic." Fatalistically, he viewed the Battle of the Little Bighorn as the Indians' one big day. He puts the battle into perspective with this practical accounting: "It'd be easy to say we were thinking only of glory on this hot June Sunday afternoon . . . but I reckon what most of the plain soldiers were thinking about was how good a nice cold bottle of beer would taste right now."

But Windolph did cover himself with glory that afternoon and on the following day. He received the coveted Medal of Honor for volunteering to expose himself to Indian fire while acting as a sharpshooter as other volunteers ran a gauntlet to retrieve water for the wounded. He suggests, unselfishly, that many more men were deserving of the medal, but they went unnoticed, or officers failed to recognize fully their achievements. With amazing ease, he rattles off their names as if the battle had just happened.

Windolph does not speak of his military career before his service in the Seventh Cavalry. Perhaps it was an oversight; more realistically, it was by design. Before enlisting in the Seventh, Windolph had been in the Second Infantry. For reasons unknown, he deserted. He joined the Seventh Cavalry, using the alias Charles Wrangell. Windolph was apprehended in 1873. Because of the desertion, his enlistment with the Seventh was canceled. In 1874 he was transferred to the Seventh and again assigned to Company H. In neither the 1930 nor the 1947 narrative does he comment on the desertion. He either blotted the incident from his memory or he was too ashamed to discuss it. Whatever the circumstances involving his desertion, Windolph found the Seventh to his liking.

Windolph exhibits an uncanny penchant for details. And despite the fact he told his story seventy years after the battle, it is an extraordinary exhibition of accuracy. I found that it collaborates in most every instance incidences produced by other informants. Errors that do creep into the text are mostly minor, such as giving Custer's age as thirty-seven (he was thirty-six) and citing the year of John Burkman's death as 1926 (it was 1925).

Windolph's account covers the first half of *I Fought with Custer*. The second half is a student's delight. The Hunts incorporated testimony, official reports, and personal accounts in examining major controversies of the battle. It is a compendium of data discussing both sides. The authors have purposely drawn no conclusions for the reader.

To trivia buffs, Windolph is best remembered for being the last surviving soldier from the Battle of the Little Bighorn. He died at Lead, South Dakota, on March 11,

1950, and was interred in the Black Hills National Cemetery at Sturgis. With the reprinting of *I Fought with Custer,* old and new students of the battle can read his story. It ranks as one of the finest accounts given by an enlisted man. Given this renewed exposure, Windolph should no longer be considered just an answer in a trivia test.

ERRATA

Photo caption opposite page 22: *for* Yellowstone Expedition in the summer of 1873 *read* Black Hills expedition in 1874.

Upper photo caption opposite page 23: *for* not long before the battle *read* 1873.

Photo caption opposite page 142: *for* Miss Matson *read* Miss Watson.

Opposite page 168: The painting shown, by Otto Becker, was not destroyed by fire; rather, the prototype on which it was based, by Cassily Adams, was destroyed by fire in 1946.

Preface

It is possible that there has never been a factual book quite like this one. The authors had two definite objectives before them; one was to present the story of the last living survivor of the Battle of the Little Big Horn, as faithfully and accurately as it was possible to do. The other was to give the reader all available source material that might throw light on the battle and the events that led up to it.

In all military history no single battle has been plagued with more mystery, more uncertainty and more bitterness. Even Thermopylae had its single survivor. But no white man of the five troops who rode with General Custer on that June day of 1876 lived to tell the tale. Records of high heroism and incredible bravery have been mixed indiscriminately with accusations of cowardice and even desertion. For seventy years men have argued and wrangled over almost every minute of those two or three hours of uncertain action that ended with the death of Custer and some 220 of his comrades on Custer Hill.

For the best part of twenty years the authors have been gathering material, collecting stories of survivors, both white and Indian, studying the battlefield, and quietly researching for lost letters, reports and documents, that might bring into relief the true happenings.

Nine or ten years ago while motoring through Denver, Colorado, I visited Brigadier General W. C. Brown, U. S. Army, retired, who had spent a lifetime as an Indian fighter and student. General Brown told me that at Lead, South Dakota, there lived a former First Sergeant of Benteen's troop of the Seventh Cavalry, who was the last living trooper who had fought with Custer's regiment in the battle.

I drove at once to Lead and spent the following week putting down the old Sergeant's story. Charles A. Windolph was then eighty-six years old, but his mind was as clear as a bell, and his memory was prodigious. During this and the following summer, under the guidance of my good friend, James Gatchell, of Buffalo, Wyoming, one of the greatest living authorities on the Northern Plains Indians, I scoured the Indian agencies and we located several Indians who had actually taken part in the battle. Together "Uncle Jim" and I went over, foot by foot, Custer's march from the Yellowstone, up the Rosebud, and to the Little Big Horn battleground.

The almost certain approach of World War II temporarily eclipsed interest in this remote little Indian war of long ago, so all thought of using the new material at that time was put away. But with the war ended, I returned to the fascinating subject. In 1927 I had published a series of magazine stories and a small book about Custer's life and death, but I had long wanted to go deeper into the battle and its causes. A telegram to Lead, South Dakota, in the early spring of 1946 brought the stirring news that Sergeant Windolph was still alive and active. I decided to have my son, who had developed an abiding interest in the tragedy, go to Lead and get as much additional first-hand material as he could from the old Top Sergeant. He had turned ninety-four on December 9, 1945, but his mind was still clear and alert, and he was able to fill in many holes in his story as he had given it to me several years before.

The first part of this book then, is Sergeant Windolph's own story. We have larded it with a few notes so that the reader may have such necessary background as is not included in the old trooper's words. These notes are indicated by a white space following the original narrative which is always noted by a numeral.

The second part of the book is made up of a great mass of source material: official reports, letters and eye-witness stories by men and officers actually in the battle, largely written when the events were fresh in their minds, and before the bitter controversies began. Every possible phase of the battle is covered and all evidence submitted.

The authors were determined from the start to take no sides, defend no lost causes or personalities; to include every scrap of information that could possibly be useful in helping the reader arrive at his own conclusions about the historic fight. To do this has required an unusual and unorthodox presentation of this source material in the latter part of the book.

Some readers may wonder why a military episode that is little more than a footnote in most history books, should be chronicled with all the detail of the mass of source material offered in this book. But at times there is far more to history than may be found between the covers of the formal history books. The legends of Custer and his death on the Little Big Horn have become a precious part of the heritage of American youth. Those, like myself, who grew up in this tradition, have an inexhaustible appetite for facts to bolster up their own arguments and theories.

On battlefields of two world wars I have seen mature officers forget for the moment the campaigns at hand, to indulge in sometime friendly, sometime bitter arguments over Reno and Benteen and Custer. Soldiers and western enthusiasts will not cease their arguments over this historic little battle as long as the profession of arms exists, and the romance of the frontier lives on.

Just one thing more before we turn the pages over to the old Sergeant. In a two-column obituary in the New York *Daily Tribune* of July 7, 1876, that carried the first full report of the battle, there is a paragraph that epitomizes the man this book is about. It reads:

"His success was a rule without exceptions, and his progress an advance almost without pauses. He was the youngest Brigadier and the youngest Major General in the army. He never lost a gun or a color and captured more guns, flags and prisoners than any other general not an army commander, and these guns and flags were all taken in action and field service. His personal appearance was singular. Colonel Newhall, who wrote *With Sheridan in Lee's Last Campaign*, describes him thus: 'Custer of the golden locks, his broad sombrero turned up from his hard-bronzed face, the ends of his crimson cravat floating over his shoulders, gold galore spangling his jacket sleeves, a pistol in his boot, dangling spurs on his heels and a ponderous claymore swinging at his side, a wild dare-devil of a general, and a prince of advance guards, quick to see and act.' . . . He died as he lived—fighting his hardest at the head of his men."

That was Custer—a Brigadier General of Volunteers at twenty-three; a Major General at twenty-five: Custer, the Darling of the Gods.

FRAZIER HUNT

Newtown,
Bucks County, Pa.
September 15, 1946

I Fought With Custer

Lead, South Dakota.

Feb. 15th, 1946.

I am very glad to have Frazier and Robert Hunt tell my story of Little Big Horn Battle and the facts that led up to it.

They have done an accurate and complete job and I am Grateful to them.

Signed

Charles Windolph

Charles A. Windolph

Former 1st Sergeant

Troop H, 7th Cavalry

Former First Sergeant Charles Windolph, last survivor of the Battle of the Little Big Horn. The old Indian fighter was 95 on December 9, 1946. This photograph was taken in 1938.

General Custer, Captain Tom Custer—who wore two Congressional Medals of Honor
—and the General's wife, taken shortly after the close of the Civil War.

Part One

Chapter 1

I Join the
Seventh Cavalry

*I*T doesn't seem possible that it was seventy years ago this June 25, 1946, that I last saw General Custer.

No, that isn't quite exact; that was the last time I saw him alive, for two days later I looked down on him lying white in the Montana sun.

That would have been June 27, 1876. And the following day, I helped bury him and his brother, Captain Tom Custer. They were put in graves alongside one another. It was hard digging there on that high ridge that bordered the Little Big Horn.

Seventy years is a long time. It's a long time to remember details and little things. But when you've been thinking back on them all those years, they don't fade away as easily as you might think. They're like cockleburs; they stick in your mind. Most of the things I'm putting down here I gave to my friend Frazier Hunt almost ten years ago. He used to come to see me here at Lead, South Dakota. I was then living with my younger daughter, Mrs. Harms. Her husband was an engineer in the mines. They moved away several years ago, and since then I've been living with my older daughter, Mrs. George C. Fehliman. Her husband is a dentist. My only son is a mining engineer in Chile. Frazier Hunt's son,

Robert, spent some time with me, early this spring. He pumped a lot of stuff out of me, too.

I was twenty-four and a half years old on that dusty, hot June day, seventy years ago, when Custer led us into the Battle of the Little Big Horn. I don't think there's any question but that I'm the last living survivor. Never again will a man who was there write about the fight.

People call it "The Custer Massacre." It wasn't any massacre; it was a straight, hard fight, and the five troops who were with Custer simply got cut to ribbons and every last white man destroyed. I say "every last white man" because there were one or two Crow scouts who claimed they saw the start of the fight, and then skedaddled. A Crow Indian named Curley said he escaped from the battlefield by putting a blanket over his head and pretending he was a wounded Sioux. I don't know whether there is any truth in that or not. I never quite believed it.

There's been all kinds of stories about that battle. Even the men who were with Benteen and Reno and lived to tell the tale, didn't come anywhere near telling the same stories about what they did, and what they saw. Some of them wanted to make heroes out of themselves or of their officers. I had only one pair of eyes, so, of course, all I can tell is what I saw myself. If it is something I only heard, I'll be sure to mark it down as that.

I want it understood right here at the start that I'm a simple man, but I've always tried to be an honest one. I've never owed any man a cent in my whole life. I've lived simply and honestly and brought up my children to believe in God. I gave each of them the best education I could. Next to my own folks, I'm prouder of the Seventh Cavalry than anything in the world. And I'm especially proud of Troop H. Funny, we used to call troops "companies" in my day.

And I'm proud to have known and fought under Captain Benteen, of "H." He was just about the finest soldier and the greatest gentleman I ever knew. And I might as well say right now that I'm a Benteen man. I'm not what they call an anti-Custer man, but I'm for Benteen all the ways from the Jack.

We all fought the good fight that June day in 1876. Just about half of the 600 men of the regiment were killed that day and the following one. I lost a lot of good friends. Most of the men and officers, too, for that matter, were fairly young. General Custer himself was only thirty-seven years old. Funny, but after the battle of the Little Big Horn there was just exactly that same number of widows back at Fort Abraham Lincoln on the Missouri. Thirty-seven was sure an unlucky number for the regiment.

But I reckon I better go back and tell what happened to me from the day I first joined the Seventh. Or better still, I'd better go back to the real start—to when I was born.

That was on December 9, 1851, in the city of Bergen, Germany. My father's name was Joseph Windolph and my mother had the pretty name of Adolphina. My father was a master shoemaker. He employed a dozen men, and he taught me the trade.

I was eighteen in the spring of 1870, and by June it looked pretty certain that Prussia was going to fight Napoleon the Third, of France. I was booked to be drafted in the Dragoons, but a few days before I was to report for duty I skipped out for Sweden. Then I hustled over to Copenhagen, Denmark, where we had some family friends. I stayed there eight or ten days, then I got a boat for America. It took us twelve days to make the trip.

I was about the greenest thing that ever hit New York. I couldn't talk more than a dozen words of English, and I had exactly $2.50 in money. I was having a pretty tough time of it until I met a cripple who could talk German. He got me a job in an Avenue A shoe shop. I worked there a couple of weeks, and then I got a job as a bootmaker in Hoboken. But the methods were all different from the way

3

I had been taught, and I wasn't getting along very well. Finally an old man who was working next to me, and who talked German, told me to join the army and learn English so that I could amount to something. He was a nice old man, and he went with me to the U. S. Army recruiting office down by the Battery.

The Civil War had been over only five years, and there were lots of unemployed men those days, but they didn't seem to want to go in the army. A good many German boys like myself had run away from the compulsory military service and the Franco-Prussian war, but about the only job there was for us over here was to enlist in the United States Army. Always struck me as being funny; here we'd run away from Germany to escape military service, and now, because most of us couldn't get a job anywhere else, we were forced to go into the army here. There were hundreds of us German boys in that same fix. I asked for the cavalry and was assigned to the Seventh.

A little batch of three or four of us were sent down to Nashville, Tennessee, and assigned to Company "H," Seventh Cavalry. Captain Benteen swore us in. I couldn't understand what he said, but I thought he was about the finest-looking soldier I had ever seen. He had bright eyes and a ruddy face, and he had a great thatch of iron-gray hair. It made him look mighty handsome. I found out later that he had been born in Virginia, but had stuck to the Union and had become the Colonel of the Ninth Missouri cavalry during the Civil War, and that he was known as one of the bravest officers in the Union Army.

I had quite a time of it during those first few weeks with "H" company. I'd had some drilling in the Manual of Arms in Germany and I caught on to the American Manual quick enough, but I did have trouble with "Port Arms." I always confused the order with "Shoulder Arms." But I learned pretty fast.

They used to call me "Dutchy." And some of the boys

called me "Sauerkraut," and then once in a while I'd get called "Heinie." But it wasn't so very long until they started using my real name of Charlie. Besides soldiering and drilling, I got to be the company shoemaker. I remember making a pair of cavalry boots for Captain Benteen. He always said they were about the finest boots he ever had. We usually called him "Colonel." Most of our captains had been full colonels in the Yankee armies. General Custer was actually only a Lieutenant Colonel in the Regular Army at this time, but he'd been a full Major General of Volunteers. Everybody called him "General." It was his Brevet rank. That was the usual custom in those days; to refer to an officer by his Brevet, or honorary, rank. It was a little confusing, though.

It was pretty dull, soldiering down there in the South. The regiment was broken up into companies, or small battalions, and our job was to smash the Ku Klux Klan, and run down illicit whiskey distillers. It wasn't much fun for energetic, spirited young men.

We'd been down there almost three years when in the spring of 1873, the grapevine spread the welcome word that the whole regiment was to be ordered north and brought together in the Dakotas. Our battalion was to be sent by boat from Louisville to Cairo, and then by train to Yankton, South Dakota. From there it would march straight north along the Missouri River right up to the Indian country, the Sioux lands. Everybody was glad to get that news. We were tired of playing soldier. We wanted some action. It'd be fun to do a little Indian fighting.

I'd learned a lot about the regiment by this time. It was supposed to be one of the top Indian-fighting outfits in the whole army. It was a fairly new regiment, as it had only been formed in 1866. They got a fancy word for that now. They call it "activated."

As I say, the Seventh was only seven years old in 1873, but it had a fine reputation. Everybody in the country knew

General Custer, and he was always bragging about what a fine fighting regiment he had. He was supposed to be the best Indian fighter in the American army. In the Civil War they'd called him "the Boy General" and he'd been a dashing, popular figure.

The regiment had spent the first four years of its life on the Kansas plains, and in Indian territory. The old-timers in the outfit could sure tell some blood-curdling Indian stories. They used to say that it was worse than straight death to get captured by Indians, because you would be slowly tortured until you gave up the ghost. They told all of us young soldiers, if we were ever wounded in an Indian fight and left behind and in danger of being captured, that we must save our last cartridge to blow out our own brains.

And here it was the early spring of 1873, and we were being sent from Nashville a thousand miles north straight into the Indian country. We'd see some service now. And we wanted it, too. We were tired of garrison duty.

We'd just like to see the bunch of Indians that would dare fight the Seventh Cavalry. All we knew or cared about was that we were going into the last of the real Indian country.

By this spring of 1873, the Plains Indians had been largely debased, beaten and driven to the great reservations that had been allotted to the various tribes. It had not been a deliberate government policy, but it had been a cruelly effective one. Treaty after treaty had been broken by the relentless pressure of white men and their civilization, constantly pushing against the ineffective resistance of the red men. Now and again the Indians had struck back, and as a rule their angry flare-ups were put down by the army—and then new and drastic treaties would be made and more land taken from them in punishment. The ink would hardly be dry on these new government commitments before the white pressure would be resumed, intrusions made—and once again the bewildered, enraged Indians would strike back, only to be subdued by the army and harsh penalties imposed on them. It was a deadly and vicious cycle the Indian found himself whirling endlessly in. . . .

A number of specific things had been responsible for the bitter feeling of the Northern Plains Indians against the white men. In 1862 a mad uproar of Indian resentment had suddenly broken out in Minnesota. Before it could be put down by General Sibley, several hundred Minnesota settlers had been killed. In retaliation the government had hung thirty-two culprits on a single scaffold and moved the Sioux tribes, guilty and innocent alike, far to the westward. The harsh and possibly unjust treatment had embittered many of the Chiefs. They saw in the forced migration another evidence of how lightly Indian treaties were kept, and how insatiable was the white man's hunger for their lands. . . .

In 1864, a certain Colonel Chivington, with a regiment of volunteer Colorado Cavalry, had suddenly moved against a large encampment of Cheyennes and indiscriminately killed some three hundred Indians. The massacre unquestionably had turned many lukewarm Indians into out-and-out hostiles. This bitterness of the Cheyennes was inflamed two or three years later when Custer led his newly formed Seventh Cavalry against Black Kettle and his band, in a sudden attack against their sleeping village on the Washita in Kansas. This so-called "battle" had brought Custer and his cavalry a burst of fame, but it was responsible for two highly important developments that must be given their proper proportion in tracing the events that led up to the great campaign of 1876. First: the Cheyennes, who are recognized as the most brilliant Indian fighters of the Plains, never forgave either Custer or his Seventh Cavalry for this whirling attack on their sleeping village in the dead of winter. Second: an aftermath of the fight—the death of Major Elliott and seventeen troopers in a distant part of the frozen field—had caused a split in both the officer and enlisted personnel of the regiment that years later was to have strange repercussions. . . . In 1867 the Union Pacific Railroad had been driven through the buffalo and Indian lands of southern Nebraska and Wyoming. The year before this, the Sioux, under Red Cloud, had blindly struck at three forts on the forbidden "Bozeman Trail," that ran northward through Wyoming from Fort Laramie on the North Platte, to the mining camps of northwestern Montana. The Fetterman massacre had brought violent protests from Indian friends in Washington and in 1867 and 1868, a peace committee, headed by General Sherman, had finally agreed that the Sioux should forever have for their own a reservation embracing the entire State of South Dakota, and for hunting purposes a vast area below the Black Hills, and to the east and north of the Big Horn Mountains of Wyoming. This was popularly known as the "Great Sioux Reservation." It covered approximately twenty-two million acres of buffalo land. Besides this land, guaranteed to be theirs in perpetuity, they were to be given certain important annuities and government aids to help them in their transition from nomads to reservation farmers. All this was part of the solemn treaty signed on April 29, 1868. . . . In the five years that had elapsed between that date and this spring of 1873, the old pressure of the advancing white men, and his civilization, had never ceased for a single moment. Rumors of gold within the "Great Sioux Reservation," and particularly within the barred and mysterious Black Hills, had whetted the insatiable appetite of the mining men. Scores of great cattle ranches had been established in the rich grass country adjoining the Sioux hunting lands to the south. Here were millions of acres of free grass that were needed by the vast steer herds that were being driven every summer northward up the Chisholm trail, from Texas. The annual north and south migrations of the buffalo had largely ceased, because the minute the herds appeared in the white man's country the slaughter was on. No less than five million of these great beasts, that spelled life to the Indians, were slaughtered in the five-year period beginning with 1870. It was almost a deliberate government policy to permit and encourage the destruction. Once the buffalo, around whose existence the whole economy of the Indian was based, was killed off the nomads had nothing to do but submit to government control and become Agency Indians, degraded, whiskey-crazed, beaten. Only the various tribes of the Sioux, and the fighting Cheyennes, refused to be broken on the wheel of civilization. A few determined leaders such as Sitting Bull, Crazy Horse, Gall, American Horse, Two Moon, White Bull, Spotted Eagle and Chief Hunk, stubbornly held out against the threats and blandishments of the whites. . . . But by the spring of 1873 they were beginning to be branded as "hostiles." That spring of '73, contrary to the treaty and pledges of 1868, a full-dress engineering survey was to be made straight across the heart of the Indian lands of South Dakota, and on westward up the valley of the Yellowstone in Central Montana. The Great Northern railway would soon push its steel arm out through this forbidden land. And Custer's famous Seventh Cavalry would furnish most of the military escort for this preliminary surveying party.

—2—

It took us several days to make the rail trip north from Cairo, Illinois, to Yankton, South Dakota. We'd make two or three stops every day to water and feed our horses, and cook our own meals. Each man would look after his own horse, and we'd usually give him a little exercise and a good rubdown. All troop horses were geldings, though once in a while an officer would have his own privately owned mare.

A trooper thought a lot of his mount, and a cavalryman would have to be pretty mean who wouldn't take good care of his horse. If we got a good chance we'd steal a little extra oats or hay for our individual mounts. My horse at this time was named Pig. That wasn't his real name, but I called him that because nothing could keep him from rolling in a mud hole when he was being watered, after we'd come in from a long ride. He was fast and he could show his heels to most of the horses in the regiment. I thought a lot of him but the army condemned him after we'd been in the Dakota country a year or two. I'll tell you later about the horse I rode in the Battle of the Little Big Horn. But one thing more about "Pig." Two or three years after the army sold him, I saw him in a contractor's six-horse team in the Black Hills. He looked so poor and abused, I'd have bought him from the contractor but I didn't have the money. I went up to him and petted him. He knew me all right. He nickered and looked at me as much as to say, "Come on, please, Charlie, get me out of here." I had ridden old Pig thousands of miles, and more than once he saved my life. I pretty near cried when I saw him that time in the Black Hills.

That first night at Yankton, South Dakota, a terrible blizzard hit us, even if it was early May. I'll never forget that storm. General Custer ordered every man to take his mount into the town, and find whatever shelter he could get for himself and his horse. We were camped a mile or two away, over by the railroad tracks. I imagine if we hadn't done that there would have been scores of men and horses frozen to death. There was no fooling about a Dakota blizzard, even that late in the spring. We learned a good lesson about northern weather right at the start.

It was at Yankton that I first saw General Custer. He was not far from six feet tall, and he must have weighed around 180 pounds. He was energetic, and it was mighty hard to wear him out. I've heard people say that when he was at West Point he was the second strongest man there.

As I remember him at that time, he was wearing long hair, something like Buffalo Bill used to wear. He had a big, wide-brimmed western hat, and long military mustaches. His hair and mustaches were yellow; tawny-colored, I suppose would be the right way to describe them. He had on high Wellington boots. They were the kind that came up to the knees, with the front three or four inches higher than the back. They were popular among the officers at that time.

General Custer wasn't the kind to mix freely with the men. In those years there was quite a gulf between the officers and the enlisted men. Some of the officers were friendly and easy-going with their troopers, but there was always a gulf. Custer struck me as being aloof and removed.

It got to be gossip among the troopers that some of the officers didn't set so very well with the General. My Captain, "Colonel" Benteen, was one of those who didn't belong to the General's inner circle. I suppose you could say about half of the officers in the regiment were close to Custer, and the rest were not. I repeat, that Benteen was distinctly not an intimate of Custer. I heard all sorts of reasons why that was true. There was one report that Benteen had turned bitter because Custer had pulled out after the Battle of the Washita, in December, 1868, in Kansas, and had left Major Elliott and seventeen men to their fate. A day or two later they were all found killed, scalped and mutilated. There was a story that Custer and Benteen had had some hard words over that. But of course I don't know how true that old story is.

So much stress has been put upon the break between Custer and Captain Benteen over this incident, that a full recital of the case may be useful. Sometime in late February, 1869, almost two months after the battle, a copy of a letter supposedly written by an officer of the regiment to a friend, who turned it over to the St. Louis *Democrat*, was received in camp by General Custer. So incensed was he that he called all the officers of the regiment to his tent, and sitting cross-legged on the seat of his table, tapping the sole of his boot with the handle of a whip, Custer read aloud the news-paper version of the letter. It read, in the purple-patch style of the era:

Fort Cobb, I.T., Dec. 22, 1868

"My Dear Friend: I wrote to you from Camp Supply, which place we left on the 7th, arriving at this post on the evening of the 18th. On the 11th we camped within a few miles of our "battle of the Washita," and Generals Sheridan and Custer, with a detail of one hundred men, mounted, as escort, went out with the view of searching for the bodies of our nineteen missing comrades, including Major Elliott.

"The bodies were found in a small circle, stripped as naked as when born, and frozen stiff. Their heads had been battered in, and some of them had been entirely chopped off; some of them had the Adam's apple cut out of their throats; some had their hands and feet cut off, and nearly all had been horribly mangled in a way delicacy forbids me to mention. They lay scarcely two miles from the scene of the fight, and all we know of the manner they were killed we have learned from Indian sources. It seems that Major Elliott's party were pursuing a well-mounted party of Cheyennes in the direction of the Grand Village, where nearly all the tribes were encamped, and were surrounded by the reinforcements coming to the rescue of the pursued, before the Major was aware of their position. They were out of sight and hearing of the Seventh Cavalry, which had remained at and around the captured village, about two miles away. As soon as Major Elliott found that he was surrounded he caused his men to dismount, and did some execution among the Indians, which added to the mortifica-tion they must have felt at the loss of the village and herds of their friends and allies, and enraged them so that they determined upon the destruction of the entire little band.

"Who can describe the feeling of that brave band, as with anxious beating hearts, they strained their yearning eyes in the direction whence help should come? What must have been the despair that, when all hopes of succor died out, nerved their stout arms to do and die? Round and round rush the red fiends, smaller and smaller shrinks the circle, but the aim of that devoted, gallant knot of heroes is steadier than ever, and the death howl of the murderous redskin is more frequent. But on they come in masses grim, with glittering lance and one long, loud, exulting whoop, as if the gates of hell had opened and loosed the whole infernal host. A well-directed volley from their trusty carbines makes some of the miscreants reel and fall, but their death-rattles are drowned in the greater din. Soon every voice in that little band is still as death; but the hellish work of the savages is scarce begun, and their ingenuities are taxed to invent barbarities to practice on the bodies of the fallen brave, the relation of which is scarcely necessary to the completion of this tale.

"And now to learn why the anxiously-looked-for succor did not come, let us view the scene in the captured village, scarce two short miles away. Light skirmishing is going on all around. Savages on flying steeds, with shields and feathers gay, are circling everywhere, riding like devils incarnate. The troops are on all sides of the village, looking on and seizing every opportunity of picking off some of those daring riders with their carbines. But does no one think of the welfare of Major Elliott and party? It seems not. But yes! a squadron of cavalry is in motion. They trot; they gallop. Now they charge! The cowardly redskins flee the coming shock, and scatter here and there among the hills on beyond. But is it the true line—will the cavalry keep it? No! No! They turn! Ah, 'tis only to intercept the wily foe. See! a gray troop goes on in the direction again. One more short mile and they will be saved. Oh, for a mother's prayers! Will not some good angel prompt them? They charge the mound—a few scattering shots, and the murderous pirates of the plains go unhurt away. There is no hope for that brave little band, the death doom is theirs, for the cavalry halt and rest their panting steeds.

"And now return with me to the village. Officers and soldiers are watching, resting, eating and sleeping. In an hour or so they will be refreshed and then scour the hills and plains for their missing comrades. The commander occupies himself in taking an inventory of the captured property which he has promised the officers shall be distributed among the enlisted men of the command if they falter or halt not in the charge.

"The day is drawing to a close and but little has been done save the work of the first hour. A great deal remains to be done. That which cannot be taken away must be destroyed. Eight hundred ponies are to be put to death. Our Chief exhibits his close sharp-shooting and terrifies the crowd of frightened, captured squaws and papooses by dropping the straggling ponies to death near them. Ah! he is a clever marksman. Not even do the poor dogs of the Indians escape his eye and aim as they drop dead or limp howling away. But are not those our men on guard on the other side of the creek? Will he not hit them? 'My troop is on guard, General, just over there,' says an officer. 'Well, bullets will not go through or around hills and you see there is a hill between us,' was the reply, and the exhibition goes on. No one will come that way intentionally—certainly not. Now commences the slaughter of the ponies. Volley on volley is poured into them by too hasty men, and they, limping, get away only to meet death from a surer hand. The work progresses! The plunder having been culled over, is hastily piled; the wigwams are pulled down and thrown on it, and soon the whole is one blazing mass. Occasionally a startling report is heard and a steamlike volume of smoke ascends as the fire reaches a powder bag, and thus the glorious deeds of valor done in the morning are celebrated by the flaming bonfire of the afternoon. The last pony is killed. The huge fire dies out; our wounded and dead comrades—

heroes of a bloody day—are carefully laid on ready ambulances, and as the brave band of the Seventh Cavalry strikes up the air, 'Ain't I glad to get out of the Wilderness?' we slowly pick our way across the creek over which we charged so gallantly in the early morn. Take care! do not trample on the dead bodies of that woman and child lying there! In a short time we shall be far from the scene of our daring dash, and night will have thrown her dark mantle over the scene. But surely some search will be made for our missing comrades. No, they are forgotten. Over them and the poor ponies the wolves will hold high carnival, and their howlings will be their only requiem. Slowly trudging, we return to our train, some twenty miles away, and with bold, exulting hearts, learn from one another how many dead Indians have been seen.

"Two weeks elapse—a larger force returns that way. A search is made and the bodies are found strewn round that little circle, frozen stiff and hard. Who shall write their eulogy?

"This, my dear friend, is the story of the 'battle of the Washita,' poorly told."

. . . When he had finished reading the bitter letter Custer is said to have pronounced that he was certain it had been written by an officer of the regiment, and that he deserved to be horsewhipped. He demanded the officer reveal himself. The story goes that Benteen shifted his revolver holster to a convenient position and announced that he was the author. What happened then has never been cleared up. But there is no question that from then on there was no love lost between the two strong personalities.

—3—

Benteen always pretty much minded his own business. He was often the third ranking officer in the regiment, even if he was only a company commander. Right after the Civil

War, when they were forming the new regiments for the regular army, Benteen had been offered a majority in the new Ninth colored cavalry, but he had accepted a captaincy in the new Seventh Cavalry. Twenty years later, and just three days before I finally left the service, Benteen was made a Major, and ordered to the Ninth colored cavalry. Can you beat that?

Most of the time we were in the field, Captain Benteen commanded a squadron. Usually he'd have one or two companies, besides his own "H" company.

He was a wonderful officer. He let the First Sergeant pretty much run the company. He wasn't always interfering and running the details. I served under Benteen for twelve full years, lacking only those three days.

One of the best descriptions of Captain Benteen is that penned by the late Major General Hugh L. Scott on page 454 of his interesting book, *Some Memoirs of a Soldier:*

"I found my model early in Captain Benteen, the idol of the Seventh Cavalry on the upper Missouri in 1877, who governed mainly by suggestion; in all the years I knew him, I never once heard him raise his voice to enforce his purpose. He would sit by the open fire at night, his bright pleasant face framed by his snow-white hair, beaming with kindness and humor, and often I watched his every movement to find out the secret of his quiet steady government, that I might go and govern likewise. For example, if he intended to stay a few days in one camp he would say to his adjutant, 'Brewer, don't you think we had better take up our regular guard mount while in camp?' and Brewer always thought it 'Better' and so did everybody else. If he found this kindly manner was misunderstood, then his iron hand would close down quickly, but that was seldom necessary, and then only with newcomers and never twice with the same person.

"Benteen's policy, which I adopted in 1877, has paid

me large dividends. The press has lately remarked that General Foch, marshal of France, probably considered now the foremost soldier in the world, commands in this same way, and from my brief association with him I am prepared to believe this is quite true. I tried to teach command by suggestion and persuasion at West Point by methods of precept and example. I tried to follow the same methods with the Indians, and at Jolo, and while my efforts along this line were not always successful, they did prove so in a significant number of cases."

—4—

Well, when we'd got ourselves shaken down after that blizzard in Yankton, S. D., we took up the 500-mile march overland, up the east bank of the Missouri River to Fort Randall, Fort Sully, and finally to Fort Rice. It was a wonderful trip. We had a wagon train, and there was a flat-bottomed steamer that kept right along with the column.

General Custer and his wife would ride at the head of the column, with scouts thrown out in front. We had flankers, and a full company closing the rear behind the wagons. I suppose we must have stretched out a mile or two. We'd mostly be in columns of fours, but there wasn't any great amount of order.

It was beautiful to ride northward in those spring days. There were lots of wild flowers, and there was a fine nip in the air.

It was wonderful to be young, and to be riding into Indian country as part of the finest regiment of cavalry in the world.

We were all mighty proud of the Seventh. It just didn't seem like anything could ever happen to it.

Chapter 2

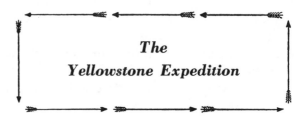

The Yellowstone Expedition

*B*REVET Major General Stanley, Colonel of the Twenty-second Infantry, was in command of the Yellowstone Expedition, although the big end of his troops was made up of the Seventh Cavalry, under General Custer. We struck almost due west from Fort Rice, crossing the creeks and rivers the best way we could. As a rule General Custer and two or three troops of cavalry would march well ahead of the column, lay out the best route, and early in the afternoon pick out the camp site for the night. Sometimes this advance guard would throw up temporary bridges and do all kinds of pioneer work. The General had a small pack of wolf hounds that followed him. He'd do a good deal of hunting on the side.

We had not gone very far west of the Missouri until we started running into buffalo. Sometimes there would be considerable herds of the odd-shaped, lumbering fellows. Lots of times you'd find an old bull with some twenty to thirty buffalo cows off by themselves. The buffalo calves were just beginning to come along about the time we started, and it was a thrilling sight to see those little yellow tykes. Their humps hadn't begun to show clearly, and they looked more like Jersey calves than anything else.

We had not been out very long until I killed a buffalo

calf, cut out the liver, and the upper hind quarters, and that night our company cook fixed up our first buffalo meat for us. It was mighty tender. There were lots of fleet little antelope, but I never killed one. Before I was through with the army, I'd killed many a buffalo. The hump of a young two-year-old is about as tender as anything you ever put your teeth into.

Once in a while we'd get a glimpse of Indians. They'd appear singly, or in pairs, way off on some hill or knoll. They acted as if they were scouting us. When the column would get a little nearer they'd mount their ponies and away they'd go. We had a little bunch of Crow Indian scouts along, and I always felt they were half scared to death of the Sioux. They were their traditional enemies and it was usually said that the Sioux were much better fighters.

Custer's head Indian scout was a young Arikara named Bloody Knife. I saw him lots of times. He was with us that next summer of 1874, when we went to the Black Hills. He was killed in the Battle of the Little Big Horn two years later.

The regiment had only one real brush with the Indians on the Yellowstone Expedition. That was on August 4, when the expedition was almost as far west as it was to go. I didn't take part in this myself because "H" troop, and a company of the Seventeenth Infantry, had been left behind on the lower reaches of the Yellowstone to guard supplies at a temporary fort we called "Stanley's Stockade."

An excellent account of the fight near the mouth of the Tongue River was written by the correspondent of the New York *Tribune* who accompanied the expedition. His story published in the *Tribune* of September 8, 1873, is herewith produced:

"Camp Near Musselshell River, Montana, August 19. —No day since the expedition started opened more monotonously than the 4th of August. . . . We left camp at the usual hour—5 o'clock in the morning. The coolness of the early morning, which had excited the hope of a relief from the oppressiveness of the preceding days, soon disappeared, and the sun rose without a single veil of cloud. I pitied the poor men and the poorer mules, compelled to march and pull through this wilderness of sage and cactus. As I rode up to the head of the infantry line before crossing to join a squadron of cavalry on the flank, I gathered something of the sentiment of the men concerning things in general and the expedition in particular. . . .

"As I galloped along I overtook Captain Hale's detachment of cavalry, which was guarding the left flank. I came up with the veterinary surgeon of the cavalry, Mr. Honsinger, a fine-looking portly man, about fifty-five years of age, dressed in a blue coat and buckskin pantaloons, mounted on his fine blooded horse, leisurely trotting along the cavalry trail. No man in the regiment took more care of his horse than he. It was an extra professional care—a love of the horse for his own sake, much less a veterinary surgeon. He had taken the horse at Yankton, in the Spring, from one of the cavalry troops—a gaunt-looking steed then, but under his fostering care he had grown fat and sleek. Poor man! he was soon to make a last long camp on the lonely banks of the Yellowstone. Without dirge or funeral note, he was slowly marching to his own grave. When I saw him again, a few hours later, he was a corpse. He had died a victim to his devotion to that noble horse. . . .

"While the infantry and the cavalry near the train were longing for any deliverance from heat, thirst and monotony, General Custer, with a squadron of cavalry several miles ahead, was having a warmer and much more lively experience. With a squadron numbering eighty men under Captain Moylan, one troop of which was commanded by his brother, Lieutenant Thomas Custer, and the other by Lieutenant Charles A. Varnum, he had started in advance of the train to find a good road. In addition to the officers named, he was accompanied by Bloody Knife, the Indian scout, an interpreter, and the regimental adjutant, Lieutenant James Calhoun. When about two miles from the camp of the preceding night, they struck an Indian trail. Indians had been seen lurking near the camp several nights previous, but we had no intimation that they were near in any considerable force. General Stanley had carefully abstained from taking the aggressive. The order was that the Indians should not be molested unless they first molested us. General Custer therefore proceeded on his march without taking note of the Indian trail, except to read the very legible caution which the pony footprints had left in the sand. He advanced with his detachment about ten miles at a fast walk, and, having descended from the bluffs to the valley below, halted in a pleasant cottonwood grove on the banks of the river, judging from the nature of the road and the terrain he had traversed that the train would not be able to go beyond that point during the day.

"It was then about 9:30 in the morning. The train could not reach this point until late in the afternoon. He therefore ordered his men to water their horses, unsaddle and picket in the woods, where the tall grass afforded very good grazing. After having posted a picket on the outskirt of the wood, commanding a view of the valley and to the entrance of the wood, officers and men lay down under the trees, General Custer taking the precaution to call his trumpeter and tell him to lie down within call. 'I had a presentiment,' said he afterward, 'that we were going to have an alarm.' The camp thus secured, General Custer and many of the men dropped into a light sleep. A quarter of a mile further down the river was another copse of cottonwood larger and more dense than the one occupied by the cavalry. It concealed, too, a heap of latent mischief of which the drowsy horsemen under the neighboring timber were little aware.

"Two hours later, that quiet, shady rest under the grateful trees was abruptly disturbed by a sight which came to the quick eye of one of the pickets. Six Indians were coming across the plain from the woods on the river below. The corporal of the picket rushed to General Custer.

" 'Indians are galloping this way, Sir.'

" 'Bring in your horses, bring in your horses,' yelled out the General, as he jumped to his feet.

"Never was an order obeyed more promptly. Every man sprang to his picket rope, and the horses were immediately brought under cover. A line of skirmishers was at once thrown out to receive with martial courtesy the advancing Indians, whose intention when within 250 yards became clearly evident. They had not come to hold a peace conference, but to steal our horses and drive out our men. They were evidently the decoy of a larger party. General Custer immediately sent word back to Captain Moylan for all the men in the woods to saddle their horses. With his dismounted skirmish line the General kept the Indians off until the horses were saddled, the men in the timber who had saddled coming out and relieving those on the skirmish line. General Custer then called for his horse, and accompanied by Lieutenant Calhoun and Lieutenant Custer, and his own orderly, rode out toward the Indians. As they advanced, the Indians retreated. General Custer, having a thoroughbred horse whose speed he had tested in many a hunt, then started in chase, taking his orderly, but telling his officers to remain where they were.

" 'Tuttle,' said the General to his man, 'just stay behind about a hundred yards; I want to go on a little and see what those Indians are up to. But keep your eyes on those woods.'

"The General started. So did the Indians. They had a good start, and General Custer resolved not to pursue them too far away from his men. After a sharp, short race he stopped on the plain, keeping well away from the suspicious woods. When he stopped the Indians stopped. It was evident that they would not be so audacious without a consciousness of strength somewhere. For ways that are dark and tricks that are vain the heathen Sioux is almost as peculiar as the

Officers and guests on the Yellowstone Expedition in the summer of 1873. 1. Gibson; 2. Godfrey; 3. Benteen; 4. Hyde; 5. Frederick Dent Grant; 6. Tilford; 7. Gen. Custer; 8. Sandy Forsyth; 10. Wallace; 11. Tom Custer; 12. Yates; 13. McIntosh; 16. Ludlow; 17. Indian Scout; 18. "Doc" Honsinger, regimental veterinarian.

From a photograph by Barry in the Denver Public Library Western Collection

General Custer, officers and ladies at Fort Abraham Lincoln, not long before the Battle.

Barry photo from Bureau of American Ethnology.
Through courtesy of Ex-Rep. Usher L. Burdick

Left: First Sergeant Windolph, taken about 1880. *Right:* Captain Benteen, taken sometime after the Battle of the Little Big Horn.

heathen Chinee. This time the trick was indeed vain. They were fighting with no novice. As soon as General Custer saw the Indian dodge, which was to use these men as a decoy to draw him into the woods, he immediately sent his orderly back to Captain Moylan to order a platoon to dismount. Before the order could get back, 250 mounted Indians, drawn up in line of battle, came out of the woods in fine military style. The Seventh Cavalry could hardly have done it better. With painted faces, heads decorated with ribbons and fillets, they sallied out with loud warwhoops. General Custer, putting more confidence in the feet of his thoroughbred than the voice of his rifle against 250 Indians, turned back to his command, calling out to his brother to throw out a dismounted line. Lieutenant Custer had anticipated the order, and was already dismounting his men. They ran forward and took places in the grass. The Indians opened a heavy fire which was quickly answered by our men with their Sharpe's carbines. In a dismounted cavalry fight every fourth man is usually detailed to hold the horses; but being short of fighting men, and the reserves being several miles back with the train, General Custer ordered every sixth man only to hold the horses, and the rest to join the skirmish line. The Indians having three times as large a force, and seeing the cavalry dismounted, followed their example and dismounted. From their advantage of numbers, they were able to extend their skirmish line clear around from river to river, so as to inclose the cavalry in a semicircle with the woods and the river at their back. Finding that the horses were exposed to fire, General Custer ordered them to be led further into the timber.

"As he fell back with his skirmish line the Indians advanced theirs, coming within easy rifle range. One of their number attracted a great deal of attention. He carried a long staff or lance with a pennant at the end. During the fire one of the Indians was wounded. Several others immediately collected around him, the man with the pennant, who most probably was the medicine man, being one of the number. Lieutenant Varnum called out to his men to fire into the party. The men fired, and the man with the lance fell. Previous to this, Bloody Knife, the guide, had earned the honor of the 'first blood,' having dropped a man from his saddle at the second fire. General Custer, with his Remington, brought down a pony. After fighting the Indians in this way for nearly three hours our ammunition gave out. General Custer sent back for the ammunition of the men holding horses. While the fight was going on, the bluffs on which the train was moving with the main body of cavalry and infantry, were behind the Indians. General Custer noticed a party of four or five Indians moving toward the bluffs. The train had not yet come in sight, having had to make a detour to head a ravine. He was at a loss at first to divine their purpose. Presently two men were seen to run up the bluff, hotly pursued by the Indians. They were stragglers from the train. He was too far away to render assistance, nor could he pursue the Indians without dividing the command and dangerously weakening it. The sad work of this small detachment was not learned until after the train had arrived.

"The strategy and cunning of the Indians were not confined to extending this skirmish line and making a diversion to cut off stragglers from the train. The cavalry horses were a great temptation. They laid an ingenious plot to capture them. Having engaged the attention of General Custer's whole force in front of the woods, they had sent a party down under the river bank to come into the rear of the woods and seize or stampede the horses. The first intimation General Custer got of this scheme was the sight of a single Indian stealthily advancing in the rear. A few well-directed shots toward him published his discovery, and checked his design. He retired very reluctantly, but somewhat quicker than he came. The boldness of this single Indian was at first a matter of surprise. It was easily explained after the fight, when an examination of the river bank showed the footprints of the fifty or more Indians which it had concealed.

"The Indians, having lost two men, were more cautious in their advances, and, finding that they could not with their heavy rifles drive the cavalry into the woods, had recourse to another favorite weapon. They fired the grass in four or five places. Fortunately there was little or no wind, and the grass was too short and too green to burn well, else this new weapon might have proved formidable indeed. The fire, however, raised a blue curtain of smoke, forming a corner segment between the fighting arcs. Failing in their attempt to raise a great fire, the redskins used this smoke line as a mask for their rifles. Advancing under cover of this curtain, they would pour a volley at our line and retreat. Our men soon discovered the dodge, and laid equal claim to the curtain. The Indians, abandoning this position, began to draw in their men.

"Now, said General Custer to Captain Moylan, 'let us mount and drive them off.' The men immediately mounted and advanced as skirmishers on a trot. Finding this was not fast enough, a charge was ordered. The men, eager for the order, gave a loud yell and put their horses into a full gallop. Though nearly 300 in number, the sight of eighty cavalry-men coming toward them like madcaps was too much for the Indians. They turned like sheep and scattered in every direction. Mounted on their fleet war ponies, with several hundred yards start, over ground with which they were familiar, they succeeded, after a close chase of three miles by our cavalry, in getting beyond pursuit. Only one of our men, Private J. R. Crow, was wounded, and he received but a slight flesh wound in the arm. One of our horses was struck in three places, none of the wounds being fatal.

"Just about the time that General Custer ordered the charge, General Stanley and those at the head of the train, which was then within three-quarters of a mile from the edge of the bluff, discovered a hatless horseman coming full speed toward the train. His hair was streaming in the wind. His horse, without bridle, seemed moved by the same fear which impelled his frightened rider. He soon reached the train, and, almost breathless from haste and fear, told his story. He had been out hunting with three or four men of Captain Yates's squadron of cavalry, which that day had been detailed as escort to the engineers. Becoming tired, he had declined to go further with the party. He picketed his horse, took off his bridle, and let him graze, then lay down himself. Had he fallen asleep he would never have waked again. While lying there he was suddenly startled by seeing two Indians coming toward the bluff. Two stragglers from the train, one of them Doctor Honsinger, were directly in their path. He saw the Indians approach and seize their bridles, he heard a shot and saw the cavalry doctor fall. He immediately jumped on his horse without bridling him and went off at full speed. He had lost his hat, his belt, and pistol, and had come near losing his life. General Stanley, who at this time had no knowledge of General Custer's fight, immediately started all the cavalry in pursuit of the Indians. Captain Hale with his squadron descending into the valley at the left; Colonel Hart with his squadron on the right and Captain French with his squadron on the center. Lieutenant Brush of the Eighteenth Infantry in command of the scouts was also ordered to charge down the valley. Arriving at the edge of the bluffs the curling smoke from the green plain, and the blackened patches of burnt grass showed that the cavalryman's story was not without foundation. A cloud of dust away off to the left showed the direction of General Custer's charge.

"Two Indians of the party who had made the diversion from the main body to cut off stragglers from the train were seen making for the 'Bad Lands.' They were hotly pursued by the cavalry and Lieutenant Brush, but under cover of the numerous ravines which afforded them a favorable opportunity of escape, succeeded in eluding their pursuers. The Indians are thoroughly acquainted with these 'Bad Lands' and their ponies are used to climbing them. In such ground they are more than a match for our best American horses. Meanwhile General Stanley had sent out the demoralized cavalryman with two or three scouts to look for the bodies of the unfortunate men. The soldier's fright had scared all sense of locality out of him and stampeded the four points of the compass. He was unable to find the place he had started from. The two bodies were subsequently found by a party of infantry. They proved to be the bodies of Doctor Honsinger and Mr. Baliran, the cavalry sutler. Doctor Honsinger was shot through the body by a Henry rifle ball. Mr. Baliran was killed by two arrows which entered his back, coming out of his stomach. Ever since we left Fort Rice, in spite of the order prohibiting straggling, many of the men have been in the habit of cutting loose from the train, to hunt game or moss agate, wandering from half a mile to two miles; but Doctor Honsinger was never known to leave the column. Mr. Baliran seldom left it. Doctor Honsinger was about the last man who would have been selected as a victim of this dangerous habit. His absence on this occasion was easily explained. The day, as I have said before, was one of intense heat. Tne Doctor's horse had had no water since morning. The river lay only a mile away. The train would evidently camp on the river bottom. General Custer, he knew, had gone on with his soldiers. A couple of miles back along the river was the surveying party with a cavalry guard. There seemed to be little danger in going to the river. He took the chances, risking his life to give his horse a drink of water. The Indians won the wager. Mr. Baliran was in company with Doctor Honsinger and going to the river for the same reason. One of our Indian scouts who could not speak English met the two as they were descending into the valley. The quick eye of the scout had seen the Indians. He stopped the Doctor and said, 'Indians, Indians.' 'No, no,' said the Doctor, 'they are cavalry, cavalry.' The scout took hold of their bridle-reins and tried to turn their horses back. They refused to be convinced and the scout left them to their fate. It must have been soon after that the Indians were upon them. The nature of the wounds showed that both men had been shot in the saddle. They had turned after seeing the Indians, and tried to climb the bluffs. The Indians had fired and brought them both down. The Doctor having the better horse had nearly reached the top of the bluff, when the ball overtook him. Strange to say, neither of the party was scalped. The Indians took Mr. Baliran's money, amounting to about $100 and the doctor's watch. The bodies were not mutilated. Perhaps the sudden departure of the frightened cavalryman for assistance, was seen, and their departure thereby hastened. Doctor Honsinger had served through the war, and had previously accompanied General Frémont on some of his expeditions. He had been a long time connected with the Seventh Cavalry, and was greatly esteemed by officers and men for his personal and professional qualities. He resided in Adrian, Michigan. Mr. Baliran was also a favorite in the cavalry. He has a wife and child in Memphis, Tennessee."

—2—

The thing that struck in our craw long after we got back to our winter quarters was the brutal killing of Doctor Honsinger, our old German-born Vet whom everybody loved, and our sutler, Mr. Baliran. Both of them were kindly, inoffensive men, and their murder rankled in our hearts. The whole regiment swore some day we would get revenge. We had to wait more than a year for our chance—and even then it slipped out of our hands.

Early in the winter of '74, Charlie Reynolds, who had been Custer's head white scout in that Yellowstone campaign of '73, was down at the big Standing Rock reservation, which is seventy miles on down the Missouri River from

Fort Abraham Lincoln. Charlie used to hang around the store just to hear what the Indians were saying, so he could report to General Custer. One day he saw a young Indian sub-chief and brave named Rain-in-the-Face, exhibiting a gold watch. Reynolds could talk Sioux, and he heard the Indian bragging how he had killed a white man and taken the watch. Charlie caught enough of the drift to recognize that it was "Doc" Honsinger's. At once he sent word to General Custer at his headquarters at Fort Lincoln that he thought he had the man who had murdered Doctor Honsinger and Mr. Baliran.

It was in the dead of winter and the thermometer stood at ten or more below zero, but the General immediately ordered Captain Yates and his own brother, Tom Custer, to take Troop F and reinforcements, and march out under sealed orders. They were to go to the Standing Rock Agency, arrest Rain-in-the-Face, and if possible bring him back alive. Several thousand Indians were around the Agency that winter, and both officers knew that a misstep might cost the lives of themselves and their little command.

In order to deceive the Indians, Captain Yates sent forty men and an officer ostensibly to an Indian camp, ten miles on below. Hiding most of his force in reserve near the store, he sent Tom Custer inside to make the arrest.

Tom Custer laid out his plan and entered the agency store with five picked men. The big log room was full of Indians, most of whom had their blankets drawn up around their heads. It was arranged that Charlie Reynolds would tip off which Indian was Rain-in-the-Face, if he could locate him among the blanketed figures.

The soldiers pretended to be buying tobacco and trinkets. Finally Reynolds nodded towards the guilty Indian. Tom Custer signalled his men, and when they were in position, he suddenly grappled Rain-in-the-Face from behind. He was quickly disarmed and handcuffed. The Indians, surprised and unorganized, had no time to move before a second squad of troopers entered and helped remove Rain-in-the-Face.

He was hustled to a designated spot, where the rest of the two troops were in battle order. The Indians, helpless without their leaders, milled about most of the night, shouting threats.

In the bitter cold of dawn the two troops started on the long, dangerous trip back to Fort Lincoln. Reaching there safely, Rain-in-the-Face was put in leg irons, and placed in a guard house with two civilian thieves. The Indian's brother pleaded for his release, offering to take his place, but Custer, of course, refused.

Then one night, two or three weeks later, the civilians sawed their way out, taking Rain-in-the-Face with them. For the next two years the Indian outlaw lived with the hostiles in their lodges along Powder River, and in the buffalo camps along the Little Big Horn. Word drifted out of the vengeance he swore he would some day take on Tom Custer. Apparently Captain Custer and not the General was the one that Rain-in-the-Face blamed for his arrest and disgrace.

Two and a half years went by, and then came that hot dusty afternoon of June 25, 1876. This time Rain-in-the-Face had his triumph. Three days later when we identified and helped bury the General and the men of his five troops, we found Tom Custer's body mutilated beyond recognition. Rain-in-the-Face was supposed to have cut out the brave Captain's heart. The only way he was identified was when Lieutenant Godfrey discovered the letters "TWC" tattooed above the elbow on his right arm.

In 1905, twenty-nine years after the Battle of the Little Big Horn, a South Dakota newspaper made the following comment on the death of Rain-in-the-Face in that year:

"News comes from Grand River, North Dakota, of the death there, Monday, of that celebrated old Sioux warrior, Rain-in-the-Face, who was one of the leaders in the Custer massacre. He was sixty-three years of age, and had been an Indian policeman for many years. The famous Sioux and David F. Barry, of Superior, were great friends, the latter having helped to get the Indian his police appointment at Standing Rock.

"Mr. Barry had known Rain-in-the-Face since 1875 or 1876, and the red man very much liked the frontier photographer in the early days. Among the many famous men, both red and white, that Mr. Barry came to know there, he has always admired Rain-in-the-Face. The Indian called the Superior man, in the Sioux tongue, the 'Little Shadow Catcher.'

" 'I was sorry to hear of the death of Rain-in-the-Face,' said Mr. Barry last evening. 'He was a great Indian, and he has been grossly maligned in some respects. It has been so widely published that it is hardly possible to contradict it now, that Rain-in-the-Face killed Tom Custer and then cut his heart out.

" 'I investigated that story, and did it early, and found that it was not true. Rain-in-the-Face has often talked with me about that report. It has worried him that the public should accept it as true. Now that he is dead, we may look for a recurrence of the libel on the old chief. He was a great warrior and a typical Sioux. He has killed many white men, no doubt, but that story of his cutting Tom Custer's heart out should not be allowed to go undisputed. There are several men living who are ready to prove what I say.' "

Chapter 3

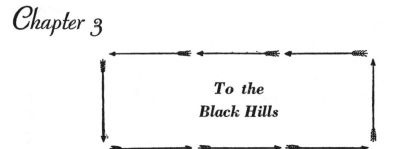

To the
Black Hills

*I*T was in June of 1874 that "H" troop, along with one or two other companies of the Seventh, left Fort Rice and marched up the west bank of the Missouri to Fort Abraham Lincoln, where most of the regiment was quartered.

That previous summer and fall, Fort Abraham Lincoln had been built on a flat plateau that lay some distance back from the river. Acrosss the Missouri, on the east bank, was the frontier town of Bismarck, North Dakota. Here was the western end of the Northern Pacific Railroad. It would be several years before a bridge would be thrown across the muddy, treacherous Missouri River, and the rails strung out along the line we had surveyed that previous summer of 1873.

For a long time there had been wild rumors of gold in the Black Hills country. They used that term "Black Hills" pretty freely in those days. Roughly speaking, even parts of the Big Horn and Laramie Mountains were included in the general term "Black Hills." But that was wrong. The "Black Hills" proper are located in the extreme southwest corner of South Dakota, and run roughly some 150 miles north and south and about fifty miles east and west. That's an area of about the size of the state of Connecticut.

They're a sort of freak of nature. They rise out of the dry dusty plains and rolling lands, almost as clean-cut as a great square building lifts itself out of a city. You might almost call the "Black Hills" a high, green oasis in a desert. They rise right out of the land and are covered with pine and fir and spruce, with beautiful little valleys dotting the river bottom. Peaks stand out here and there—Harney's Peak sticking its proud head over 9,000 feet into the clear, blue sky.

The "Black Hills" were like a great castle, surrounded by high walls that seemed to have no gates in them. It was as if the Almighty had set this place aside, and put a sign on it that read: "No white men wanted here!"

That's the way the Indians thought about it, anyway. For generations it had been a sort of sacred Indian hide-out. Explorers and army surveyors and engineers had traveled around it, but none of them had really penetrated it. It was supposed to be "bad medicine" even to enter that territory near the forbidden mountains.

But if you want to keep people out of any place, don't spread the report that there's gold there. That's what was happening.

And now the Seventh Cavalry was being sent in there by General Sheridan to make a thorough exploration of its forbidden interior. To us troopers it was a good deal like going on a prolonged picnic. We'd be seeing country probably no white man had ever put his foot in.

The "Black Hills" were definitely ceded to the Indians in the Treaty of 1868, but that made little difference to the restless gold-hungry miners and pioneers, living in frontier forts 400 miles eastward on the Missouri, or southward on the North Platte. Now and again Indians would show up with little bags of gold, and mysteriously hint that they had found them over there somewhere—over there in the "Black Hills" country. As a matter of fact, the probabilities are that the Indians had waylaid some unfortunate miner returning from the Montana or Idaho diggings, murdered him and taken his gold. To cover up the crime the culprits would hint that they had found the gold in the mysterious Indian country of the "Black Hills." And the magic word "Gold!" would once again travel by the frontier grapevine from one settlement to another.

Most of the gold talk naturally was in the West, but even far away New York City now and again caught the magic word. On March 9, 1872, the New York *Tribune* carried the following letter:

"To the Editor of the *Tribune*.

"Sir: The reported discovery of gold in the Black Hills is attracting much attention throughout the West, and if the statements in regard to the matter prove to be as well founded as they seem, the discovery will be one of great national importance. For several months past the Indians and whites connected with Spotted Tail's tribe of Sioux have shown rich specimens of gold-bearing quartz, but until a very recent date they have persistently refused to make known the exact locality where it was obtained. It has long been believed that gold would ultimately be found in large quantities in the Black Hills, but as the entire country surrounding was in the undisputed possession of the Sioux, no effort could, until recently, be made to verify these impressions. At different times, adventurous frontiersmen have penetrated this almost wholly unknown region, and have brought back specimens of gold that certainly left no doubt of the existence of the precious metal in paying quantities.

"As far back as 1867 the people of Dakota were firm in the belief that the Black Hills were rich in gold and other minerals. In the year named an expedition was organized by Byron M. Smith for the purpose of exploring that region, and people from the East went to Yankton to join it, but the Government, instead of furnishing an escort of cavalry, as was expected, ordered it to disband. In 1868, Captain

P. B. Davey of Minnesota started a similar scheme, but the Government again refused to allow an expedition of the kind to enter the Indian country, believing that the result would be a general Indian war. Last season a party of men having the same object in view assembled at Cheyenne and proposed to explore the Big Horn River, but were compelled to disband for the same reason. . . . It is now generally believed that the Government will throw no further obstacles in the way of an expedition exploring this region. . . ."

D. H. O.

Sioux City, Iowa, February 27, 1872

In 1872 a strange and imaginative newspaper man by the name of Charlie Collins began dreaming out a vast "Black Hills" colonization scheme. Collins was editor of the booming Sioux City, Iowa, *Times*. Three years before this, Collins, along with John P. Hodnett, then U. S. Assessor for Dakota Territory, had planned an Irish-American colony on the Missouri River, opposite the spot where the White River empties into it. The plan was for this anti-British group to be settled and all set to invade Canada when the time was ripe. It was a Fenian scheme and it eventually died of its own fanaticism. Collins then turned to his wild scheme of invading the forbidden "Black Hills" and establishing a settlement there. He advertised this project in his paper during the Spring and Summer of 1872, and scores of boomers, drifters and romantic adventurers enrolled. The start was to be made on September 1, 1872. But the army stepped in, and General Hancock, in command at Fort Snelling, near St. Paul, issued an order to all commanders along the Missouri: "Any expedition organized for the purpose of penetrating the Black Hills, must be immediately dispersed, the leaders arrested and placed in the nearest military prison." Thus died the private and fantastic "Black Hills" expedition of 1872.

The outfit that left Fort Lincoln for the Black Hills on July 2, 1874, was almost as formidable an outfit as the one we had the year before on the Yellowstone surveying expedition. General Custer was in command, and he had ten companies of the Seventh Cavalry, one company from each of the Twentieth and the Seventeenth Infantry, a three-inch field rifle, two Gatling guns, a detachment of Indian scouts, numerous white guides, interpreters, civilian teamsters, packers and herders. We numbered in all around a thousand men. We had 110 six-mule team wagons, and we were ready for bear. Brevet Colonel Williams Ludlow was sent along as chief engineer and we had several scientists from the East, and a young newspaper correspondent for a Chicago paper, named Charles E. Curtis. He had a good deal to do with what happened later, when they let the cat out of the bag.

Custer's favorite Indian scout, Bloody Knife, was along. And there was also Charlie Reynolds, who was one of the best-known guides and Indian men in the whole West, next to old Jim Bridges. Those three men, Bloody Knife, Charlie Reynolds and Custer, were again and again tied in together. That is, until their luck ran out.

Of course I don't remember all the details of that "Black Hills" expedition. I know we marched about 400 miles westward and to the south, camping late afternoons where we could get wood and water. That'd always be along some creek or river. General Custer was good at picking out camp sites. He did most of that work himself. He'd usually ride way ahead of the column, and lay out the line of march and the crossings, and pick the spot where we'd camp. He was a good plainsman, right enough. He had an eye for it.

We had a long column, and we moved out with our wagons four abreast. It was a pretty sight to see those canvas-covered army Studebakers, each with its three teams of

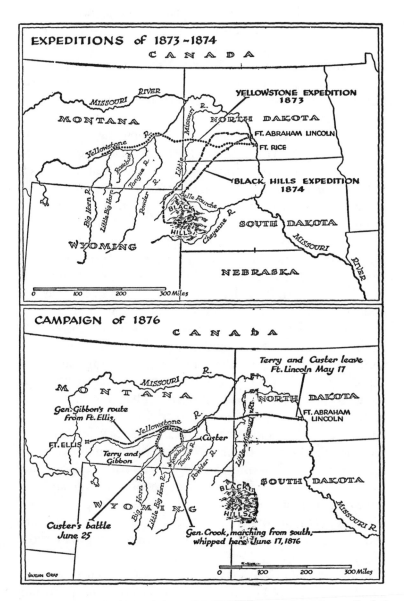

Maps showing all three of the Custer Expeditions; 1873, 1874 and 1876

government mules. We had civilian "mule skinners." The infantry was their special guard, but we were always ready for any Indian surprise attacks. We had 300 head of beef cattle, and they were driven behind the wagon train. There was always at least one cavalry company in the rear guard. It was a big outfit; a thousand men and horses, 700 mules and 300 steers.

We didn't see any buffalo for several days, but there was a world of fleet little antelope. We had sixty days to make the trip to the Hills, explore the region and get back to Fort Abraham Lincoln. Some days we'd make thirty miles, but now and again when the going was bad we wouldn't make more than fourteen or fifteen.

It was fun in the long evenings, when we'd taken care of our horses, and the guards were posted, and everything was shipshape. It was getting higher country all the time as we went west, and that meant cool nights, even in the middle of July. We'd make great campfires and almost every evening there'd be a band concert. General Custer was mighty proud of our Seventh Regiment band. They were mounted on white horses and he had them along on all his expeditions and campaigns. They'd never fail to play the regiment's own song "Garry Owen." That was an old Irish battle song that Custer had adopted for Seventh's own. I faintly remember some of the other tunes they used to play on that trip. One of them was "The Mocking Bird." And then there was "The Blue Danube." We had a mighty fine band, and on the nights when the moon was out and the stars cracking in the sky, and the air was crisp and cool, it was something to stretch out before a big open log fire and listen to the music. Soldiering wasn't half bad those times.

Colonel Fred Dent Grant, the President's oldest son was along with us, too. He had no official position but just came for the fun of it. The Colonel used to get a little tipsy. But that didn't do anybody any harm. There were also two civilian miners from Bismarck who were brought along as experts. More about them later.

It seems to me we'd been out about three weeks, when we left the hot, dry country up near the headwaters of the Little Missouri River, and headed straight south until we hit the headwaters of the Belle Fourche. The Belle Fourche is really the North Fork of the Cheyenne River, and it forms the northern boundary of the Black Hills. The southern border of the Hills is made by the South Fork of the Cheyenne. Between these streams, rises this strange formation of hills and high valleys, woods and lovely parks, shut off from the rest of the world by steep cliffs and green mountains.

We were now traveling slowly down the West side of the Black Hills. Scouts finally found an opening, and we turned sharply to our left, or east, and entered the forbidden land. It was a paradise of flowers and cool, sweet air, and clear running streams. You never saw so many wild flowers in your life as there were that first day. And the grass reached almost to our stirrups. It was like heaven, after the hot, dry days on the Dakota plains.

General Custer, who as usual was riding ahead with a couple of troops, came upon smoldering campfires that showed that three Indian tepees had recently been there. He sent Bloody Knife ahead with several Indians. Soon they galloped back with information they had located the Indians. Custer surrounded the little group and brought back four bucks with him to our camp. The head was a minor chief named One Stab, whose squaw was a daughter of Red Cloud. Custer promised them food if they helped him, but they seemed to be in a hurry to leave, and before they could be checked they mounted their ponies and were off. Custer sent troopers after them but the only one they could catch and bring back was One Stab. He was told he would be given all the bacon, sugar and coffee that two ponies could carry if he'd act as a guide. He agreed, but in order to make it stick Custer had four troopers guard him night and day. It was a good thing we had One Stab with us for the next three or four days because it was hard to find our way through those narrow valleys and canyons of the Black Hills. When One Stab finally left he got his two pony loads of grub, as Custer had promised. His band were the only Indians we saw while we were in the Hills proper.

A couple of days after we had entered the Black Hills we passed over a divide and rode into Castle Creek Valley. It was pretty and green there, too. We weren't hurrying matters. Every day the two miners would be out with their picks and shovels and pans. Troopers were prospecting, too, and you couldn't hear much else talked about but gold. Everybody was sure the creek bottoms must be full of gold, and you'd hear all sorts of wild rumors of big nuggets and findings.

But I believe the first real gold that was panned was found by the miner named Horatio Nelson Ross. If I remember rightly, that was on the afternoon of July 30. We were camped for several days in one spot while General Custer was exploring south of Harney's Peak. I suppose we were twenty-five miles or so south of what is now Lead. Lead, South Dakota, is where the great Homestake Mine was discovered in the early Eighties. More gold has been taken out of that mine than any other mine in the world. I ought to know, because I worked for the Homestake for forty-eight years. I still live at Lead. It's a great place.

We sure were excited when word spun around our camp that Ross had really found gold. I suppose that word "gold" is the most exciting word in the language. Men will do more crazy things, and more brave things, and more cruel things for it than for anything else. Just holler "Gold!" "Gold!" a couple of times and men will stampede like Texas longhorns used to when they were driven north up the old Chisholm trail.

Gold to most men means sudden wealth, big times,

The Inter Ocean.

VOL. III. NO. 156.   CHICAGO, FRIDAY MORNING, AUGUST 28, 1874.

THE GOLD FEVER.

Intense Excitement in the City Yesterday Over the News from the Black Hills.

The Mining Offices and Bullion Dealers Invaded by Anxious Inquirers.

General Sheridan Warns Miners and Prospectors to Keep Away from the Scene,

As by Treaty that Section is Exempt from Settlement by the Whites.

Some Doubts as to Whether All the Gold Region is Within the Reservation.

Reminiscences of the Invasion of the Big Horn Country by the Gold-Seekers.

The Existence of Gold in the Black Hills Known to the Fur Traders for Years.

What a Catholic Missionary Told General Sheridan Fifteen Years Since.

Interesting Interviews with Missouri River Traders and Explorers.

THE BLACK HILLS COUNTRY.

DISTANCES.

From Chicago to Bismarck, 1,660 miles.
From Bismarck to Black Hills, by the route followed by General Custer, 420 miles.
From Bonle City to Harney's Peak about 185 miles, the proposed route being along the valley of the White River.
From Harney's Peak to Fort Laramie, 146 miles.
The dotted line represents the route pursued by Custer's command to Harney's Peak. He returns by much the same road.

Facsimile of front-page account of the discovery of gold in the Black Hills: Chicago *Inter Ocean*, August 28, 1874 whiskey and gambling and women. It means fortune and adventure and all the things they never had. The gold fever is like taking dope. You're helpless when it strikes you.

That's the way most of us felt in those days at the end of July in 1874. I had a great friend in "H" company who at that time was our trumpeter. His name was Everett Edward, and we used to call him "Dutchie." He'd been a gold miner in California in 1849, and during the Civil War he'd been a Lieutenant in a Negro regiment. He hadn't hit it very well in the California gold rush and he was fit to be tied when he heard about Ross finding gold here in the Black Hills. We got the cook of "H" company to loan us a pan, and we found a pick and shovel, and hurried off by ourselves. And we found gold, too. We panned out a number of tiny specks. But it was gold right enough.

I get excited when I think about it even now—seventy-two years later. We had it bad. "Dutchie" filled me full of all kinds of stories. We'd come back here and get rich. We might even "go over the hill." You have to have money to get yourself an outfit, and money was something we didn't have. But we knew you couldn't keep white men out of these hills once word of the gold discovery got out to the world.

All the soldiers in the United States couldn't hold back the tide then. You could sign all the Indian treaties you could pack on a mule, but they wouldn't do any good. Men would get through. They'd go after gold in spite of hell and high water.

We had some newspaper men along and they had a story big enough to suit them. It'd help make them famous, even if it would do a lot of harm. Lots of the people connected with the discovery would pay for it with their lives.

Charlie Reynolds rode out late on the evening of August 1st or 2nd with the newspapermen's dispatches and the report from General Custer.

He was a wonderful man, that Charlie Reynolds. We

used to call him "Lonesome Charlie" because he never talked very much and seemed to like to be by himself. He was the silent kind. I suppose you might say he was on the moody side. I never did know much about him but I've been told that he was born in Warren County, Illinois, in March, 1844. Like a lot of boys around that time, he joined up with an emigrant train going West. I think he was sixteen then—so that would make it 1860 when he first touched the Plains country. I heard he served three years in a Kansas regiment during the Civil War; then for a time he settled down in Atchison, Kansas. From then on he started living in the Indian country, trapping and hunting buffalo. I first saw him in the summer of '73, when he was chief scout and guide of the Yellowstone Expedition.

He was all nerve, afraid of nothing, and he had a good head on his shoulders. This day in the Black Hills—I believe it was August 1—when he volunteered to try to get those dispatches through, it didn't look like he had more than an even chance at the best of getting through alive. He had to ride more than a hundred miles southwest through danger-ous Indian country before he reached Fort Laramie, Wyo-ming. He did it alone, riding at night and hiding by day. He took the story of Black Hills gold to the world. And he paid for it with his life on that terrible day of June 25, two years later.

I read once about how every one who touched an Egyp-tian King's tomb was doomed to die a violent death. Seems to me that the Indians must have put some curse like that on the white men who first touched their sacred Black Hills at this time.

Custer got a lot of notoriety from his Black Hills ex-pedition, and the discovery of gold. But he never had any luck after that.

On August 10, 1874, the New York *Tribune* carried a front-page story regarding the Hills:

"Headquarters Black Hills Expedition, Eight and a Half Miles South-East of Harney's Peak, Dakota Territory, August 2:—

"On the 30th day of July we halted about noon in a pleasant valley, within ten miles of Harney's Peak. One of our miners took his pan, went to the stream, and washed out a pan or two of earth taken right from the grass roots. There was gold there, but it was merely a color, requiring careful manipulation and an experienced eye to find it. The few glittering grains, with a slight residue of earth, were carefully wrapped up in a small piece of paper and put in the miner's pocketbook.

"The next day the expedition remained in camp and the miners had a chance to renew their search. The result was the discovery of a good bar, yielding from five to seven cents per pan, which could easily be made to pay if water were more plentiful there. On the succeeding day the expedition made a march of but five miles and found another excellent camp, in which General Custer decided to remain for four or five days. Ross and McKay, in a literal sense, found this their golden opportunity. Along the creek, running down the valley, very good colors were found in the loose dirt, none of which were worth less than half a cent a pan, and some worth three or four cents. A hole was then sunk in a promising bar to the depth of six feet. Water intruded and embarrassed the work; but the earth panned out as high as ten cents. The miners were not able to reach the bed rock on account of the water. An examination of the gulch for two or three miles showed the existence of a succession of gold bars of equal and some perhaps of greater value. Time proved insufficient, however, to test them all, or yet to define the limits of the gold belt even in this special locality. . . .

"The last pans taken out on Custer Gulch—for so the miners call it—averaged ten cents a pan, but this was from the richer bars. The general yield would average less. Mr.

March of the Custer column to the Black Hills in the summer of 1874.

Barry photo from Bureau of American Ethnology through courtesy
Ex-Rep. Usher L. Burdick

From a photograph in the National Archives, Washington, D. C.

Left: "Lonesome Charley" Reynolds, Custer's Chief of Scouts, who was killed fighting in the valley with Reno, early in the afternoon of June 25. *Right:* Rain-in-the-Face, who has been accused of mutilating the body of Capt. Tom Custer.

Ross is of the opinion that the gulch where the hole was sunk would yield $50 a day to the man, and in some places $75."

The cat was now out of the bag. There was no holding back the men with the far-away look in their eyes—and the word "gold" on their lips.

That following Spring and Summer, of 1875, white miners trooped into the Hills, despite every effort made by the Army to keep them out. White man's civilization was again on the march, and nothing could stop it. Benteen's Troop "H" was dispatched into the Black Hills to round up and bring out miners. A number were rounded up and escorted out, but immediately frontier civil courts would turn the men loose, and they would return to the hills as soon as they could get a fresh outfit. No less than 11,000 miners and camp followers of one kind or another were credited with passing through the brand-new settlement of Custer City that single year of 1875. . . .

Regarding Troop "H's" unhappy task of herding the miners from the new "diggins," there is an interesting item in the *Army and Navy Journal* of October 2, 1875. It reads:

"Black Hills—A number of the recently returned Black Hillers who had reached Yankton from Fort Randall, met for the purpose of giving a formal expression to their feelings about men and things. Mr. Geo. Loper was made chairman of the meeting and A. R. Miller, secretary. A series of resolutions prepared and presented by Mr. A. H. Hale, were passed as follows:

"Resolved. That our heartfelt thanks and lasting gratitude are due to Colonel F. W. Benteen and the men of his command, who accompanied us on our homeward march, for their unremitting kindness and courtesy toward us, and a thousand valuable favors voluntarily and respectfully bestowed; that the gallant commander and his worthy men will ever hold a high place in our esteem and a sacred spot in our affections.

"Resolved. That we feel under deep obligations to the Quartermaster at Fort Randall, Captain Pierce, for his disinterested and kind-hearted efforts to relieve our necessities and assist us on our journey.

"Resolved. That the route from the Black Hills to Fort Randolph for loaded wagons on account of the abundance of good wholesome water, convenient timber and superior grass, is preferable to any route to the Black Hills we are acquainted with; and with the bridging of five or six small streams would be in our opinion the best route attainable.

"Resolved. That our confidence in the mineral resources of the Black Hills is unabated—that gold exists there in paying quantities—and we declare our purpose to return there prepared to engage in mining just as soon as we can do so under authority of law.

> W. B. Long, Geo. Loper, J. A. Loper, Roger Gaffner, A. H. Hale, Sam Thomas, James Quigley, William Tillson, A. R. Miller."

An attempt was made that summer of '75 to buy the Black Hills from the Indians, and make legal this onslaught. But the Indians were in no mood to believe anything the commissioners told them, and it was impossible to make a deal of any kind. . . . A feeling of utter despair and despondency cast its spell over even the "friendly" reservation Indians. Maybe the radical things Sitting Bull and Crazy Horse and Gall and Two Moons and the other wild Chiefs, far back in the buffalo lands around the Powder and Big Horn were preaching, maybe they made sense. The free Indian was doomed. They were all to be made reservation Indians. That meant all the colorful old life would be gone forever, the buffalo hunts, the feasts, the sun dances, the visiting, and the pleasant horse-stealing wars, all the old life would be no more. Maybe those radical Chiefs were right.

Maybe they'd all better make one big battle against the whites. It would be better to die a free Indian than live on as a degraded, helpless "treaty" Indian. . . . So evident was the hostile feeling in that fall of 1875 that an order was submitted by the Commissioner of Indian Affairs, Edward P. Smith, to the Secretary of the Interior, Z. Chandler, who in turn submitted it to the Secretary of War, General Belknap. A subsequent communication from the Secretary of the Interior to the Secretary of War, dated December 1, 1875, read as follows:

"I have the honor to inform you that I have this day directed the Commissioner of Indian Affairs to notify said Indian, Sitting Bull, and the others outside their reservations, that they must return to their reservations before January 31, 1876; and that if they neglect or refuse so to move, they will be reported to the War Department as hostile Indians, and that a military Force will be sent to compel them to obey the order of the Indian Department."

It was all legal and proper—and all equally impossible to comply with, even if the Indians had so desired. It is to be doubted if the messengers who started out with the order even bothered to reach Sitting Bull and his outlaws, wintering in the cut banks and protected cottonwood groves of the Powder River, and in the snowbound river valleys to the west. And if the word had reached them it would have been next to impossible for the hostiles to have moved their camps, and made their way back to the reservations in the dead of winter and in the short time allowed. . . . So the army was at last to have its day. The patience of Sheridan and Sherman and the others had been exhausted. This time there would be no foolishness. A great pincer movement would be undertaken, and the hostile Indians caught in the jaws of the trap. From the North Platte, near the Nebraska-Wyoming line the old Arizona Indian fighter, General

47

George Crook, "The Grey Fox" would be sent north to the headwaters of the Tongue, with no less than a thousand men. From Fort Ellis and Fort Shaw in western Montana good old General Gibbon, he of the Iron Corps of Gettysburg fame, would move eastward along the north bank of the Yellowstone, and somewhere around the mouth of the Powder he would contact Terry's west-bound column, with Custer's Seventh Cavalry. These two, under the over-all command of Terry, would hunt down the hostiles and destroy them. This time there would be no chance of interference from the tenderhearted Indian friends in the East. This time the hostiles would either go back to their reservations to stay, or they would lie forever on distant battlefields where violent death overtook them.

Chapter 4

The March from
Fort Lincoln

*G*ENERAL CUSTER was not at Fort Abraham Lincoln when we arrived there late in April, 1876. Of course that aroused a lot of talk and suspicion.

Company "H" with two other troops of the Seventh Cavalry had been down in Louisiana that Winter of 1875–6. We of "H" had been posted in pleasant, sunny New Orleans.

Towards Spring we were ordered to proceed by rail up to St. Paul, and then on west to the Northern Pacific rail head at Bismarck, North Dakota. Fort Lincoln was across the Missouri River, and that was where we headed for.

We found plenty of excitement when we made camp on the plateau, a little west of the fort enclosure. You could hear more wild rumors than a dog has fleas. When you jiggled all those rumors down, you got about this: we were soon to start on a big expedition up the Yellowstone to round up the hostiles and drive them back to their reservations. If they would not go peacefully we were to make good Indians out of them.

There was a lot of suspicious talk going around all over the place. Custer was still in the East, and you could hear a hundred tales of how he was being kept away from the expedition because he had got under the skin of President

Grant. A lot of the troopers didn't care much for Custer, but it looked as if Major Reno would command the regiment if Custer didn't arrive. And most of us didn't know or care a great deal about Reno. Of course we knew he had been a Colonel of a Pennsylvania cavalry regiment at the end of the Civil War, but he'd never fought Indians, and he didn't seem to be very popular with either the men or the officers. If I remember correctly he was a West Pointer and was three or four years ahead of Custer. It was pretty clear that there wasn't much love lost between the two men.

Everything was uncertain those late April and early May days while the regiment was being whipped into marching shape. We had quite a few recruits, and a bunch of fresh young horses, so there was plenty to do to break in both of them. One thing that people get wrong about the recruits was that about half of the 150 new men we had were men who either had Civil War service or had already served a five-year hitch in the army. Most of the rest were plenty green. A good many of them were German boys. They made fine soldiers once they were trained.

I think it was about May 10 that General Custer suddenly showed up. General Terry was with him. Terry was of slight build and wore whiskers. He was a gentle, kindly man who never strutted or roared. Nothing at all like the quick-moving, dashing young Custer. Terry was a Brigadier-General of the Regular army and so he ranked Custer by two grades.

Word ran around camp that General Terry was to command the whole expedition, but that Custer was to have his old regiment. Custer was as happy as a boy with a new red sled. He put a lot of zip into us.

That spring of 1876, Democratic politicians in Washington were busy as beavers trying to unearth anything that would embarrass President Grant, facing the end of his second term. In November there would be a Presidential election, and any sort of powder would be good enough to serve as ammunition against Grant. A letter General Hazen had written to Congressman James Garfield in January, 1872, and printed in the New York *Tribune* was dug up. This letter stated that John S. Evans, post trader at Fort Sill, Indian Territory, was paying $1,000 a month to Caleb P. Marsh of New York, for the privilege of holding the lucrative post tradership. The intimation was that Marsh was splitting the graft with Secretary of War General Belknap. For four years this letter had rested quietly in the files of the *Tribune*, but now it was dug up and made the principal item in the indictment of Grant's Secretary of War, and in the subsequent Senate impeachment trial of the Secretary. Grant had sent a letter in his own handwriting to the Senate announcing the resignation of General Belknap a few minutes before the Senate had voted the impeachment trial—but the trial went ahead just the same. . . . Custer, sentimental Democrat that he was, had, while vacationing in New York, talked a little too freely about post traderships and graft— even going so far as to intimate that Orville Grant, the President's young brother, had been paid a thousand dollars to secure a post tradership. Custer had refused to accept a shipment of corn packed in sacks bearing the stamp of the Indian Department, and smelled graft in the subsequent army order for him to go ahead and accept the grain.

Back at Fort Lincoln in March a telegram was sent to him ordering him to appear as a witness against Belknap before the Heister Clymer Senate Committee. Custer, busy with the details of the coming expedition against the Sioux, which he was to command, tried to beg off by promising to send sworn answers to any questions asked. But Clymer was out for blood, and Custer was ordered to come to Washington. The upshot of all this was that Grant was so angered at Custer's hearsay accusations, that he ordered General Sherman not only to place Brigadier General Terry, in command of the Department of the Dakotas, as head of the expedition, but to deprive Custer of the right to go with his own regiment. Custer, humiliated and distraught, having arrived in St. Paul, sent the following dispatch to the President:

"I have seen your order transmitted through the General of the army, directing that I not be permitted to accompany the expedition about to move against the hostile Indians. As my entire regiment forms a part of the proposed expedition, and as I am the senior officer of the regiment on duty in the Department, I respectfully, but most earnestly request that while not allowed to go in command of the expedition, I may be permitted to serve with my regiment in the field. *I appeal to you as a soldier to spare me the humiliation of seeing my regiment march to meet the enemy and I not to share its dangers.*"

It was too much for the hero of Appomattox. Custer was to have back his beloved regiment. . . . Custer's wire to Grant was dated May 6. Two days later he and General Terry left St. Paul together for "the Wild Missouri."

—2—

Everything was all set for the big expedition to move out early Monday morning, May 15. But Sunday afternoon a heavy downpour and windstorm hit the camp and turned it into a lake of mud. The heavy six-mule wagons were bogged down and the whole outfit soaked and miserable. General Terry postponed the start until Wednesday, May 17.

That morning it was foggy and dull, and nobody was in a very good humor when the bugles sounded reveille at 4 o'clock. Soon as the men breakfasted and formed up, the heavy wagons led off in a column of fours. There were more than one hundred and fourteen of them, each drawn by six government mules. They hauled around two tons each. Next came the small two-horse wagons that were under contract by the government. They'd each hold around a ton. All the drivers were civilians.

The wagon train was headed west, the wheels of the heavy outfits making big ruts in the rain-soaked ground. General Terry suggested that Custer parade to the fort so that the worried women and children there could see for themselves what a strong fighting force it was. The band on white horses led off and we paraded around the inner area. Then the married men and officers were allowed to leave their troops and say good-by to their families. In a few minutes "Boots and Saddles" was sounded, and the troopers returned to their companions. Then the regiment, its guidons snapping in the morning breeze, marched off, while the band played over and over again "The Girl I Left Behind Me."

You felt like you were somebody when you were on a good horse, with a carbine dangling from its small leather ring socket on your McClelland saddle, and a Colt army revolver strapped on your hip; and a hundred rounds of ammunition in your web belt and in your saddle pockets. You were a cavalryman of the Seventh Regiment. You were a part of a proud outfit that had a fighting reputation, and you were ready for a fight or a frolic.

We made only fourteen miles that first day, and early in the afternoon camped on Heart River. After we got bedded down the paymaster turned over to each troop commander the payroll. We were paid off by companies and there was a lot of grumbling by the men. The paymaster had come up the river three days before, but General Custer wouldn't let him do his job until we were well away from Bismarck and the gambling and red-light district. I suppose it saved many a bad head, and the trouble of rounding up some of the worst drunks. But the men resented the fact they didn't get to go on their regular spree.

About half of that payroll found its way into the hands of the squaws and Sioux children when the dead troopers were stripped and mutilated a little over a month later on the Little Big Horn. I remember finding a little clay pony in an abandoned Indian camp the following spring. There was a worn five-dollar bill folded up and tied on the clay pony for a blanket. I was always sure that it had come out of the pocket of some dead trooper, who had been paid off that afternoon of May 17 on the Heart River. We got $13 a month in those days.

Mrs. Custer and Lieutenant Calhoun's wife, who was the General's sister, had ridden out with the column that first day. But the next morning when the column left, the two women rode the fourteen miles back to Lincoln with the paymaster and his guard. That was the last time Mrs. Custer ever saw her husband. It was the picture she carried in her heart for nearly sixty years, until she died in New York City in 1933.

I can almost see him myself in my mind's eye. He was wearing a broad western hat, with a low crown and wide brim. It was grayish in color. He'd had his long yellow hair cut just before we left, and he had on a buckskin suit, with fringe. He had two short-barreled "bull-dog" revolvers and a Remington sporting rifle, carried in a scabbard. It's my recollection that he carried a hunting knife in a fringed buckskin case.

I don't remember whether he was riding Vic or Dandy. I know that he had both horses along, and the one he didn't ride would be led by his old hostler, John Burkman, whom we used to call "Old Nutriment." He didn't have any extra sense, but he sure looked after the General's horses. Just exactly one month later, on the day of the battle, I know that Custer rode Vic. He was a sorrel with four white stockings and a blaze in his forehead. He was a wonderful horse. I might as well tell you now while I think of it, that years later we used to hear reports that Vic had been captured on the Little Horn, and had been taken up to Canada by one of the Indians who had escaped there with Sitting Bull. On the day of the battle the General's other horse, Dandy, was back with John Burkman in the rear guard. Eventually Dandy was sent out to Monroe, Michigan, to General Custer's father. He used to ride him on Decoration Day parades, and on such occasions. He was a fine horse too. The General had bought both Vic and Dandy when he was down in Kentucky in the early Seventies. They were Kentucky thoroughbreds.

This John Burkman couldn't read or write and he didn't have many friends in the outfit. Most of the time he'd be with the General's two horses or with his string of hunting dogs. Custer went in for dogs pretty heavy. If I remember rightly Burkman joined Troop "A" of the Seventh along about 1870. He'd been in the Civil War and was just about Custer's age. Somehow or other Custer took a shine to the silent trooper and soon had him assigned to look after his own horses and dogs.

A number of years ago some one told me that Old Nutriment came to a tragic end. After the Little Big Horn, when his enlistment was over, he headed for Billings, Montana. That was about as close as he could get to the Indian battlefields. In the Yellowstone Expedition of '73 Custer had had a little fight near where Billings is now located, and the old fellow seemed to get satisfaction in being close by. He certainly worshiped Custer's memory. He'd go around with an old army pistol strapped to his hip and if any one made the slightest remark against Custer, John would threaten to kill him. John built a little shack for himself on the edge of Billings, and for many years he batched there. Finally he got a pension as an Indian Wars veteran, and things got a little better for him. Since he couldn't read, time passed mighty slow, and he had only one or two friends. In the end poor old John shot himself. I think that was along about 1926.

But to get on with my story. We were back there on the little Heart River and the regiment was marching away, while Mrs. Custer was watching it from a hilltop. It must have made a great sight. Each troop had horses all of the same color. I believe when the regiment was formed in Kansas in 1866, that the General went to a lot of trouble to have each troop mounted on distinct colors.

I can still call them off, even at this late date. "H," my own troop, rode blood bays. "B," "D," "I" and "L" also were mounted on bays. "C," "G," and "K" had sorrels. "A" had coal blacks. And Lieutenant Edgerley's "E" troop had grays. We used to call "E" the Band Box troop. "M" troop was the only one that had mixed colors. The band rode white horses. I remember the drummer had a horse that would run away every time he mounted him, except when he put his drum on him. Then that old white horse would stand as still as a wooden horse.

Oh, it was a fine regiment, right enough. And there wasn't a man in it who didn't believe it was the greatest cavalry outfit in the entire United States Army.

That was an especially rainy May, and we struck bad going almost from the time we left Fort Abe Lincoln. We made camp early that second afternoon, and I don't think we covered more than eleven or twelve miles. I recall we'd no more than set up our pup tents than we had a heavy rain. A cold spring rain is mighty discouraging for both men and horses on a long march.

From the start of the expedition the same general plan was followed in making camp. Whenever possible a camp site would be located along a stream; usually there'd be plenty of wood and good grass nearby. The regiment had been divided into two wings of six troops each, Major Reno and Captain Benteen commanding. As we'd move on to the camp site the wings would make up the two sides of an oblong, with the flank of each wing resting on the river or creek bank. Next to the river, and between the wings, the Headquarters would be set up. The upper end of the oblong would be filled with the wagons.

Picket ropes would keep the lines straight for each company. We'd dismount, unsaddle and lead our horses to water. Then we'd stake them out to graze, under a guard. Then we'd set up our four-man pup tents, and place our saddles and gear nine feet in front of the tents. The company cooks would be preparing supper. We had our own beef herd along, and always they'd slaughter enough beeves for the following day's use.

After chow we'd bring in our horses to the picket line in front of the tents. The ropes would be tied to three wagons. Of course we had guards posted, and a main guard of four non-coms and twelve or fourteen privates.

It didn't take us very long to get into the swing of things, and most of the times everything went off just like clock work. Now and again we'd hit a bad creek or river crossing, and pioneer troops would have to build a temporary bridge. We had an awful smart young army engineer along with us. His name was Lieutenant Maguire and he was mighty clever. We had two light wagons filled with axes, picks and shovels, and bridge timbers and planks. Most of the creek bottoms were hard, but now and again we'd run into soft shoulders and mud bottoms and we'd have a hard time of it.

Custer was usually far out ahead with one or two troops. He was mighty good at laying out the best trails and crossings, and picking camp sites. There'd always be a battalion of three troops in the rear guard, and a battalion riding on each flank. The two wings, under Reno and Benteen, were each divided into two battalions, and the senior officer of each was put in command. That way we had four battalions and we were ready for any surprise or emergency.

After we'd been out just about two weeks, we hit the valley of the Little Missouri and found excellent grass and clear sparkling water. There was big talk of Indians, and Terry sent Custer and three or four troops to scout up the Little Missouri and really find out conditions. Custer got back towards evening, after riding close to fifty miles, but he found no trace of hostiles. Next day after Custer's return, we continued the march, but the country was rough and broken and we didn't make many miles. That same thing was true for the next two or three days.

It was along about this time that scouts from Colonel Gibbon's Montana column reached us. They'd marched all the way from Fort Ellis over near where Bozeman, Montana, now stands. The idea was for us to connect with them.

It took us two or three days of hard travel before we marched over the divide into the valley of the Powder River. The river was a couple of hundred feet wide here, which was some twenty miles from where it emptied into the Yellowstone. All the rivers below the Yellowstone flowed northward into the big river.

We made camp on the Powder and General Terry and an escort rode northward to the mouth. General Gibbon was there, and also the flat-bottom river steamer, the *Far West*. It'd left Fort Lincoln long after we had. It had forage and supplies, and three companies of the Sixth Infantry on board. Major Moore was in command of the soldiers.

The *Far West* was an old stern-wheeler and Captain Grant Marsh could pretty near sail her over dry land. He was a wonderful pilot. Before we were through with this campaign that old *Far West* would push its way two or three hundred miles farther westward up the Yellowstone than any river steamer in history had ever done. Then "Cap" Marsh would drive her right up to the forks of the Little Big Horn and the Big Horn.

Joseph Mills Hanson's colorful book, *The Conquest of the Missouri*, describes accurately the *Far West*, and the exciting trip of the sturdy flat-bottomed boat from Bismarck to this junction of Generals Terry and Gibbon at the mouth of the Tongue River:

"The *Far West* had been built for the Coulsons at Pitts-

Captain Grant Marsh, of the supply ship *Far West,* who played an important part in the campaign of 1876, that culminated in the Battle of the Little Big Horn.

Steamer *Far West,* the most famous of all the river boats on the Missouri and the Yellowstone in the middle '70's and early '80's.

Barry photos from the Bureau of American Ethnology through courtesy of Ex-Rep. Usher L. Burdick

Capt. Keogh's mount, "Comanche," the only living thing found on Custer Hill, when the tragedy was discovered on the morning of June 27.

Curley, the Crow scout, whose claim that he witnessed the annihilation of Custer and his five troops, has never been successfully disputed.

From a photograph by Barry in the Denver Public Library Western Collection

burgh in 1870. She was 190 feet long, 33 feet beam and her draught, when loaded to her full capacity of 400 tons, was 4 feet, 6 inches, while unloaded she drew 20 inches. Thirty passengers were all her cabin could accommodate. Her motive power consisted of two 15-inch diameter engines of 5-foot piston stoke, built by the Herbertson Engine Works of Brownsville, Pa., and she carried three boilers. She was also provided with two steam capstans, one on each side of the bow, being the first boat ever built with more than one, though afterward all Missouri River steamers were similarly equipped. Light, strong and speedy, she was eminently a vessel for hard and continuous service. During her long tour of duty that summer the Government paid $360.00 per day for her use.

"At Yankton, where the *Far West* had spent the winter, she began loading with Government stores for Fort Lincoln and the troops in the field as soon as she could be brought to the levee after the ice went out, and with a full cargo she left Yankton about the middle of May. The trip to Fort Lincoln was quick and uneventful, and she reached the post on May 27, to find that the expedition had started for the Yellowstone ten days before.

"The few persons remaining at the fort, including the families of the absent troops, hailed the appearance of the boat with rejoicing. It was the first break in the monotony of their existence since the departure of the column, and the day of her arrival was treated by them as a holiday. The wives of the officers in Custer's regiment all came down to the river and made themselves at home on the boat while she was unloading, as was customary at the isolated frontier posts. Captain Marsh was busy throughout the morning superintending the discharge of cargo, but he instructed the steward to prepare as dainty a luncheon as the larder of the boat would afford, and spread it in the small cabin for the ladies.

"When informed of this pleasant attention, they were

much pleased and accepted it gratefully. Before they took their seats, Mrs. Custer sent to Captain Marsh an invitation to preside at the table, which he, being very busy, had not intended doing. But he heeded her urgent request and, hastily making himself as presentable as possible, joined them at the board. Mrs. Custer and Mrs. Algernon E. Smith, wife of a lieutenant in the Seventh with whom Captain Marsh was unacquainted, seated themselves beside him and were at particular pains to treat him cordially. When the agreeable meal was concluded and the captain was about to withdraw, Mrs. Custer and Mrs. Smith took him aside and asked him if they might accompany the boat to the Yellowstone, Mrs. Custer stating that her husband had authorized her to go if Captain Marsh was willing.

"The captain was much taken aback at this request, as under the circumstances he believed that such a trip would be both dangerous and uncomfortable for them. He pointed this out, showing them how limited were the accommodations of the *Far West* and what inconveniences they would have to put up with. As they still remained undiscouraged, he at last fell back upon a feeble subterfuge and mendaciously expressed regret that he had not brought his own comfortable boat, the *Josephine*, declaring that, if he had, he would gladly take them along. Finally seeing that it would be impossible to gain his consent, the ladies reluctantly gave up their plan, though with evident disappointment. It was well that the captain stood firm, for had he yielded to their wishes through a mistaken sense of courtesy and allowed them to go, all the heart-breaking suspense and horror of those days so soon to follow, might well have bereft them of reason.

"During the afternoon the supplies waiting at the fort for the cavalry were taken on board, consisting of forage such as oats and bran, commissary goods, medical supplies, tents, tarpaulins and other quartermaster's stores, and small arms ammunition. The total weight of the new cargo was about 200 tons, as much as it was safe to carry into the

Yellowstone since it brought the boat to a draught of thirty inches or more. The next morning the *Far West* started up the river. At Fort Buford the escort came on board, consisting of Company B of the Sixth infantry; Captain Stephen Baker, commanding, and John A. Carlin, First Lieutenant. The company numbered about sixty men and they made their quarters as usual on the main deck, the officers taking cabins above. The other three companies of the battalion, under Major Moore, had already marched up the east bank of the Yellowstone for Stanley's Stockade. The *Far West* at once followed, and in a few days reached the rendezvous to find Major Moore and his command already encamped there.

"The Major had received despatches from General Gibbon, who was coming down the left bank of the river, and on the arrival of the *Far West* he forwarded them, as well as one from himself, to General Terry. His courier traveled eastward along the old Stanley trail and encountered Terry just west of the Little Missouri, still several days' march from the Yellowstone. Learning from the despatches the location of Gibbon and also that the supply steamer had arrived, Terry diverted the march of his troops up the valley of Beaver Creek toward the mouth of the Powder, where the junction with Gibbon could be sooner accomplished, and sent back instructions to Major Moore to have the *Far West* meet him there. Captain Marsh proceeded thither, and tied to the bank on the 7th of June.

"Toward evening of that day, several skiffs were seen floating down the river. Upon sighting the steamer they pulled in and were found to contain Major Brisbin, Captain Clifford and others of Gibbon's command—Captain Clifford carrying despatches for General Terry. They had floated thirty or forty miles meeting no Indians on their journey. The next morning while the crew were engaged in cutting wood, a body of horsemen was discerned rapidly approaching through the valley of the Powder. When they drew up on the bank they proved to be General Terry and his staff escorted by two troops of cavalry, who had ridden down in advance of the main column, leaving the latter in camp about twenty miles up the Powder. The General immediately came on board to make his headquarters, and he gave Captain Marsh a cordial welcome, congratulating him on his prompt arrival. After reading Captain Clifford's despatches, Terry sent couriers to Gibbon with orders to leave his command and himself come down to meet the boat, which would steam up until he was encountered.

"The following morning the *Far West* got under way and went up until she reached a point about fifteen miles below the mouth of the Tongue River where a trooper hailed her from the shore. She came in and General Gibbon was found, accompanied by cavalry and the company of twenty-five mounted Crow Indians, who, under Lieutenant J. H. Bradley, had served him efficiently as scouts during his march from Fort Ellis. The two generals who had so long been planning for the junction now successfully accomplished, greeted each other at the bow of the *Far West* and then repaired to the cabin to discuss future movements. Finding that Gibbon's main body was resting but a short distance above, General Terry instructed Captain Marsh to steam up to their camping place. This was reached about noon and Terry invited all the officers on board, where a reunion affording opportunity for pleasant exchange of experiences occurred between them and the members of Terry's staff. After lying at the camp for some two hours, Gibbon and his officers took their leave and the boat returned to the Powder, where Terry also left for Custer's camp, after instructing Captain Marsh to return to Stanley's Stockade and bring all the supplies there up to the Powder, where a new depot was to be established. He also sent orders to Major Moore to bring his troops to the same point. By the 15th of June, Captain Marsh had accomplished these transfers and held his boat at the Powder, ready for further work."

Chapter 5

March Up
the Rosebud

WHEN General Terry got back to our camp on the Powder, twenty miles from its mouth, he ordered Reno to take six troops and scout up the Powder, and then cross the divide on west to the Tongue, and then follow northward down that little river to its mouth. You remember, all these rivers south of the Yellowstone, flowed north and emptied into it.

"H" and the remaining five troops headed down the Powder and eventually arrived at the southern bank of the Yellowstone. The wagons had a tough time, and it wasn't until Custer had taken a troop and scouted out a good road, that the heavy wagons could make it. Custer was mighty good at this kind of work. He had a nose for scouting and finding the best trails, all right.

I remember we stayed around our camp there at the mouth of the Powder for five or six days. This would bring us to the morning of June 15. We'd been out from Fort Lincoln a full month now, less two days. Here at the mouth of the Powder we started training pack mules and we had a lot of fun doing it. They were the ordinary army wagon mules. We had a few experienced packers with us, but I think they must have been pretty disgusted trying to teach us how to throw the Diamond hitch. The mules were just as green as the men. But both of us learned. We first tried out our mules with sacks of grain and water kegs, and we had a lot of fun laughing at the other fellow. Eventually we all learned fairly well, but right up to the big battle itself, we had some trouble with the mules and pack saddles. The Spanish leather *aparejos* were easier to handle than the army pack saddles, with their forked cross-pieces.

When we had been in this country three years before with Stanley's Yellowstone surveying expedition, we'd marched on the north bank of the Yellowstone. We were now marching on the south bank. On the morning of the sixteenth we arrived at the mouth of the Tongue. Here we would make our supply depot and camp, and we were kept busy sorting out the things we would leave behind. They would include all our wagons and teams, our tents and officer's baggage and all supplies and equipment except what we carried on our saddles and on our pack mules. The *Far West* was to go on up stream with us, and carry extra supplies on board.

After we'd been in camp about three days, an Indian scout came in with a letter from Major Reno, who had reached a spot near the mouth of the Rosebud. That was about twenty miles on westward, up the Yellowstone. We started marching there at once.

There were rumors that Reno and his six troops had found hot Indian trails and that there were plenty of Indians on to the south and east, eighty or ninety miles away. Things were getting a little exciting now. We'd have some real fighting soon.

Major Reno on his long ten-day Indian search from the Powder, had Mitch Boyer along as his head scout. Boyer was a half-breed Crow and was recognized as one of the finest scouts in Plains country. He had been with General Gibbon on the long march from the Fort Ellis country, and he and young Lieutenant Bradley, who was in charge of

Gibbon's scouts, had pretty well located the Indians. General Gibbon unquestionably had been able to give General Terry fairly accurate accounts of where the Indians were encamped. It seemed reasonable to suppose that the hostiles had by now moved westward from the Tongue and were either on the upper Rosebud or on farther west on the Little Big Horn at this time. It was difficult to get more than a vague idea of their numbers, but Boyer figured there were not less than 800 warriors in one band that were moving westward. At this period the best estimate seemed that altogether there would be around 1,500 fighting hostiles to whip. It was known that several thousand Indians had left the reservation late that winter, or early in the spring, and there were some who felt that there would be many more Indian warriors than were generally expected. . . . What was completely unknown and unsuspected was that on the morning of June 17, when Major Reno and his six troops of the Seventh Cavalry were at the furthest point up the Rosebud, just forty miles on south near the headwaters of the stream, General Crook and over 1,000 troopers were being given a sound lacing by the Sioux and Cheyenne hostiles, under the partial command of the great Crazy Horse. Sitting Bull, the irreconcilable medicine man of the Uncapapa Sioux, was there also. Crook's expedition against the hostiles not only was stopped in its tracks on June 17, but the highly touted Crook was sent reeling back to his camp on Goose Creek—near where Sheridan, Wyoming, is now located. . . . Eight days later, and only eighteen miles "the way the crow flies" from Crook's unhappy battleground on the headwaters of the Rosebud, the same Indians that humiliated his splendid expedition would annihilate Custer and almost half his magnificent Seventh Cavalry. Surely it was the Indian's day.

—2—

It was around 8 o'clock in the morning when we broke

camp at the mouth of the Tongue and marched up the Yellowstone, and joined Reno and his six troops that had been on the long scout.

I remember one thing that happened as we were leaving the Tongue. Our Seventh Cavalry band was mounted on white horses, and as we were short of good mounts the bandsmen were left behind, while the horses were taken over as remounts to replace horses that had been worn down. While the column was pulling out, the dismounted band stood on a little knoll near the big river and played "Garry Owen" as the regiment rode by. It was something you'd never forget.

It was good to see our old pals again, when the whole regiment got together there on the Yellowstone, near the mouth of the Rosebud. We made camp about four o'clock that afternoon. I believe it was June 21. There was plenty of excitement around camp that night. We all knew that there was a big conference on board the *Far West* with General Terry and Custer and Gibbon figuring out what we would do next.

Early Wednesday morning, Captain Benteen told us to get ready for a long march. We'd start that day at noon. We were to take fifteen days' rations with us. We'd have twelve mules for each troop and we'd carry hard tack, coffee and sugar for the full fifteen days, and bacon for only twelve days. Each trooper would carry 100 rounds of carbine ammunition and twenty-four rounds for his pistol. What he could not carry on his person he'd pack in his saddle bags. There were twelve of the biggest strongest mules, with the Spanish *aparejos*, carrying an additional 24,-000 rounds of carbine ammunition for the entire regiment.

From *The Conquest of the Missouri* the following interesting details are taken:

"The supplies for the Seventh Cavalry were drawn from the hold of the *Far West* early on the morning of Thursday,

March Up the Rosebud

June 22. . . . Hours before sunrise Captain Marsh was about directing the discharge of cargo and keeping his thirty deckhands rushing, and when, at the first streaks of dawn, the bugles echoing reveille roused the sleeping soldiers, the fifteen days' supplies were ready for issue on the bank. After the bustle of breakfast was over the camp quieted for a few hours while the men arranged their belongings for the hard march ahead. A number, including the officers, seized the opportunity for writing letters to dear ones at home. For many of them, alas, these were to be the last messages of love they would ever send on earth. Though the morning was glorious, and though the soldiers were veterans, accustomed to hail the approach of action with enthusiasm, strangely enough a sense of depression seemed to pervade the camp and not a few of the letters voiced this feeling. It was as if a premonition of coming catastrophe was in the men's hearts which they could not shake off. General Custer himself was affected by it and so were many of his officers.

"It is only fair to say, however, that the dejected spirits of several of the gallant cavalrymen may have resulted from a more substantial cause than premonition of coming ill. This is mere conjecture, but the fact remains that through the small hours of the previous night, more than one of them had remained awake to attend a meeting of absorbing interest in the cabin of the *Far West*. Captain Marsh was there, also Captain Tom Custer, Lieutenant Calhoun, Captain Crowell of the Sixth Infantry, and others, and the matter which kept them from their blankets on the eve of a hard campaign was one which rarely fails in its attraction to an American—poker. . . . Captain Crowell arose from the board a winner by several thousand dollars. Perhaps the thought of the perils they were about to face tended to make the participants reckless, but, be that as it may, Captain Marsh remembers that poker game on the eve of the Little Big Horn campaign as one of the stiffest ever played on the rivers, and he has witnessed some wherein fortunes were won and lost.

"Once during the morning, while busy about his manifold duties, the captain came face to face with Charlie Reynolds. The features of the scout were haggard with pain, and the captain asked him solicitously about the felon on his hand.

" 'No better,' answered Reynolds. 'Doctor Porter can't seem to cure it and my hand is no use.'

" 'See here, Charlie,' exclaimed the captain, 'I wish you would give up going with General Custer and stay on the boat. It will be a hard march for you in your condition and you can't do any fighting anyway with that hand.' The gallant fellow flushed and straightened.

" 'Captain,' he said earnestly, 'I've been waiting and getting ready for this expedition for two years and I would sooner be dead than miss it.'

"It was useless to argue with such a spirit and when the column left, Captain Marsh regretfully saw Reynolds start with it, never to return."

—3—

It was noon on June 22 when we broke camp, and started our march up the Rosebud. Just before we packed our mules, Benteen ordered us to take along an extra supply of salt. That meant that we might be living on mule or horse meat before we got back. I suppose we all knew by this time that we'd be hitting it into dangerous country. But as I look back, I don't believe many of the troopers were very worried. We knew there'd be some hard fighting, but a soldier always feels that it's the other fellow who's going to get it. Never himself.

That morning word had spread about the camp that mail was going to be sent back home, and that this would be the last chance to get off letters. Of course, I didn't have anybody to write to, but the officers and many of the men hurriedly scribbled letters to their dear ones.

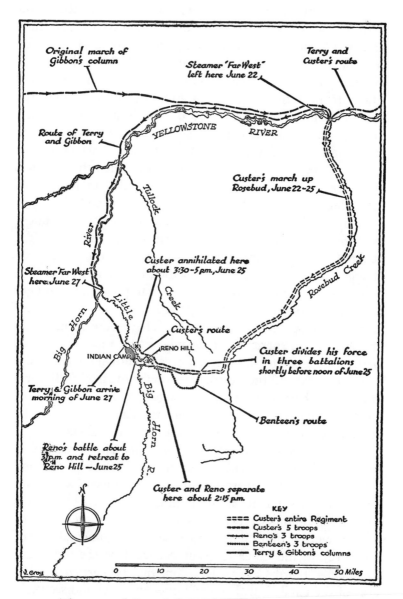

The route of Custer's forces from June 22 to June 25

I've been told that soon after the column started all the letters were gathered together by Captain Marsh, carefully put in a leather mail pouch. The pouch would be taken by a skiff to Fort Buford, at the mouth of the Yellowstone. Sergeant Fox, with twenty years' service behind him and about to be retired, agreed to attempt the dangerous trip, with two privates. The troops on the boat, and those left behind on the shore, cheered as the three soldiers stepped into the skiff and pushed it out into the swirling yellow current. They had gone a bare fifty feet when the boat was overturned. Before help of any kind could reach them all three men disappeared, along with the mail sack.

Captain Marsh sent boats as quickly as possible, but it was too late. The rescue skiffs returned to the *Far West*, secured boat hooks and quickly rowed back. For hours they dragged the river for the three bodies, but none were found. Strangely enough they did hook the mail pouch and brought it to the little steamer. Carefully the letters and official documents were spread out and dried. They were returned to the sack, and experienced men who knew the river and its perils were asked to volunteer. Three unknown heroes finally came forward and they were able to take the mail to Buford, and from there it eventually reached Bismarck and Fort Lincoln. Many of the letters were the last ones ever to be received by members of the families of the soldiers.

We marched off in columns of fours, and I recall that on a little rise of ground on the west, Generals Terry and Custer and Gibbon were seated on their horses, with their orderlies to their rear, as the regiment marched by. It was sort of an unofficial review. Custer's two sergeant color bearers were behind him; one carried the regimental flag of the Seventh; the other sergeant carried Custer's old battle flag of his Third Cavalry Division, that he carried the last year of the Civil War. I can still close my eyes and see those three Generals taking the review.

When the last troops had gone by, Custer said good-by

to Terry and Gibbon and with his adjutant and his two color bearers and bugler, galloped the full length of the regiment, and took his place at the head of the long column. He made quite a figure, even if he wasn't wearing his yellow curls. He had plenty of dash. And he was mighty proud of his regiment.

There has been so much controversy over whether or not Custer disobeyed the written orders that General Terry had given him that morning of June 22, that it might be well to quote here the exact orders:

> "Headquarters Dept. of Dakota,
> (in the Field)
> Camp of Mouth of Rosebud River
> Montana, June 22, 1876.

"Colonel: The brigadier general commanding directs that as soon as your regiment can be made ready for the march, you proceed up the Rosebud in pursuit of the Indians whose trail was discovered by Major Reno a few days since. It is, of course, impossible to give you any definite instructions in regard to this movement; and were it not impossible to do so the department commander places too much confidence in your zeal, energy and ability to wish to impose on you precise orders, which might hamper your action when nearly in contact with the enemy. He will, however, indicate to you his own views of what your action should be, and he desires that you should conform to them unless you shall see sufficient reason for departing from them. He thinks you should proceed up the Rosebud until you ascertain definitely the direction in which the trail above spoken of leads. Should it be found (as it appears to be almost certain it will be found) to turn towards the Little Horn, he thinks that you should still proceed on southward, perhaps as far as the headwaters of the Tongue, and then turn towards the Little Horn, feeling constantly, however, to your left, so as to preclude the possibility of the escape of the Indians to the south or southeast passing around your left flank.

"The column of Colonel Gibbon is now in motion for the mouth of the Big Horn. As soon as it reaches that point it will cross the Yellowstone and move up at least as far as the forks of the Little and Big Horns. Of course its future movements must be controlled by circumstances as they arise; but it is hoped that the Indians, if upon the Little Horn, may be so nearly enclosed by the two columns that their escape will be impossible. The department commander desires that on your way up the Rosebud you should thoroughly examine the upper part of Tullock's Creek; and that you should endeavor to send a scout through to Colonel Gibbon's command with information of the result of your examination. The lower part of this creek will be examined by a detachment from Colonel Gibbon's command.

"The supply steamer will be pushed up the Big Horn as far as the forks, if the river is found navigable for that distance; and the department commander (who will accompany the column of Colonel Gibbon) desires you to report to him there not later than the expiration of the time for which your troops are rationed, unless in the meantime you receive further orders.

> Very respectfully, your obedient
> servant, Ed. W. Smith
>
> Captain, Eighteenth Infantry, A.A.CC

Lieut. Col. G. A. Custer,
Seventh Cavalry"

—4—

That afternoon, of June 22, we rode some fourteen miles, and then made camp on the west bank of the Rosebud. The going had been fairly rough and we had some difficulty with our pack mules. All the mules were bunched together, with the rear-guard troops closing in behind them. When we'd break camp, each troop would have to pack its own mules. There was so much trouble with packs coming loose and holding up the outfit that General Custer put an officer in charge of the pack train. He had to put down on a list the order of the troops that had done the best job of packing. Then Custer assigned the next day's order of march according to that list. The troops that had done the worst job were in the rear and so had to eat the alkaline dust.

We hit the trail at 5 o'clock sharp that second morning.

Around noon we began to pass signs of big Indian camps. As I remember, we made around thirty-three miles that day. The next day we rode hard too. There was no foolishness. Custer had a bunch of Ree and Crow scouts ahead with him, and he kept them covering the ground far off both flanks of the column.

We were in Indian country now, right enough. There were all kinds of signs that hundreds of Indians had been here. I remember that in one single day we passed three big areas where hostile encampments had been made. There were dozens of wickiups. And in one place we halted there had been a sun-dance lodge. The scalp of a white man was still hanging from the ridge pole. They figured it was that of a man who had been with Gibbon's Montana column. I believe it was the third day out when we passed that sun-dance lodge.

On the third day, we made better than thirty miles and went into camp at sundown. In late June up here in this northwest country, that means around 9 o'clock.

We'd finished our supper and were just starting to rest when we got word that we'd start again. It hadn't been much of a supper. We were all fairly tired, men and horses alike, but we weren't anywheres near being worn out. Each of us had started with a twelve-pound bag of oats tied on to our saddles and we were almost to the end of them. But we'd let our horses graze as much as we could and with two

or three pounds of oats a day our mounts were doing fairly
well. Most of them were strong young cavalry horses.

It was dark as pitch when we started out again, around
11:30 that night. You couldn't see twenty feet ahead of you.
The best we could do was to follow along behind the troop
ahead, letting the rattle of the tin cups and carbines on the
saddles guide you. The dust was pretty heavy but it was
such a dark night that a little more or less trail dust didn't
make any difference.

I think we must have stumbled along in the dark for
around three hours, when a halt was ordered. None of us
had had much sleep for several days, so we were glad
to lie down and grab a little rest. When daylight came
around 3 o'clock we made coffee, but the water was so
alkaline we almost gagged on it.

It was around 8 o'clock when we got orders to saddle
up. We marched about ten miles, when we were halted
in a sort of ravine. We'd been told to make as little noise
as possible and light no fires. There'd been no bugle calls
for a day or two. The sun was at our back, so apparently
we were headed straight west now, towards the Little Big
Horn. I learned later that the Indians called it "Greasy
Grass." I never did know why.

We had hardly halted before General Custer rode off
with the Indian scouts and Charlie Reynolds and Lieutenant
Hare, who had charge of the Indians. I don't know just
what happened, but I've been told that the General made
his way to the highest point of land in the vicinity called
"Crow's Nest." There he tried to locate the big Indian
village that the scouts said was in the Little Horn Valley,
some twelve or fifteen miles on to the west. Just as dawn
was breaking they'd made out smoke from the village and
the dust from the pony herd. Those Indians could see better
with their naked eye at that time of morning than the officers
could in broad daylight with their high-powered field glasses.

Judging distances and objects in the high country is very tricky business.

About the time that General Custer came back from his scout, word went around that Indians had found a box of hard tack that had dropped from one of Captain Yates' mules. Two or three troopers who had been sent back to pick up the box had reported seeing two hostiles trying to open it, with their tomahawks. This meant that the Indians had us under observation.

Apparently Custer had figured on hiding the command in the ravine, during the day, and then attacking the big Indian village on the Little Big Horn at daybreak the next morning. That would have been the 26th and would have been just about the time that Gibbon's column with General Terry along, was supposed to hit the junction of the Big and Little Horns. Years later I read that order General Terry gave Custer just before we started up the Rosebud and it seems that the 26th was just about when it was calculated the two columns—Custer's and Gibbon's—could close in on the Indians.

But here it was Sunday morning, June 25. We were still more than twelve miles from the Little Horn and the Indian village, but the Indians knew where we were and all about us.

I remember that I was riding a horse called "Roman Nose," and while we were resting there in the wooded ravine waiting for orders, a man named McCurry came over to me and said he'd like to trade his horse for mine. His horse was called "Tip" and he told me that he was a little hard for him to handle and that he'd like to trade. I was proud of being a good rider in those days, and I figured I could ride anything you could put a saddle on. I suppose I was a little flattered by him wanting to trade his tough horse for my gentle one, so I told him it was all right with me if it was agreeable with Captain Benteen.

I went to look him up and get his permission, and I found him with General Custer and several of the officers at a conference. I approached as near as seemed respectful and while I was waiting to catch Benteen's attention, I couldn't help but overhear part of the conversation.

Charlie Reynolds, the famous white scout—who was never to see the sun set that day—was talking, and I heard him say that there was the biggest bunch of Indians he'd ever seen over there. Finally I heard Benteen say to Custer: "Hadn't we better keep the regiment together, General? If this is as big a camp as they say, we'll need every man we have."

Custer's only answer was: "You have your orders." I never did get to ask Benteen about that horse trade. So I rode old Roman Nose into the battle.

It was a little before noon when our troop was formed up. Captain Benteen had been the first commander to report to Custer that his troop was ready to march and so "H" company was given the post of honor at the head of the column.

Nobody was doing any talking when the word was passed to mount. Custer was ahead with those two flags of his. There was a little Italian trumpeter named Martini with him, along with Adjutant Cooke and the two sergeants. Martini belonged to "H" and he was a friend of mine. Trumpeters were mounted on white horses so they could be easily picked out, if they had to sound the "Rally!"

We were tired and dirty and hungry. Our horses hadn't had a drink of good water since the day before and we weren't much better off.

It'd be easy to say we were thinking only of glory on this hot June Sunday afternoon seventy years ago, but I reckon what most of the plain troopers were thinking about was how good a nice cold bottle of beer would taste right now.

We knew right enough that this was *the day*. This was

IT. This was what we had been training for and working for all these years.

Captain Benteen used to say: "The government pays you to get shot at."

And I suppose the dumbest, greenest trooper in the regiment figured that this day he'd get shot at plenty.

Chapter 6

Into the
Jaws of Death

*I*T was around noon on this fatal Sunday of June 25 when we crossed the divide between the Rosebud and the Little Big Horn. We were riding straight west, with the regiment in column of march, the troopers of each company riding four abreast. There was possibly fifty or sixty feet space between companies.

Suddenly the column halted, and pretty soon Lieutenant Cooke, who was the regimental adjutant, rode up and I heard him say to Benteen that he was to take his own company "H" and "D," under Captain Weir and Lieutenant Edgerly, and "K" under Lieutenant Godfrey, and bear off to the left and scout the hills that were pitching and bucking as far as you could see. He was to fight anything that he came across and if he saw no Indians on the first ridge he was to keep on going south and west.

I didn't know then but I found out later that General Custer kept troops "I," "F," "C," "E" and "L" under his own immediate command. He gave Major Reno a battalion consisting of troops "M," "A" and "G," with most of the Indian scouts under Lieutenants Varnum and Hare. Major Reno also had Charlie Reynolds, Herendon and the interpreter Frank Grouard. Captain McDougall with troop "B" had charge of the rear guard and pack escort. That last was under Lieutenant Mathey, and consisted of six men and a Corporal from each of the twelve troops. That meant that, along with the civilian packers, there were more than 130 armed men in the pack train.

Here was the Seventh Cavalry with a total of some 600 men, split up into four outfits. We were Indian hunting in a rolling, mountainous country, far removed from all civilization. We knew that twelve to fifteen miles west of us there was a considerable force of hostiles, but we had little accurate knowledge of how many warriors we would meet, or whether they would run or fight. Apparently the Indian scouts and experienced old guides knew that there were several thousand of the hostiles, but it is my belief that Custer and most of our officers thought they'd have to whip somewhere between a thousand and fifteen hundred. And they expected most of these to be poorly armed and poorly led. From experience they figured the Indians would fight only a rear-guard action, while the women, children, old men and pony herds got away. But in place of a maximum of 1,500 Indian warriors, it developed that there were possibly twice that number about to face Custer's total of 600— or five to one.

Apparently Custer had planned to stay in hiding in the ravine we had reached a little after ten o'clock that Sunday, and then attack the village at daybreak on the morning of the 26th. That would more or less have dove-tailed into Terry's idea of boxing the Indians. But when he found the hostile scouts had discovered his column, he figured there was nothing to do but attack at once before they could vamoose. And in justice to Custer I imagine that when he now sent Benteen and the three troops off to the hills on the southwest, it was sort of a half-hearted attempt to carry out Terry's orders to keep scouting on south of the Indian trail that led from the Rosebud westward to the Little Horn.

Anyway, Benteen and his trumpeter led off on the left-oblique with our three troops. Pretty soon Benteen called

Lieutenant Gibson, who was in temporary charge of my own troop, "H," and told him to take a man or two and scout on ahead. Benteen was riding maybe a hundred yards or so in front of the battalion, while Lieutenant Gibson now rode a quarter mile or so on ahead of him.

It was rough, rolling country we were going over, and it was hard on the horses. Lieutenant Gibson kept signaling back from each successive hilltop that he could see no signs of Indians. Even to the troopers in the ranks, it looked as if we were on a wild-goose chase. And it wasn't long before we were bearing off to our right, towards the trail Custer and Reno had followed in their march westward towards the Little Big Horn.

I suppose we must have been going up and down those rugged hills for the best part of two hours before we turned back on the Custer trail. I think we covered somewhere around seven or eight miles. That doesn't sound very much, until you take into consideration how hard-going it was. I know we were all glad to hit that little valley again.

We must have gone two or three miles along the well-marked trail (shod cavalry horses, you know, cut up the grass so a half-blind man could follow them) when we came to the headwaters of the little stream that flowed on west. Like most places of this nature, it was a sort of morass, and we pulled up and let our horses water in small groups. They hadn't had a drink since late on the previous afternoon. This took a few minutes: then we went on down the tiny creek towards the west. I recall we saw the lead pack mules breaking for the morass just as we were pulling out. Two or three of them got out of control, and were so greedy for water they got stuck in the bog. It showed how slow the pack train was, for here we'd been on this miserable scout over in the hills to the south for a couple of hours and yet we were still ahead of the packs when we reached this spot on the Custer-Reno trail. It's only fair to explain that the mules were not regular pack mules, but animals that had been taken out of the wagon teams. Many of them had been poorly packed, and they had sore backs and were pretty tired. They had gone close to twenty-four hours without water.

About the time we were leaving the water hole we began to hear firing way on ahead. Captain Weir lead off his company, although he was second in line of march. But Benteen was at least a hundred yards in advance of him. We all knew we'd be in a fight before long.

Shortly after leaving the morass we passed a burning tepee. We figured it had been set on fire by our Indian scouts who were riding with either Custer or Reno. We were trotting briskly now, and there was a good deal of excitement. Horses seem to know when they're heading into trouble the same as men do and some of the mounts were anxious to run away, tired as they were.

I figure it was about this time that we saw a trooper coming towards us at the fast trot. I recognized him as Sergeant Kanipe of Tom Custer's "C" troop. He had an order from General Custer for Captain McDougall to hurry across country and bring on the pack mules as fast as he could. He told Benteen what his orders were and the Captain motioned him back down the trail to where the pack train could be found. As Sergeant Kanipe trotted by us, he waved and shouted something about having the Indians on the run.

Sergeant Daniel A. Kanipe was born April 15, 1853, at Marion, N. C., and enlisted in Troop C, Seventh U. S. Cavalry, August 7, 1872. He had barely turned twenty-three at the time of the battle. In Kanipe's own account of the fight, published in the magazine of the *Historical Society* of Montana, he says:

"Reno and his men went at a swift gallop down Mud Creek across the Little Big Horn River and down the valley toward the south end of the Indian camp. General Custer followed the same route that Reno took, for a short distance, then turned squarely to the right charging up the bluffs on the banks of the Little Big Horn, where he saw a number of Indians. . . .

"When we reached the top of the bluffs the Indians had disappeared, but we were in plain view of the Indian camps, which appeared to cover a space of about two miles wide and four miles long on the west side of the river. We were then charging at full speed.

"Reno and his troops were again seen to our left, moving at full speed down the valley. At sight of the Indian camps, the boys of our five troops began to cheer. Some of the horses became so excited that their riders were unable to hold them in ranks, and the last words I heard General Custer say were, 'Hold your horses in, boys, there are plenty of them down there for us all.'

"Custer and his troops were within about one-half mile of the east side of the Indian camps when I received the following message from Captain Thomas Custer, brother of the General:—'Go to Captain McDougall. Tell him to bring pack train straight across the country. If any packs come loose, cut them and come on quick—a big Indian camp. If you see Captain Benteen, tell him to come quick—a big Indian camp.'

"On my route back to Captain McDougall I saw Captain Benteen about half way between where I left General Custer and the pack train. He and his men were watering their horses when first seen. Captain McDougall and the pack train were found about four miles from the Indian camp. The pack train went directly to the bluff where I left Custer's five troops. When we reached there we found Reno with a remnant of his three troops and Benteen with his three troops."

—2—

We hadn't gone on very much farther before we saw

a second figure in uniform riding towards us. He was Trumpeter Martini of my company, who had been assigned that morning as special orderly trumpeter to General Custer. I learned afterwards that he had a message from Custer to Benteen, that had been scribbled out on a field order pad and signed by Lieutenant Cooke the Adjutant. It read: "Benteen, come on. Big village. Be quick. Bring packs. P. S. Bring pack, W. W. Cooke."

Martini was a salty little Italian who had been a drummer boy with Garibaldi in the fight for Italian independence. Captain Keogh, an Irishman commanding Troop "I," who was riding this day with Custer, had also fought with Garibaldi.

I knew Martini very well because he belonged to "H." We used to tease him a lot but we never did after this fight. He proved that he was plenty man. His horse was spouting blood from a bullet wound in his right hip but Martini didn't know anything about it. Benteen ordered him to rejoin his company. I always figured that Benteen thought that since Sergeant Kanipe had already taken word back to Captain McDougall to bring on the pack train as fast as they could come, there was no use sending more word to him. Anyway, Martini's horse was played out and it was all that he could do to keep up with us.

Early in 1922, Lieutenant Colonel W. A. Graham, at that time collecting data for his study of the Battle of the Little Big Horn, located the Italian-born Martini in Brooklyn, and from the retired trooper obtained his full story. It was published in the U. S. *Cavalry Journal* in June, 1923, and since it is an important link in the tragic chain of events most of it is reprinted here:

"A little before 8 o'clock on the morning of June 25, my captain, Benteen, called me to him and ordered me to report to General Custer as orderly trumpeter. The regiment was then several miles from the Divide between the Rosebud and the Little Big Horn. We had halted there to make coffee after a night march.

"We knew, of course, that plenty of Indians were somewhere near, because we had been going through deserted villages for two days and following a heavy trail from the Rosebud, and on the 24th we had found carcasses of dead buffalo that had been killed and skinned only a short time before.

"I reported to the General personally, and he just looked at me and nodded. He was talking to an Indian scout, called Bloody Knife, when I reported, and Bloody Knife was telling him about a big village in the valley, several hundred tepees and about five thousand Sioux. I sat down a little way off and heard the talk. I couldn't understand what the Indian said, but from what the General said in asking questions and his conversation with the interpreter I understood what it was about.

"The General was dressed that morning in a blue-gray flannel shirt, buckskin trousers and long boots. He wore a regular company hat. His yellow hair was cut short; not very short—but it was not long and curly on his shoulders like it used to be.

"Very soon the General jumped on his horse and rode bareback around the camp, talking to the officers in low tones and telling them what he wanted them to do. By 8:30 the command was ready to march and the scouts went on ahead. We followed slowly, about fifteen minutes later. I rode about two yards back of the General. We moved on at a walk until about two hours later we came to a deep ravine, where we halted. The General left us there and went away with the scouts. I didn't go with him but stayed with the Adjutant. This was when he went up to the 'Crow's Nest' on the Divide, to look for the Sioux village that Bloody Knife had told him about. He was gone a long time and when he came back they told him about finding fresh pony tracks close by and that the Sioux had discovered us in the ravine. At once he ordered me to sound officers' call and I did so. This showed that he realized now that we could not surprise the Sioux, and so there was no use to keep quiet any longer. For two days before this there had been no trumpet calls and every precaution had been taken to conceal our march. But now all was changed.

"The officers came quickly and they had an earnest conference with the General. None of the men were allowed to come near them, but soon they separated and went back to their companies.

"Then we moved on again, and after a while, about noon, crossed the Divide. Pretty soon the General said something to the Adjutant that I could not hear, and pointed off to the left. In a few minutes Captain Benteen, with three troops, left the column and rode off in the direction that the General had pointed. I wondered where they were going because my troop was one of them.

"The rest of the regiment rode on, in two columns—Colonel Reno, with three troops, on the left, and the other five troops, under General Custer, on the right. I was riding right behind the General. We followed the course of a little stream that led in the direction of the Little Big Horn River. Reno was on the left bank and we on the right.

"All the time, as we rode, scouts were riding in and out, and the General would listen to them and sometimes gallop away a short distance to look around. Sometimes Reno's column was several hundred yards away and sometimes it was close to us, and then the General had motioned with his hat and they crossed over to where we were.

"Soon we came to an old tepee that had a dead warrior in it. It was burning. The Indian scouts had set it afire. Just a little off from that there was a little hill, from which Girard, one of the scouts, saw some Indians between us and the river. He called to the General and pointed them out. He said they were running away. The General ordered the Indian scouts to follow them but they refused to go. Then the General motioned to Colonel Reno, and when he rode up the General told the Adjutant to order him to go down and cross the river and attack the Indian village, and that he would support him with the whole regiment. He said he would go down to the other end and drive them, and that he would have Benteen hurry up and attack them in the center.

"Reno, with his three troops, left at once on a trot, going toward the river, and we followed for a few hundred yards and then swung to the right, down the river.

"We went at a gallop, too. (Just stopped once to water the horses.) The General seemed to be in a big hurry. After we had gone about a mile or two we came to a big hill that overlooked the valley and we rode around the base of it and halted. Then the General took me with him and we rode to the top of the hill, where we could see the village in the valley on the other side of the river. It was a big village, but we couldn't see it all from there, though we didn't know it then; but several hundred tepees were in plain sight.

"There were no bucks to be seen; all we could see was some squaws and children playing and a few dogs and ponies. The General seemed both surprised and glad, and said the Indians must be in their tents, asleep.

"We did not see anything of Reno's column when we were up on the hill. I am sure the General did not see them at all, because he looked all around with his glasses, and all he said was that we had 'got them this time.'

"He turned in the saddle and took off his hat and waved it so the men of the command, who were halted at the base of the hill, could see him and he shouted to them, 'Hurrah, boys, we've got them! We'll finish them up and then go home to our station.'

"Then the General and I rode back down to where the troops were, and he talked a minute with the Adjutant, telling him what he had seen. We rode on, pretty fast, until we came to a big ravine that led in the direction of the river, and the General pointed down there and then called me. This was about a mile down the river from where we went up on the hill, and we had been going at a trot and gallop all the way. It must have been about three miles from where we left Reno's trail.

"The General said to me, 'Orderly, I want you to take a message to Colonel Benteen. Ride as fast as you can and tell him to hurry. Tell him it's a big village and I want him to be quick, and to bring the ammunition packs.' He didn't stop at all when he was telling me this and I just said, 'Yes sir,' and checked my horse, when the Adjutant said, 'Wait, orderly, I'll give you a message,' and he stopped and wrote it in a big hurry, in a little book, and then tore out the leaf and gave it to me.

"And then he told me, 'Now, orderly, ride as fast as you can to Colonel Benteen. Take the same trail we came down. If you have time and there is no danger, come back; but otherwise stay with your company.'

"My horse was pretty tired, but I started back as fast as I could go. The last I saw of the command they were going down into the ravine. The gray horse troop was in the center and they were galloping.

"The Adjutant had told me to follow our trail back, and so in a few minutes I was back on the same hill again where the General and I had looked at the village; but before I got there I heard firing back of me and I looked around and saw Indians, some waving buffalo robes and some shooting. They had been in ambush.

"Just before I got to the hill I met Boston Custer. He was riding at a run, but when he saw me he checked his horse and shouted, 'Where's the General?' and I answered, pointing back of me, 'Right behind that next ridge you'll find him.' And he dashed on. That was the last time he was ever seen alive.

"When I got up on the hill, I looked down and there I saw Reno's battalion in action. It had not been more than ten or fifteen minutes since the General and I were on the hill, and then we had seen no Indians. But now there were lots of them, riding around and shooting at Reno's men, who were dismounted and in skirmish line. I don't know how many Indians there were—a lot of them. I did not have time to stop and watch the fight; I had to get on to Colonel Benteen; but the last I saw of Reno's men they were fighting in the valley and the line was falling back.

"Some Indians saw me because right away they commenced shooting at me. Several shots were fired at me— four or five, I think—but I was lucky and did not get hit. My horse was struck in the hip, though I did not know it until later.

"It was a very warm day and my horse was hot, and I kept on as fast as I could go. I didn't know where Colonel Benteen was, nor where to look for him, but I knew I had to find him.

"I followed our trail back to the place we had watered our horses and looked all around for Colonel Benteen. Pretty soon I saw his command coming. I was riding at a jog trot then. My horse was all in and I was looking everywhere for Colonel Benteen.

"As soon as I saw them coming I waved my hat to them and spurred my horse, but he couldn't go any faster. But it was only a few hundred yards before I met Colonel Benteen. He was riding quite a distance in front of his troops, with his orderly trumpeter, at a fast trot. The nearest officer to him was Captain Weir, who was at the head of his troop, about two or three hundred yards back.

"I saluted and handed the message to Colonel Benteen and then I told him what the General said—that it was a big village and to hurry. He said, 'Where's the General now?' and I answered that the Indians we saw were running and I supposed that by this time he had charged through the village. I was going to tell him about Major Reno being in action too, but he didn't give me the chance. He said, 'What's the matter with your horse?' and I said, 'He's just tired out, I guess.' The Colonel said, 'Tired out? Look at his hip,' and then I saw the blood from the wound. Colonel Benteen said, 'You're lucky it was the horse and not you.' By this time Captain Weir had come up to us and Colonel Benteen handed the message to him to read and told me to join my company.

"He didn't give me any order to Captain McDougall, who was in command of the rear guard, or to Lieutenant Mathey, who had the packs. I told them so at Chicago in 1879 when they had the court of inquiry, but I didn't speak English so good then, and they misunderstood me and made the report of my testimony show that I took an order to Captain McDougall. But that is a mistake.

"They gave me another horse and I joined my troop and rode on with them. The pack train was not very far behind them. It was in sight, maybe a mile away and the mules were coming along, some of them walking, some trotting, and others running. We moved on faster than the packs could go, and soon they were out of sight, except that we could see their dust."

—3—

But to get back to where I left off.

We could hear heavy firing now. Before long we passed several Crow or Ree scouts, driving a few head of Indian ponies, and they shouted "Soldiers," and pointed towards the bluffs that were rising towards the north. We knew that we were close to the valley of the Little Big Horn, and that somewhere in this neighborhood there was hard fighting going on.

Benteen ordered us to draw pistols and we charged up the bluffs at a gallop, expecting at any moment to run into hostiles. When we reached the brow of the first set of rolling hills the river valley suddenly opened up below us to our left. It was a sight to strike terror in the hearts of the bravest men. Down there in the valley maybe 150 feet or more below us, and somewhere around a half mile away, there were figures galloping on horseback, and much shooting. Farther down the river there were great masses of mounted men we suspicioned were Indians. We were going at a fast clip ourselves, and we had no more than caught swift glimpses of this tragic battlefield below, when we saw mounted and dismounted soldiers on the knoll of a hill on to the northward. We rode swiftly towards them.

—4—

I think I'd better stop long enough right here to tell what happened to our comrades with Reno. Remember it was around 12:15 noon when Reno was given his three troops and seventeen Crow and Ree scouts and three white scouts. Custer, with his five troops, led off in column on the right, while Reno was on his left. Benteen, with his three troops, had been told to go "valley hunting" in the rough hills over to the south and west. Of course being with Benteen I didn't see anything that happened to either Custer or Reno during the next five hours, but I've heard the story, or stories, so many hundreds of times that I'm going to try to tell it the simplest way I can. But I want it understood that I was not along and that I'm repeating what survivors told me.

When the two battalions started moving down the dry creek bottom towards the valley of the Little Big Horn they would at times be within fifty yards of one another; at other times they might be two hundred yards apart. They were both trotting westward towards the Little Big Horn. . . .

It was about 2 o'clock when the two columns reached a burning tepee, containing the body of the Indian warrior who had been killed exactly one week before in General Crook's disastrous battle with the Indians, less than twenty miles away. One of the white scouts riding ahead shouted back to Custer that a number of hostiles were just ahead of him. They were making no effort to fight but were keeping well out of rifle range.

Custer now motioned Major Reno to cross the little creek they were riding down, and the General instructed his adjutant Cooke to order Reno to cross the Little Big Horn two miles farther on west, and then, swinging to his right, charge the Indian village, and that the whole outfit would support him. That last phrase has been one of the most gnawed-over bones of contention of all the disputed points of the tragedy that was about to happen. . . .

Reno led his little group of 120 men and the handful of guides and scouts at a fast trot, crossed the Little Big Horn ford, delaying only long enough to water his thirsty horses and reform in troop formation on the west side of the river. This west side was a fairly flat valley, possibly a half mile to a mile wide, that led to a low plateau on to the west. On the opposite or east side of the Little Big Horn rose a range of hills one hundred and fifty or more feet high, forming the so-called Wolf Mountains.

At several places in these steep cliffs coulees ran down to the river bottom from the bluffs above. The river was, at this time of the year, from a hundred to a hundred and fifty feet wide, running clear and cold, with a gravelly bottom. For almost three miles on the west bank of the river were pitched the various Indian camps. They were strung out and each of the five tribes of the Sioux or Dakotas, the Cheyennes, and small bands of Blackfeet and Arapahoes were camped in their own circles, with possibly as much as a quarter mile separating them.

On to the west there were several immense pony herds, guarded by Indian boys and squaws. Altogether there may have been as many as one third of all the Sioux tribesmen here—possibly close to 10,000 out of 30,000. That would figure out somewhere between 2,000 to 3,000 warriors.

And this may be as good a time as any to clear up the popular misconception regarding the arms of the hostiles. It has been generally accepted that all the red warriors were armed with the latest model repeating Winchester rifles and that they had a plentiful supply of ammunition. For my part, I believe that fully half of all the warriors carried only bows and arrows and lances, and that possibly half of the remainder carried odds and ends of old muzzle-loaders and single-shot rifles of various vintages. Probably not more than 25 or 30 per cent of the warriors carried modern repeating rifles.

And one other point: Indian boys from fourteen years old up, accompanied the warriors and took part, especially in the latter stages of the fighting. The soldiers, incidentally, were armed with single-shot 45–70 caliber Springfield carbines, an accurate and deadly weapon up to 600 yards. But when fired rapidly the breech became foul and the greasy cartridges often jammed and could not be removed by the extractor. This meant that the empty shell had to be forced out by the blade of a hunting knife. This very fact was responsible for the death of many a trooper this hot Sunday, and may actually have been the indirect cause of the great disaster.

Each trooper also carried the latest model six-shot, single-action Colt army pistol. All the soldiers had been ordered to carry 100 rounds of rifle ammunition and twenty-four rounds of pistol ammunition, either on their person or in their saddlebags. As the troopers dismounted and each fourth man became a horse holder, many of the horse mounts were stampeded and thus thousands of rounds of much-needed ammunition were lost, especially to the men with Custer.

But to get back to Reno. He had crossed the river and had his troops in line in columns of fours, with the Indian

Frederic Remington's drawing for *Century Magazine,* showing each fourth trooper leading horses to safety when his comrades dismounted and fought on foot. This was done when Reno's men struck the Indian camp at the opening of the Battle.

Indian squaws hurriedly breaking camp. This famous picture by Frederic Remington, now in the Museum of Fine Art of Houston, Texas, depicts what undoubtedly happened on the early afternoon of June 26, 1876.

scouts on his left. Soon Indian horsemen were seen riding madly to and fro in the valley and shortly the southern end of the Indian camps came into view. Reno now had his three troops and scouts thrown out in skirmish line, covering possibly the full width of the narrow valley.

There was heavy but wild firing from the Indians ahead, who were being reinforced by hundreds of mounted hostiles. The horses of three of the troopers became unmanageable and dashed straight towards the Indian lines; two troopers, G. H. Meyer and Roman Rutten, managed to circle their horses and, although wounded, join their comrades. The third trooper, G. E. Smith, rode straight to his death.

Realizing that his charge towards the Indian hordes would end in almost certain disaster, Reno now ordered his troops to dismount and fight on foot. Even before this order came, scores of Indians had swung to the southwestward and pressed against the Crow and Ree scouts. These were forced to give way.

Things were looking bad for Reno, and he ordered his skirmish lines to fall back to the edge of a heavy grove of cottonwoods that followed a bend in the river, and jutted out halfway across the valley. The horses were led into the woods, while the thin line of men held three sides of the grove. Some ninety men were holding not less than 250 yards of line. Hundreds of mounted Indians were now half-circling the skirmish line, riding close in, firing from under their ponies' necks and then galloping away. Reno's men were now either firing from a prone position or were using the bank of a dry creek bed as a barricade and rifle rest.

In taking up this new position Sergeant O'Hara of Troop "M" had been killed—the first man on the skirmish line to die. Apparently Reno had a fairly defendable position and some people think that if he had pulled in his lines, and consolidated his position, he might have held out here for an indefinite length of time—or at least as long as his ammunition lasted. But the savage yells, the heavy firing, the smoke and dust and fear all combined to fog his judgment.

Suddenly Custer's favorite scout, Bloody Knife, was shot through the head and his brains scattered over Reno. Then the Negro scout Dorman fell, and soon Charlie Reynolds was shot through the head.

Reno, figuring that his only chance lay in getting to high ground across the river, shouted for his men to mount in company formation. Two troop commanders heard the order and amid confusion and excitement had their men mount and line up in column of fours.

The third troop, "G," under Lieutenant McIntosh, himself part Indian who had been adopted by General McIntosh, was in the woods and did not get the order until the two other troops, with Reno riding at their head, were racing up stream, trying to find a place to cross the river. All order and discipline were gone.

Lieutenant McIntosh, finally getting his troopers in some semblance of a column, pulled out from the woods, far behind the fleeing troops. In the mad rush nineteen men were left behind, including Lieutenant De Rudio and the white scout Herendon.

Nobody will ever know how any man escaped alive from this mad retreat. All we are sure of is that the charging troops broke through the cordon of mounted Indians, and followed a buffalo path to the river. Here they somehow managed to jump their horses over a four- or five-foot bank, plunge across the stream, and scramble up a narrow trail in the steep hills to the east.

Hundreds of Indians fired indiscriminately into the panic-stricken soldiers, and the wonder is that any troopers escaped. No motion picture could be as fantastic as this wild milling of frightened men and horses.

Young Lieutenant Benny Hodgson was shot through the upper leg and his horse killed under him as he jumped him off the west bank of the stream. Grabbing hold of a trooper's stirrup, he was dragged across the river and then cut down by a second bullet, just as he reached the safety of the east bank.

In all, twenty-six troopers and scouts and three officers were killed, either in this ride through the Indian gauntlet, or back at the edge of the woods. Of nineteen men left behind, seventeen crossed the river and reached Reno Hill on foot within two hours. Lieutenant De Rudio and Private O'Neill did not join us until thirty-six hours later. They came right through where I was on guard.

It was now somewhere around 3:30 in the afternoon.

Reno, shaken and unnerved, had reached the hilltop and here his frightened troopers were joining him. He was whipped and completely disorganized.

Remember, all this about Reno's fight in the Valley is what I've been told, because I saw none of it with my own eyes.

Chapter 7

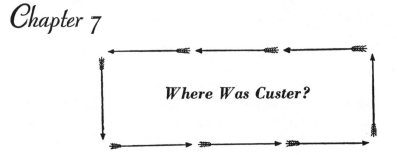

Where Was Custer?

I'LL never forget that first glimpse I had of the hilltop. Here were a little group of men in blue, forming a skirmish line, while their beaten comrades, disorganized and terror stricken, were making their way on foot and on horseback up the narrow coulee that led from the river, 150 feet below. We recognized Major Reno and Lieutenant Varnum. I believe both of them had lost their hats and now had handkerchiefs tied around their heads to protect them from the blazing Montana sun.

I saw Lieutenant Varnum reach up and shake hands with Lieutenant Godfrey of "K" troop, who was Varnum's regular company commander. And I heard him say something about a hard fight and that they'd got a damn good licking.

It's no use pretending that the men here on the hill, from Reno down, were not disorganized and downright frightened. They'd had a lot of men killed, and it had only been the grace of God, and the bad aim of the Indians, that had let them escape across the river with their lives.

But it wasn't at all certain that they could keep them now. For there were hundreds of Indians still down there in the valley, maybe a half mile from where we were standing. They were still firing at stragglers trying to cross the river and reach the little command here on the hilltop.

Cool, capable Benteen more or less assumed command. Major Reno had just come through a terrible experience, and at the moment was glad to have Benteen, his junior, take over.

Quickly Benteen dismounted his own three troops and ordered us to form a skirmish line. Reno's men had expended most of their ammunition so we were told to divide ours with them.

We had Benteen's 120 men intact and there were around sixty men who'd been in the valley fight with Reno. And even before we got the kinks out of our legs from our long hours in the saddle, we were asking one another, "Where's Custer?"

Officers and men alike were trying to solve the riddle. What had become of Custer and his five troops? We knew from Trumpeter Martini who'd come back with that last message for Benteen to hurry forward with the packs, that Custer had ridden northward over these rolling hills to the east of the Little Big Horn. Some of Reno's men told in excited tones how from the valley below they had seen Captain Yates' white horse troop on a bluff on our side of the river, maybe a mile or so down the river, to the north. Others said they had seen Custer and one or two men looking down from a hilltop. Trumpeter Martini figured it was maybe a mile on farther downstream, to the northward from our hill, to the spot where he'd been ordered to report to Benteen.

Apparently Custer was now much farther on to the northward and was this moment hotly engaged. But no one was certain. All we knew was that he had disappeared with almost half the regiment. And luckily for unhappy Reno, we had come up just in time to save him from what might have been complete destruction.

We could see the river valley down below from where we were spread out in a circular skirmish line here on Reno Hill. Some of the poor troopers were still being cut down by the swirling mass of Indians. There was shooting, and dust, and savage yells—then suddenly most of the Indians began galloping downstream. That's to the north, and before long we could hear heavy firing from down that way.

Reno and Benteen and two or three of the officers held a little conference, and we saw Lieutenant Hare, who had had charge of Reno's Indian scouts, suddenly mount Godfrey's horse and head back down our trail to the southward. Maybe it was fifteen or twenty minutes, or possibly a half hour, before he came up at a trot with several pack mules, loaded with ammunition boxes. The rest of the dozen ammunition mules slowly dribbled in, and before long the pack train itself came up. We now had 24,000 rounds of rifle ammunition, food and a new force of not less than 130 armed men.

Except for an odd hostile shot, fired from a distance, there was no firing near us now. The Indians apparently had left for the north. We could hear the sound of distant firing echoing down through the hills and valleys from that direction. Custer must be down there.

—2—

It was now maybe 4:30 and the sun was still fairly high in the sky. We troopers didn't know what was going on, but I remember that Captain Weir suddenly rode off to the north alone, and a minute later, Lieutenant Edgerly, second in command of "D," followed with the whole troop. The pack mules were coming up about this time and there was a lot of speculating going on. As I recall, Reno had seven wounded men, some of them in pretty bad shape. But altogether he now had around 310 effective, which was a little more than half the total number in the regiment. Custer had around 220 men with him.

It's pretty hard to estimate time under such circumstances, but as I've tried to reconstruct the situation over the years, I believe it must have been around 5 o'clock when Reno and Benteen ordered the whole outfit to move northward, in the general direction Captain Weir and his troop "D" had taken a good half hour before. The wounded men who could mount were put on horses, but the others were carried in blankets by details of six troopers on foot. It was slow and painful work, and I've always figured that most of the officers thought it was a questionable move.

We'd gone less than a mile when we got in sight of Weir's troop. Way off to the north you could see what looked to be groups of mounted Indians. There was plenty of firing going on.

Pretty soon it looked as if the Indian masses were coming towards us. It didn't take long to realize that this was true. Here we were stretched out all over the hell's half acre, a troop on this hill knob, another in this little valley and over there a third troop. Behind, at a slow walk, came the pack trains, the wounded men and the rear guard.

Reno and Benteen both sensed the danger and ordered a withdrawal. The advance troops were dismounted and fought as skirmishers. Soon the Indians were pressing hard, and it was only good luck and the hard courage of Lieutenant Godfrey's troop, fighting stubbornly on foot, that kept disaster from overtaking us. We were able to regain Reno's Hill while Troop "K" kept back the Indians until the men, retreating slowly, got close enough to the hilltop to make a dash for it.

It was now possibly 6:30 in the afternoon, with three hours of daylight still to go. Hurriedly Reno, with Benteen helping him with advice and suggestions, posted his forces for the coming attack. In the center in a slight depression the horses and mules were staked out, and an inadequate little field hospital was established. But it was impossible to shield the men and stock from the Indians firing from a hilltop off to the east. Animal after animal was killed, and men

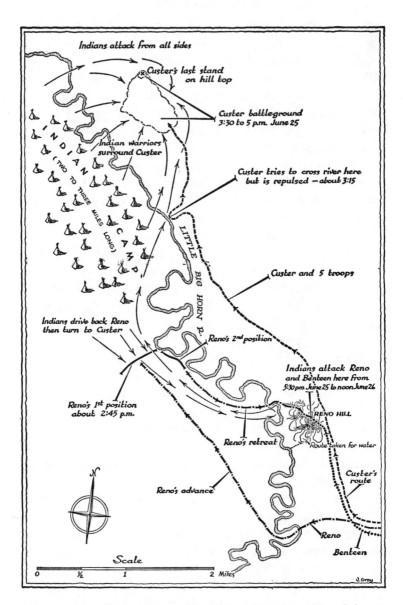

The route of Custer's five troops and of Reno's retreat, and the
hilltop where death overtook Custer

were hit. It was tough not to be able to do something about it.

My own Troop "H" was posted to the south, in a dangerous position, bordering the river. There was higher ground behind us and we were as helpless as the animals and wounded men to protect ourselves from fire. But we were not yet fully aware of our peril as we hurriedly piled up such inadequate barricades as we could find. We used pack saddles, boxes of hard tack, and bacon, anything we could lay our hands on. For the most part it wasn't any real protection at all, but it made you feel a lot safer.

We'd hardly got settled down on our skirmish line, with "H" men posted at twenty-feet intervals, when the Indians had us all but completely surrounded, and the fighting began in earnest. There was no full-fledged charge, but little groups of Indians would creep up as close as they could get, and from behind bushes or little knolls open fire. They'd practice all kinds of cute tricks to draw our fire. Maybe a naked redskin would suddenly jump to his feet, and while you drew a bead on him he'd throw himself to the ground. Then they'd show a blanket or a headdress and we'd blaze away, until we learned better.

I always figured if the Indians had used their heads and made a charge on us from all directions at the same time, they could have swept over us. But they didn't. An Indian's way of fighting was to follow his own devices. If he could "count coup" on an enemy with his long "coup stick" he was even prouder than if he killed a man. One Indian ran in close to our lines to touch one of our dead men with his "coup stick," and we filled him full of lead before he could get away. At that time the Indians were pressing "H" hard, and we were in grave danger of being overrun.

—3—

The sun went down that night like a ball of fire. Pretty

soon the quick Montana twilight settled down on us, and then came the chill of the high plains. There was no moon, and no one ever welcomed darkness more than we did.

The firing had gradually died out. Now and again you'd hear the ping of a rifle bullet, but by 10 o'clock even that had stopped. But welcome as the darkness was, it brought a penetrating feeling of fear and uncertainty of what tomorrow might bring. We felt terribly alone on that dangerous hilltop. We were a million miles from nowhere. And death was all around us.

Across the river and down below in the valley of the Little Horn, where so many of our men lay dead, we could see great fires and hear the steady rhythm of Indian tomtoms beating for their wild victory dances. The Indians apparently must have had great success everywhere this Sabbath day. But now and again you'd hear what sounded like the high-pitched wailing of the squaws, crying to the Great Spirits for their departed dead.

All through the short, black night the orgy went on down below in the river valley. It struck fear in our hearts, just as the mystery of Custer's disappearance made our blood run cold each time we tried to solve it. Where was Custer? What had happened to him?

Surely he must have met with some sort of defeat and then had ridden on downstream towards the junction of the Little and the Big Horn. Gibbon's column, with General Terry, would be arriving there soon.

Had Custer reached there, with such of his five troops as had escaped the fighting that had occurred three miles on to the north from where we were lying?

They could not all be killed. Not Lucky Custer, and those five gallant troops who rode with him.

Why had he abandoned us? In those three bloody hours before darkness had saved us, we had had no less than a dozen men killed and three times that number wounded.

You could hear them crying out for water all through

the short night. It would be death to try to reach the river, even in the covering darkness. We had been busy too, digging shallow holes with our mess kits, our steel knives and forks and with our fingers. We would not have to face the daylight without at least some little protection. It was pitifully inadequate but it was something.

Off to the east pink and yellow light began to show. Dawn was breaking.

Two shots sounded from the hilltop behind us. Soon there was firing all around.

—4—

It had rained a little during the night and some of us had taken our overcoats from the cantles of our McClelland saddles and put them on. It was cold here on this bleak hilltop, too, and those old army bluecoats felt good.

My buddy, a young fellow named Jones, who hailed from Milwaukee, was lying alongside of me. Together we had scooped out a wide shallow trench and piled up the dirt to make a little breastwork in front of us. It was plumb light now and sharpshooters on the knob of a hill south of us and maybe a thousand yards away, were taking pot shots at us.

Jones said something about taking off his overcoat, and he started to roll on his side so that he could get his arms and shoulders out, without exposing himself to fire. Suddenly I heard him cry out. He had been shot straight through the heart.

The lead kept spitting around where I lay. Up on the hilltop I could see a figure firing at me from a prone position. Looked like he was resting his long-range rifle on a bleached buffalo head. I tried my best to reach him with my Springfield carbine but it simply wouldn't carry that far.

A few minutes after Jones was killed, a bullet ricocheted from the hard ground and tore into my clothing. About this time the surgeon came up and took a look at Jones. He asked me if I wasn't wounded. I said no, that I was all right. "Put your hand inside your shirt," he ordered. I did, and when I pulled it out it was bloody. That ricocheted bullet had given me a slight flesh wound. The surgeon wanted to bind it up but I told him there were plenty of badly wounded men to take care of.

A minute or two later another bullet from the hilltop tore into the hickory butt of my rifle, splitting it squarely in two. I was plenty mad because my army carbine wouldn't let me return the compliment. Somehow I always figured that the sharpshooter who had killed Jones, hit me and split my rifle butt, must have been either a renegade white man, or a squaw man of some kind or another. He could shoot too well to have been a full-blood Indian.

Along about this time our thirty or forty wounded men began crying out again for water. "H" troop held the hill here on the southwest. There was a draw that ran down the west side of the hill to the river. It was rough and exposed and it looked like a dead cinch that any one who tried to work his way down that draw to the river would be killed. Indians concealed in bushes across the river were firing up at us, and they had every foot of this draw and the river bank covered. But we had to do something for those men who were wounded and crying for water.

Finally Captain Benteen called for volunteers. I think there were seventeen of us altogether who stepped forward. He detailed four of us from "H" who were extra good marksmen to take up an exposed position on the brow of the hill, facing the river. We were to stand up and not only draw the fire of the Indians below, but we were to pump as much lead as we could into the bushes where the Indians were hiding, while the water party hurried down to the draw, got their buckets and pots and canteens filled, and then made their way back. It just happened that the four of us who were posted on the hill were all German boys: Geiger,

Meckling, Voit and myself. None of us four were wounded, although we stood exposed on that ridge for more than twenty minutes, and they threw plenty of lead at us. Several of the water party, however, were badly wounded, although we kept up a steady fire into the bushes where the Indians were hiding. Each of us was given a Congressional Medal of Honor.

But lots of times the men who most deserve the medals don't get them, because no officer happened to see their deed of valor or, if he did see it, failed to turn in a recommendation for a decoration. Fact is that many men that day deserved the highest of decorations for their bravery. There was Sergeant Paul, for instance, who led the charge we made a little later. And there were "Crazy Jim" Seivers and Dan Newell, and Slaper and others. I got more than my share of credit that day. After we'd got the water up for the wounded, Benteen told me he was making me a Sergeant—promoting me on the field of battle. I was always proud of that.

Speaking about that charge we made; sometime that morning the Indians were crowding us pretty hard. "H" was the most exposed of any of the troops, and it looked as if the hostiles were massing for a sudden charge. Benteen had been walking up and down the line urging the men to hold fast, not to waste their fire, and to keep cool.

I remember saying to him: "Colonel, you better get down, sir, or you'll get killed."

"Don't worry about me," he answered grimly. "I'm all right." He sure had a charmed life that day.

But things looked bad, and finally Benteen hurried to the north side of the lines and asked Major Reno for reinforcements. He made it clear that the Indians were about to charge his line, and that if they were able to sweep over it the whole outfit would be destroyed. Reno told him to take as much of "M" troop as he could gather. Those men certainly looked good to us.

Soon after they came up Captain Benteen led the charge.

Yelling and firing, we went at the "double quick" and the Indians broke and ran. When we had cleaned them out for a hundred yards ahead of us, we hustled back to our holes. Once again we settled back to the business of getting fired at, with men hit at intervals, and with the poor horses and mules taking a terrible beating in their hollow. It must have been along about this time that Benteen called me to attention and made me a Sergeant. We'd had one sergeant and two men killed and twelve wounded in "H" troop alone.

—5—

I suppose it was early in the afternoon when the firing seemed to quiet down. Now and again bullets would come tearing in, but gradually they became fewer and fewer. Then below across the Little Horn heavy smoke began drifting southward. Pretty soon it became clear that the Indians were firing the grass. That seemed odd, unless they were getting ready to leave.

The gunfire had almost ceased and some of us left our trenches and stood in little groups on the brow of the hill. Then something happened that I'll never forget, if I live to be a hundred. The heavy smoke seemed to lift for a few moments, and there in the valley below we caught glimpses of thousands of Indians on foot and horseback, with their pony herds and travois, dogs and pack animals, and all the trappings of a great camp, slowly moving southward. It was like some Biblical exodus; the Israelites moving into Egypt; a mighty tribe on the march.

We thought at first that it must be some trick: that the Indians were only removing their families from danger and that the warriors would soon return and try to overwhelm us. Patiently we waited in our little trenches. The long June afternoon dragged on. The firing had all but ceased. The smoke in the valley had blown away, and the last Indian had gone.

Where Was Custer?

While guards kept their posts, the rest of the men led such horses as were not killed down the steep draws to the river. It was the first drink they had had since early afternoon the day before. Gently we buried our dead in the shallow trenches we had dug for the living.

Then Reno ordered the whole camp to move as close to the river as possible. We would get as far away as we could from the terrible stench.

There was plenty of water now for the wounded. And towards evening the company cooks made us the best meal they could. At least we had hot coffee and plenty of bacon and soaked hardtack. It was our first meal in thirty-six hours.

Then night came down. We were weary, but while those on guard were awake and alert, the rest of the command slept. But it was an uneasy sleep.

We still had heard no word from Custer. We began to suspicion that some terrible fate might have overtaken him. What it was we could only guess.

Chapter 8

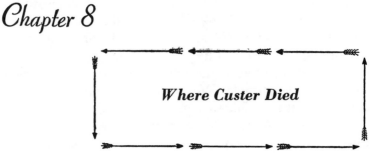

Where Custer Died

*T*HE sun was well in the sky that next morning of the 27th, when we saw dust rising slowly from down the valley to the northward. That surely would be our relief. Possibly Custer would be with Gibbon's men.

We watched two or three mounted men ride southward towards us, then cross the river and start up the coulee that Reno's men had scrambled up that wild afternoon of the 25th. Our buglers had blown calls to attract their attention when they had first come in sight. Soon they would be with us.

The officers gathered in a group and scores of the troopers stood to one side. A young officer flung himself off his horse. The whisper went around among us that he was Lieutenant Bradley, chief of scouts, of Gibbon's column. He asked for Lieutenant Godfrey, his old friend, and then quickly he told his story.

Early this morning, scouting in the hills on the east side of the Little Horn, Lieutenant Bradley had come across a battlefield dotted with the white bodies of dead men. He had counted more than 190 dead. He was certain Custer was among them. Apparently no white man had escaped. One or two Crow scouts, notably young Curley, had re-

ported at the steamer *Far West* at the junction of the Little
Horn and Big Horn the day before. There had been no
interpreter on hand, but Curley had convinced the officers
that all the white soldiers who rode with Custer had been
killed.

At dawn Lieutenant Bradley and a few men had started
out to search for the field of the tragedy. Curley was right.
No soldier or white men had escaped.

A little later the slight figure of bearded General Terry,
with his staff and a small escort, arrived on the hill.

There were tears running down his cheeks when he
spoke. I think most of us had tears in our eyes, too. More
than 200 of our comrades had met violent death, and now,
naked and unburied, were lying in the hot Montana sun
three miles to the northward.

Reno ordered Benteen to take a few officers and fourteen
troopers of "H" and ride to the battlefield. I was one of
those troopers. Captain Weir and Lieutenants Varnum and
Edgerly rode with us. We trotted quietly up and down the
folding hills to the northward.

We were all thinking of how Custer and his five troops
must have ridden close to where we were riding now; how
he must have scouted to the brow of the hills here, and
swiftly viewed the great camp below; how he had first sent
back Sergeant Kanipe with an order for Captain McDougall
of the rear guard to hurry across country with the train,
cutting loose any packs that came undone; how a little
farther on, when he began to realize the overpowering number of Indians he would have to fight, he had sent Orderly
Trumpeter Martini with the note to Benteen to "Hurry.
Big Village. Bring packs"; how he had ridden straight north
probably trying to find a trail that could lead him off to
the left down to the river, so that he could cross and pitch
into the village. We passed that coulee now, and since Custer
had not crossed the river here, it was clear that he probably
had run into an ambush of Indians and been forced on to

the northward. We could understand now why the hundreds of Indians left in the valley after they had routed Reno had suddenly ridden northward. They had been told of Custer's approach across the river.

Suddenly we caught glimpses of white objects lying along a ridge that led northward. We pulled up our horses. This was the battlefield. Here Custer's luck had finally run out.

From the way the men lay, it was clear that first one troop had been ordered to dismount and fight as a skirmish line. Then a second troop had been posted a little farther on and to the east. Then a third and fourth troop. And finally there on the knob of the hill lay some thirty bodies in a small circle. We knew instinctively that we would find Custer there.

We rode forward at a walk. Most of the troopers had been stripped of clothing and scalped. Some of them had been horribly mutilated.

Custer was lying a trifle to the southeast of the top of the knoll—where the monument is today. I stood six feet away holding Captain Benteen's horse while he identified the General. His body had not been touched, save for a single bullet hole in the left temple near the ear, and a hole on his left breast. He looked almost as if he had been peacefully sleeping. His brother Tom lay a few feet away. He was terribly mutilated.

Scattered over the field were the swollen bodies of dead horses. But there were not many of them. It seemed clear that the Indians, sweeping up the draws and coulees on all sides, had stampeded the mounts while the men were fighting dismounted. From every direction hordes of crazed Indians must have attacked with the wild courage that their desperation and hate gave them. Nothing could check their mad charges.

Captain Benteen found a bit of wood, hollowed out a hole, found an empty shell, wrote Custer's name on a bit

CUSTER'S DEATH.

The Herald's Special Report from the Field of Battle.

MARCH OF THE CO-OPERATING COLUMN.

Graphic Picture of the Arrival at the Scene of Disaster.

RESCUE OF RENO'S COMMAND

Where the Yellow-Haired Leader Lay in the Embrace of Death.

FRIENDS AND COMRADES AROUND HIM

The Savages Respect the Body of Him They Knew So Well.

THE DEAD CORRESPONDENT.

Reno's Desperate Fight Against Overwhelming Odds.

Words That Shall Go Sounding Down Through Ages.

On Fame's eternal camping ground
Their silent tents are spread;
And glory guards with solemn round
The bivouac of the dead.

CUSTER'S BATTLE FIELD, LITTLE HORN, June 25.}
Via Bismarck, D. T., July 6, 1876.}

Couriers are about to leave with General Terry's despatches, and I take advantage of the opportunity to send a hasty and necessarily imperfect account of the battle. I write from the scene of Custer's magnificent but terribly fatal charge, from a plateau on which, but a few hours since, I saw at a glance 316 heroic soldiers of the Seventh United States cavalry lying where they fell as the hands of savage foe, cold and dead. Near the top of a little knoll in the centre of this plateau lay Custer himself; and it touched my heart to see that the savages, in a kind of human recognition of heroic clay, had respected the corpse of the man they knew so well. Other bodies were mutilated; Custer's was untouched—a tribute of respect from such an enemy more real than a title of nobility. He lay as if asleep, his face calm and a smile on his lips. Near him were eleven dead officers. Captain Miles Keogh was on his right, and his brother, Captain Thomas Custer, on his left. Almost at Custer's feet lay a fair, beautiful boy of nineteen. He was young Reed, Custer's nephew. He was visiting the General at the time he was ordered on this expedition, and insisted upon coming with him. In the field, a little way off, lay Boston Custer, another of the General's brothers. Within a few feet of each other the three brothers had fallen, and on the skirmish line was the body of Lieutenant Calhoun, the husband of Custer's sister. Mrs. Calhoun lost here a husband, three brothers and a nephew. Kellogg, the special correspondent of the NEW YORK HERALD, was found on the skirmish line, near to Calhoun. Upon this scene of action, made memorable by such sacrifice, one column, commanded by General Gibbon, came just in time to rescue Colonel Reno, menaced with the fate that had more rapidly overtaken Custer. Assailed in some poor entrenchments by 4,000 Sioux, excited by the blood of Custer's men, Reno and what remained of the gallant Seventh cavalry must have fallen as their comrades did had not the appearance of General Gibbon's column at the mouth of the Little Horn alarmed the enemy and caused their precipitate retreat.

GIBBON'S MARCH.

In order to keep clear the story of these events I must recur to the movements of the column with which it was my duty to march. I will first recite the circumstances which led immediately to its march hither.

General Gibbon's command marched up the Yellowstone River on the north side from opposite the

THE WAR ON THE SIOUX.

Map Showing the Yellowstone Region, the Sites of the Battles and the Routes of the United States Troops, as Originally Planned by Crook, Terry, Gibbon and Custer.

Facsimile of the first account published in New York of the battle of the Little Big Horn

of paper and placed it in the shell, and shoved it deep in the hole in the piece of wood. Then he pushed this into the ground at Custer's head. It would make sure that the burial party would identify Custer's body.

Slowly we left the knoll and started back to the living. I tried to find the body of my German friend, Trooper Finkle, the tallest man in the regiment. But I could not identify him.

The following morning we went back to Custer Hill and buried as well as we could, the naked, mutilated bodies of our comrades. It was a gruesome task.

—2—

That night when we got back to Reno Hill from finding the bodies of Custer and the 212 men who had ridden with him, we carefully removed our fifty-two wounded soldiers and two Crow scouts down to the valley and across the river. The next afternoon they were carried on pallets made of blankets swung between two long poles, with a mule at each end, the twenty miles up Little Horn to the steamer at the junction with the Big Horn. Early the morning of the 29th, the old steamer started down the Big Horn, down the Yellowstone and then down the Missouri on its trip to Fort Abraham Lincoln, across the river from Bismarck, North Dakota.

Besides the fifty-four wounded men, lying on deep beds of freshly cut grass on the deck, the *Far West* bore the single living thing found on the Custer battlefield—Comanche, the dun-colored mount ridden that day of death by Captain Keogh. He had seven battle wounds, but he lived for fifteen more years, the pride and special care of the regiment.

Late that summer the seven troops remaining of the once magnificent Seventh Cavalry found their way back to Abe Lincoln, where we were refitted and our lost troops recruited. And in the summer of 1877 we once again took to the field, taking part in the final rubbing out and capture of Chief Joseph and his Nez Percés.

But it was a little war compared with the great Sioux outbreak of the previous year. Never in all Indian history had there been such a fight as that on the Little Big Horn. It truly had been the Indian's day. Never again—save for a moment in 1891 when they dreamed an Indian Messiah had come back—were they to stand against the white man and his driving civilization.

Custer may have made a mistake to divide his command that Sunday afternoon of June 25, but the gods themselves were against him.

It was the Indians' day. Their one and only day.

Epilogue

I am now an old man living in the deep shadows.

Next to my family I love my old regiment more than anything else in the world. And I shall die believing Colonel Benteen was one of the noblest soldiers who ever lived.

I worship his memory almost as much as I do the Stars and Stripes. He was a true friend!

He made me a Sergeant on the field of battle on June 26, 1876. He recommended me for the Medal of Honor that I was given. In 1880 he made me First Sergeant of "H." I served with him until 1883—twelve years in all—when my old sweetheart from Germany came to this country with my father and mother. I asked her to marry me, and I remember as if it was yesterday how she pointed to my First Sergeant's chevrons and said, "Charlie, you must choose between the army and me." I chose her and I never regretted my choice.

For a time after I left the army I ran cattle, but I lost money at it. Then I worked three years for the Army Quartermaster Corps. Then I took a job as a harness maker with the Homestake mines here in Lead, South Dakota, in the heart of the Black Hills that I had helped open with General Custer back in 1874. For forty-eight years I worked for the mine. Eight years ago I retired on a pension.

General Custer made his mistakes, but he was a great and brave soldier, too. There were simply too many Indians for him that June afternoon, seventy years ago.

Part Two

Contemporary Narratives Bearing on the Custer Fight

So many are the controversies regarding every phase of Custer's Indian wars, and particularly the Battle of the Little Big Horn, that the authors have decided to include in this book a number of official reports, letters, stories of eyewitnesses, and various other items of source material. Much of this special material has never before been given general circulation.

At times it has been difficult to decide whether or not to print certain rather long and complementary documents that help to light up phases of the whole intriguing story. But to the Custer enthusiast they may prove of absorbing interest.

Our primary duty has been to present, simply and accurately, the story as told to us, the co-authors, by Sergeant Windolph. No other man who actually took part in the battle lives to collaborate or refute the details as he told them. His will forever be the final spoken word of the battle. To act as his faithful amanuensis has been our first task.

We have accepted as our second duty the printing of every important sidelight that we have been able to find. We definitely have no axes to grind. We are pleading no cause. We are neither protagonist nor antagonist of any single point of view.

And so we move now into what might be called the Controversial Supplement. Sergeant Windolph is in no wise responsible for the pages that follow.

Chapter 1

Did Custer's Black Hills Expedition Bring On the Sioux War of 1876?

*I*T has often been said that the two professional miners who accompanied Custer to the Black Hills in the summer of 1874 dug his grave for him.

Custer, of course, was only carrying out General Sheridan's orders when he led his beautifully planned and equipped expedition into the forbidden hills. But there is no evidence that Custer was not eager to go, and it is believed that he helped inspire Sheridan's imaginative mind to the need of exploring this unknown and highly attractive piece of earth.

Both the Sioux and the Cheyennes had set great store by the integrity of the Black Hills. They had for several generations peopled them with their most sacred gods, and they had considered them inviolate against any white intrusion.

As the endless pressure of the whites continued against the Plains Indians, the Black Hills became more and more in their minds a sacred hunting ground and retreat that the encroaching settlers would never dare enter. To them the thought that white men would some day tramp over these forbidden hills and own and inhabit them, was as repugnant as the desecration of an altar would be to a priest.

The Indians themselves were partially responsible for the growing idea that there was gold to be had for the asking in the Black Hills. Indians around army trading posts would flaunt their buckskin pouches of the "dust," which in all probability they had taken from the scalped body of some luckless miner. When asked where they had found the metal they would grunt and motion in the general direction of the Hills. To the gold-hungry hangers-on it became more and more certain that this barred and sacred Indian stronghold was loaded with the precious metal.

Pressure for the government to do something about these isolated Black Hills became more and more insistent. The Indians were making little or no use of them, it was claimed. They had no right to them in the first place. Here on their outskirts, down on the Platte River and eastward on the Missouri, were hundreds of strong, eager men, jobless men, adventurous men. Let an expedition go into the Black Hills and then let the world know how rich or poor its prospects were, they argued. Nature would take care of the rest.

So it was that Sheridan and Custer planned their great expedition. Save for the Yellowstone Expedition of the previous year, Custer had had no real action since the Battle of the Washita in December, 1868. It would be a fine adventure for him. It would bring him new fame and glory.

At 8 A.M. on July 2, the expedition set out from Fort Lincoln. Twenty-eight days later gold was discovered. For Custer it was the culmination of the great exploration. But let his official report tell its own story. (In this, as in all subsequent reports, the italics are those of the editors.)

"Hdq. Black Hills Expedition
Eight and ½ miles southeast of Harney's Peak
Aug. 2 1874
"Assistant Adjutant-General
Department of Dakota, St. Paul, Minn.
"My last dispatch was dated July 15, and sent from Prospect Valley, Dakota. . . .
"As there are scientists accompanying the expedition

who are examining into the mineral resources of this region, the result of whose researches will accompany my detailed report, I omit all present references to that portion of our explorations till the return of our expedition, except to state, what will appear in any event in the public prints, *that gold has been found at several places and it is the belief of those who are giving their attention to this subject that it will be found in paying quantities. I have upon my table forty or fifty small particles of pure gold, in size averaging that of a small pin-head and most of it obtained today from one pan-ful of earth. As we have never remained longer at our camp than one day, it will be readily understood that there is no opportunity to make a satisfactory examination in regard to deposits of valuable minerals. Veins of lead and strong indications of the existence of silver have been found. Until further examination is made regarding the richness of the gold, no opinion should be formed.*

"Veins of what the geologists term gold-bearing quartz crop out on almost every hillside. All existing geological or geographical maps of this region have been found incorrect. This will not seem surprising when it is remembered that both have been compiled by guesswork and without entering the country attempted to be represented. The health of the command continues excellent. I will begin my northward march in four days from this date. I do not expect to arrive at Fort Lincoln until the 31st of August.

G. A. Custer
Bvt. Maj. Gen. U. S. A., Commanding Expedition"

"Headquarters Black Hills Expedition
Bear Butte, Dak., August 15 (via Bismarck)
"My last dispatch was written on the 2nd and 3rd instant, and sent from the south fork of the Cheyenne, from a point on the latter nearest to Fort Laramie . . .
"In entering the Black Hills from any direction, the

most serious, if not the only obstacles, were encountered at once near the outer base. This probably accounts for the mystery which has so long existed regarding the character of the region. Exploring parties have contented themselves with marching around the exterior base and, from the forbidding aspect of the hills as viewed at a distance, have inferred that an advance toward the interior would only encounter increased obstacles.

". . . There is no doubt as to the existence of various minerals throughout the hills, as this subject had the special attention of experts who accompany the expedition and will be reported upon in detail. I will only mention the fact that iron and plumbago have been found and beds of gypsum of apparent inexhaustible extent.

"I referred in a former dispatch to the discovery of gold. Subsequent examinations at numerous points confirm and strengthen the fact of the existence of gold in the Black Hills. On some of the water-courses almost every panful of earth produced gold in small, yet paying, quantities. Our brief halts and rapid marching prevented anything but a hasty examination of the country in this respect; but in one place, and the only one within my knowledge where so great a depth was reached, a hole was dug eight (8) feet in depth. The miners report that they found gold among the roots of the grass, and, from that point to the lowest point reached, gold was found in paying quantities. It has not required an expert to find gold in the Black Hills, as men without experience in mining have discovered it at an expense of but little time or labor. As an evidence of the rich pasturage to be found in this region, I can state the fact that my beef herd, after marching upward of six hundred (600) miles, is in better condition than when I started, being now as fat as is consistent with marching condition. The horses of the command are in good working condition. I have never seen so many deer as in the Black Hills. Elk and bear have

also been killed. We have had no collision with hostile Indians.

G. A. Custer
Brevet Major General, Commanding Expedition
To Assistant Adjutant General
  Department of Dakota, Saint Paul"

Custer's reports were given wide circulation. Published almost simultaneously with them were vivid and extravagant reports by special newspaper correspondents who accompanied the expedition as General Custer's guests. From one end of the country to the other sounded the magic cry of Gold! Gold!

"Lonesome Charlie" Reynolds on reaching Fort Laramie, on the Platte River, after his dangerous solo ride with dispatches and telegrams, from the lower edge of the Black Hills, gave out an interview on August 3. He cautiously said, "For several days the miners have been successful in obtaining gold colors." But that was enough to set off wild hopes.

A little later General "Sandy" Forsyth, who accompanied the expedition, wrote in a personal report to General Sheridan:

"The two miners we have with us tell me that they found 'color' in every pan of dirt they washed near Harney's Peak; that the diggins there in Custer's gulch will pay $10.00 per day now; that they only had two or three days in which to prospect, as we kept moving so fast, but that in their opinion, when the Eastern Hills are rightly prospected, gold will be found in abundance. I am inclined to think so, for the very roots of the grass would pan five cents to the pan in our camp near Harney's Peak."

And thus was the scene set for the drama that was to take place two years later.

Chapter 2

Was Grant's Harsh Rebuke Responsible for Custer's Death?

*T*HE winter of 1875–76 Custer and his lovely wife spent in New York City. Custer had many friends there who entertained him lavishly. Barrett, the actor, was one of his most devoted admirers, and the colorful general often visited the actor in his theatre dressing room.

Custer enjoyed a special intimate relationship with the powerful *New York Herald*. At this time it was extremely critical of President Grant, soon to end his second administration under a rising cloud. The great commander and magnanimous victor over Lee had found the job of running the government in the difficult period of reconstruction, too much for him. His nerves were filed to the raw by the constant newspaper heckling and political needling. When the youthful general eventually added his voice to the chorus of critics, it was too much for the President.

Chronologically the story unfolds as follows:

In 1870, Secretary of War Belknap suddenly removed from the lucrative job of post trader at Fort Laramie, Wyoming Territory, a man by the name of Ward. The appointments of post traders had long been in the hands of the army, and General Sherman vigorously protested the high-handed action of the War Secretary. Whereupon Belknap had the law changed, so that the post traderships would be in the hands of the Secretary of War. Soon a ring, headed by two political friends of Belknap's, Hedrick and Rice, started a wholesale business in selling post traderships.

General Hazen protested the fact that goods at army posts were high-priced on account of the graft that had to be paid for appointments to trader posts. He claimed that at Fort Sill, in Oklahoma, the trader had to pay $12,000 a year to one Caleb P. Marsh in New York to hold his job as post trader.

In the fall of 1874 the Democrats won control of the lower House, and the next year the House Committee of Expenditures, playing politics to the hilt, ordered an investigation. On March 2, 1876, it made the following report:

"That they found at the very threshold of their investigations such uncontradicted evidence of the malfeasance in office by General William W. Belknap, then Secretary of War, that they find it to be their duty to lay the same before the House.

"They further report that this day at 11 o'clock A.M., a letter of the President of the United States was presented to the committee accepting the resignation of the Secretary of War, which is hereto attached, together with a copy of his letter of resignation, which the President informs the committee was accepted about 10 o'clock 20 minutes this morning. They therefore unanimously report and demand that the said William W. Belknap, late Secretary of War, be dealt with according to the laws of the land, and to that end submit herewith the testimony in the case taken, together with the several statements and exhibits thereto attached, and also a rescript of the proceedings of the committee had during the investigation of this subject: and they submit the following resolutions, which they recommend shall be adopted:

Resolved: That William W. Belknap, late Secretary of

War, be impeached of high crimes and misdemeanors while in office.

Resolved: That the testimony in the case of William W. Belknap, late Secretary of War, be referred to the Committee on the Judiciary, with instructions to prepare and report, without unnecessary delay suitable articles of impeachment of said William W. Belknap, late Secretary of War.

Resolved: That a committee of five members of this House be appointed and instructed to proceed immediately to the bar of the Senate, and there impeach William W. Belknap, late Secretary of War, in the name of the House of Representatives and of all people of the United States of America, of high crimes and misdemeanors while in office, and to inform that body that formal articles of impeachment will in due time be presented, and to request the Senate to take such order in the premises as they deem appropriate."

Chairman Heister Clymer had heard that Custer knew of irregularities in the trader post at Fort Lincoln, involving money paid for the tradership, and ordered him to appear at the hearings in Washington. On March 15, Custer, now back at Fort Lincoln, wired the Department Commander, General Terry, at St. Paul, that he had been ordered to Washington and asked for instruction. Terry telegraphed back that, since his departure at this time might delay the expedition, Custer might ask for the privilege of answering the Committee's questions by letter rather than appearing in person.

Custer promptly telegraphed this request to Chairman Clymer, who refused it, and ordered him to appear in person. There was nothing for Custer to do but go, and on March 29 Custer presented himself before the House Committee on Expenditures. After being sworn in, Custer was questioned about the post traders at Fort Lincoln, and then the name of President Grant's younger brother, Orvil, was brought into the picture. Here is a transcript of the testimony:

"Q. Have you ever had any conversation with Orvil Grant, or his partner, Bonnafon, with regard to their interest in military and trading posts?—A. Yes, sir; I have had several conversations with Mr. Bonnafon and with Mr. Grant.

"Q. Be kind enough to state what they were in the habit of telling you about it.—A. The first time I met them I was traveling from Saint Paul to my post, Fort Abraham Lincoln, four or five or six hundred miles, and Mr. Bonnafon and Mr. Grant were on the same train, and as they desired to travel from Fort Lincoln by wagon, or other similar conveyance, and about the only means of conveyance were those in possession of the military, they explained to me that they were then on a visit to certain Indian trading-posts, in which they were interested. They mentioned the posts, four or five in number; I don't know that I can state them accurately; but Fort Belknap, Fort Peck, Fort Berthold, and Standing-Rock I think were the four posts they named, and Mr. Grant asked me if I would furnish him an ambulance to make the trip. Mr. Bonnafon explained that they were about to take possession of these posts, and were going up to overhaul the stock and see what was wanted, and he asked me if I could recommend some young man who was familiar with Indian habits, whom they could employ, and I did recommend one. Mr. Bonnafon gave me to understand that he was equally interested with Orvil Grant in these four places that they named. I think, at that time, there were other persons occupying the tradership, and they were going up to effect the transfer. I have mentioned Fort Berthold as probably one of those posts; but when Mr. Grant got back to Bismarck he found there was some difficulty about his retaining or controlling the posts himself; at any rate, he telegraphed to Mr. Delano that one Captain Raymond must be appointed trader at Fort Berthold. Mr. Delano telegraphed back at once that the appointment would be made, and Raymond showed the telegram to several persons in Bismarck, and claimed that he paid Grant $1,000 for getting the appointment for him.

"Q. You say that Mr. Grant was going to make a trip up to those posts, and asked you for transportation; did you give it to him?—A. I did.

"Q. Why?—A. I told him I would not give it to him as a trader, but that to any member of the President's family visiting there, out of courtesy to the President of the United States, I would render any facility I could.

"Q. How long were they gone on that trip?—A. About the time that Mr. Grant left the post on the trip, I left, also, on some duty, and I am not certain how long he was absent, but it must have been several weeks, as the trip involved several hundred miles' travel. . . .

"Q. Do you know anything about the extension of this Great Sioux reservation across the east bank of the Missouri River?—A. Yes, sir.

"Q. That was done by the proclamation of the President in January last year and by another proclamation in April? —A. Yes, sir.

"Q. What was the effect of that proclamation upon the value of the traderships among that river?—A. It greatly enhanced their value by making them a more perfect monopoly, by removing all opposition and rivalry.

"Q. Did it dispossess any people who had acquired title to lands there?—A. I cannot say that it dispossessed people who had acquired title, because I am not sufficiently familiar with the legality of their title, but I know that it dispossessed people who claimed that they had a title, and who, no doubt, but for this, would eventually have acquired title. That is my understanding.

"Q. Please state in general terms what you believe to have been the effect of this law of June, 1870, giving the appointment of post-trader to the Secretary of War. What has been its effect upon the condition of the officers and men and on the *morale* of the troops and the Army?—A. Well, I don't believe it has affected the *morale* of the troops or the officers. . . . The effect has been to greatly embarrass them and add to the inconveniences of frontier life, which, even under the most favorable circumstances, are very great, as the troops and officers are required to pay what would be considered in the States exorbitant prices for everything, owing to the immense distances that goods have to be transported. That is the case always, but this law placing the appointment in the hands of the Secretary of War, and then being used in the manner that he has used it, by putting these appointments at the disposal of a certain ring, and taxing the profits in this way, by these exactions, all of which had to come out of the pockets of the soldiers and officers has, as I said before, greatly increased the inconveniences and expense of living on the frontier.

"Q. The old system was to have a sutler or sutlers appointed by a council of administration?—A. Yes, sir; the three senior officers at the post, except the commanding officer, constituted a council of administration. They nominated a man for the position of sutler, and that nomination was approved by the commanding officer of the post and then by the department commander; and that constituted the appointment, and in that way it would be impossible for operations like these to be carried on.

"Q. And then if the man selected was exorbitant in his charges they had a right to give license to another, so as to bring him to reason?—A. Yes, sir.

"Q. Under the present law they have no such control over the trader?—A. No, sir; not only that, but if known to purchase elsewhere what we required for our own table we have been called to account. I have known the post-trader at Fort Lincoln to go out and stop an officer's wagon, driven by his servant, and inspect the wagon to see what was in it, and threaten to use his influence with the Secretary of War because we traded with a town five miles distant, where we got things about half his prices.

"Q. Were those facts ever reported by you in any way to the Secretary of War?—A. No, sir, they were not; because I was just as suspicious of the Secretary as I was of the sutler.

"Q. Had you any doubt that the sutler would have had influence to have himself sustained in his exactions?—A. No, sir, I had no doubt. You asked me if I ever reported these things to the Secretary of War; I did report about this officer I mentioned. I considered that a test case, and I saw then that the Secretary of War was going to stand by the sutlers.

"Q. And he did stand by them?—A. He stood by them as long as he could.

"Q. Where does this Mr. Seip come from?—A. He claims to have come from Baltimore.

"Q. Had you ever known him before he was appointed there?—A. No, sir; and I do not want to know him again.

"Q. Is he there now?—A. He will be here tomorrow or next day and he will tell you the whole story.

"Q. He said that he divided with Hedrick and Rice?—A. Yes, sir; and he said that after dividing the profits, $15,000 a year, he never had more than $2,500 or $3,000 left, and he was getting tired of it."

A little later in the testimony the President of the United States was brought squarely into the picture:

"Q. The allegation is that that order extending the Great Sioux reservation was made by the President of the United States out of care for the welfare of the Indians there, so as to prevent them from having unlimited supplies of rum. I wish you to state whether, in your judgment, that order accomplished that design?—A. No, sir; I don't believe that the Indians got one drink less by the extension of the reservation.

"Q. Do you believe that that was the real object of issuing the order?—A. Well, I would rather not answer that question.

"Q. The effect of it was, however, in addition to improving the morals of the Indians, to improve the profits of the traders, was it not?—A. I think the profits of the traders left the morals of the Indians a long way behind. That was the general impression along the river, that the order was for the benefit of the traders.

"Q. Do you know of any persons having been sent off any of the reservations, who tried to deal there, so as to prevent any interference with the exclusive privileges of Orvil Grant and Bonnafon?—A. There was a case farther up the river, in which I think a man named Tom Thum was removed on those grounds, and I think the reservation was enlarged at a point up the river for the same purpose.

"Q. What reservation is that?—A. It is the reservation on which Fort Peck is situated.

"Q. That was extended to prevent opposition?—A. That is my impression, although I do not know it; and the current story there is, that Thum was about to be removed and his privileges as a trader entirely taken away, and he obtained some affidavits showing that there were some frauds in the Indian Department in which Leighton Brothers and Orvil Grant were mixed up, and he showed them the affidavits, and they allowed him to continue his trade.

"Q. What were the alleged frauds?—A. It was something in connection with furnishing a certain amount of corn to the Indians at one of the agencies; and the same amount of corn was used to go through a certain form, at one place, and get a receipt, and then it would be carried along and delivered at another place. I had a case of it at my post. There were about eight thousand bushels of corn delivered at my post, in Indian sacks, and I sent down and notified the trader that I would not receive them. They were marked 'Indian Department,' and I notified my quartermaster not to have anything to do with the corn.

"Q. Explain how that fraud was attempted.—A. Well, for instance, suppose that a contractor who furnishes forage to the military authorities at Fort Abraham Lincoln should have a contract to furnish forage at an Indian post several hundred miles up the river. He puts the forage in sacks. It is to be inspected at a certain point down the river by Indian Inspectors; they inspect it, and report that the contractor has started with so much corn for such an agency; and it must be marked with the Indian brand. Now, if the contractor can make an arrangement with the Indian agency where he is going to deliver it, to certify that that amount has been delivered, he can take the corn and go where he pleases with it. This man happened to bring this corn to my post. He brought eight thousand bushels there in Indian sacks, which showed inspection by the Indian inspectors and I declined to receive it; it was reported to the department headquarters and the matter was carried to Washington, and an order came back from the Secretary of War or War Department that the forage in those sacks must be received.

"Q. Although you were satisfied that it belonged to the Indian Department and had been sold to them?—A. Well, I was satisfied that it was a very suspicious circumstance, to say the least of it, and it opened the way for frauds. To show you how the Indian traders and Army traders are all mixed up, the contractor for this corn that was delivered at my place got Mr. Seip, the post-trader, to act as his agent to receive it. Seip stood by to see that it was weighed. They had some difficulty and one of the clerks from my post went to Saint Louis to look over the papers and he saw the bill sent by Mr. Seip to this Indian contractor, and found an item of $50 paid the sergeant who weighed or hauled the corn. Now, the Government pays the sergeant, and the only inference we could draw was that the sergeant was paid for making false weighs. We had it all weighed over again and every sack that had been under the sergeant's supervision fell short twelve to fifteen pounds.

"Q. You refused to receive this corn because it was paid for as Indian supplies?—A. It, in my opinion, would not have been marked as such unless it had been paid for. I never knew of such a case.

"Q. Then you reported these facts to the War Department?—A. No, sir: I reported to General Terry. He reported to General Sheridan, General Sheridan reported to General Sherman, and then the matter, in regular order, was sent to the Secretary of War, and there came back an order, through the regular channels, to receive it.

"Q. You got that order and then you did pay for the corn?—A. Yes, sir; vouchers were given in payment.

"Q. Have you any doubt that that corn was paid for twice by the Government?—A. I believe that it was paid for twice; but I cannot prove it any better than I have told you, because when they gave me the order to receive it, I considered that I was relieved from all responsibility in the matter."

A month later new facts came to Custer's attention that led him to send the following telegram to the Committee Chairman, Clymer, to be included in the record:

"Saint Paul, Minn., May 6, 1876
"General Terry, commanding the Department of Dakota, informs me that the report I forwarded from Fort Lincoln, regarding certain corn delivered at that post for the use of the Army, in Indian sacks, was received at his headquarters in this city, and after due investigation was acted upon finally by his authority; and that it was he and not the late Secretary of War who sent the order to Fort Lincoln directing that, under certain restrictions, intended to protect the Government, the corn in question should be received. The receipt

of the order was reported to me and I at the same time derived the impression that the order emanated from the War Department. As I would not knowingly do injustice to any individual, I ask that this telegram may be appended to and made part of my testimony before your committee.

G. A. Custer"

—2—

Custer was in for it now. As an officer in the regular army he could be accused of openly playing politics—and against the honor and dignity of his old army commander and present Commander-in-Chief, the President of the United States. On April 4 Custer was recalled for additional testimony. With this over he expected that he would be excused from further duty and be permitted to return to Fort Lincoln. Time was running short. He would soon be riding out with the great expedition, that he was personally to lead.

The bitterness regarding the whole case had no boundaries. Grant and Belknap, of course, had their ardent defenders. On April 8 the discreet *Army and Navy Journal* carried the following interesting paragraph that shows how high tempers were:

"A special despatch to the *New York World*, dated Washington, March 30, says, 'General Custer was the hero of a severe caning affair, in which E. W. Rice, a claim agent here, was the worsted party. Rice has long been an intimate friend of General Belknap's and is believed by a good many to have been the medium through whom a large part of the post-tradership money passed from the buyers to General Belknap. General Custer's testimony tended to prove this, the General testifying among other things, that he had been told that in a certain instance a post-tradership was secured through the payment of $5,000 to Rice. He replied by a newspaper card, in which he said that if General Custer did say that any money was ever paid to him (Rice) for a post-tradership he was a liar. Tonight Custer met Rice on G street and gave him a very severe caning.' "

On April 17, the actual impeachment trial of Belknap began. Custer thought he certainly would be permitted to leave at once, but he failed to figure on the politicians. He was ordered to remain in Washington, at the call of the Committee. No pleadings could sway the bitter-enders.

Sheridan on April 28 wired Terry at St. Paul that he should arrange to send some one other than Custer in charge of the coming expedition. And the following day Sheridan sent a second telegram suggesting that Terry himself go as commanding officer.

Custer, desperate and completely stymied, now approached the new Secretary of War, Alonzo Taft, who in turn took Custer's request to leave directly to the President. But Grant had his dander up. Young Custer could sweat it out in Washington for a while. Custer turned to Sherman. The army commander agreed Custer could return to Fort Lincoln, but first he must get formal permission from the President.

Custer hurried to the White House. All afternoon he cooled his heels in the anteroom. Finally he sent a note to the President. No comment. Finally the Adjutant General walked through the reception room and when Custer told him his story, he took Custer's request to see him directly to the President. Grant now sent out word that he would not see him.

Sherman had gone to New York, and Custer, in desperation, went to the office of the Adjutant General. Here he obtained written authority to start for his post and took the night train west.

Custer arrived in Chicago on the morning of the 4th and he was met by an aide of General Sheridan's, who notified him that he was under arrest and detention in Chicago. Grant however had not sent this order. It had come from Sherman.

Custer now sent a long telegram to Sherman in which he explained how he had tried to see the President, how he had tried to call on him (Sherman) and finally how the Adjutant General had approved of his departure. Sherman took the wire to the President and late that afternoon he wired Sheridan that he had just come from seeing the President and that he had ordered Custer to return to his post *but that he was not to accompany the expedition.*

Custer, arriving in St. Paul, appealed to the kind-hearted and cool-headed Terry for help. There seems little doubt but that Terry helped him draft the following wire to the President, with his own tempered endorsement:

> "Headquarters Dept. of Dakota
> St. Paul, Minn., May 6, 1876
> "The Adjutant General
> Division of the Missouri, Chicago
> I forward the following:
> To His Excellency, the President:
> (Through Military Channels)

"I have seen your order transmitted through the General of the Army directing that I be not permitted to accompany the expedition to move against the hostile Indians. As my entire regiment forms a part of the expedition and I am the senior officer of the regiment on duty in this department I respectfully but most earnestly request that while not allowed to go in command of the expedition I may be permitted to serve with my regiment in the field. I appeal to you as a soldier to spare me the humiliation of seeing my regiment march to meet the enemy and I not share its dangers.

> /s/ G. A. Custer

"In forwarding the above I wish to say, expressly, that I have no desire whatever to question the orders of the President or my military superiors. Whether Lieutenant

Colonel Custer shall be permitted to accompany the column or not I shall go in command of it. I do not know the reasons upon which the orders given rest; but if these reasons do not forbid it, Lieutenant Colonel Custer's services would be very valuable with his regiment.

/s/ Alfred H. Terry,
Commanding Department"

Sheridan, in Chicago, immediately sent the dispatch on, with the following endorsement:

"Chicago, Ill., May 7, 1876

"Brig. General E. D. Townsend
Washington, D. C.

"The following dispatch from General Terry is respectfully forwarded. I am sorry Lieutenant Colonel Custer did not manifest as much interest in staying at his post to organize and get ready his regiment and the expedition as he now does to accompany it. On a previous occasion in eighteen sixty-eight I asked executive clemency for Colonel Custer to enable him to accompany his regiment against the Indians, and I sincerely hope that if granted this time it may have sufficient effect to prevent him from again attempting to throw discredit on his profession and his brother officers.

/s/ P. H. Sheridan, Lieutenant General"

All of which was too much for the rugged old soldier in the White House. On May 8 he wired through Sherman his permission. He could not forget the bright young Major General who had thrown his division across Lee's path on that April day near Appomattox, just ten years before.

"Headquarters of the Army
Washington, May 8, 1876

"To General A. H. Terry, St. Paul, Minn.:

"General Sheridan's enclosing yours of yesterday touching General Custer's urgent request to go under your command with his regiment has been submitted to the President, who sent me word that if you want General Custer along he withdraws his objections. Advise Custer to be prudent, not to take along any newspaper men, who always make mischief, and to abstain from personalities in the future. . . .

/s/ W. T. Sherman, General"

That night Custer and Terry left for the Missouri River in a special car. Custer was to go on the great expedition after all—and he was to have his beloved regiment. But he was not to command the expedition.

This did not mean that by some swift move, some bold stroke, he might not swing himself into glory once more; that he might not again ride his famous luck, regain his old dashing popularity with the nation, and his high place in the heart of his old commander, Phil Sheridan.

Grant had been stern with him. But Custer had his regiment back and there was action ahead.

No man will ever know for certain how much all this had to do with Custer's actions and decisions on the Little Big Horn forty-seven days later.

Chapter 3

Did Custer Disobey
Terry's Last Orders?

*T*HREE high officers, all Custer's superiors, wrote their own individual reports of the campaign that ended with the Battle of the Little Big Horn. They were the three men responsible, up to the moment that Custer started his march up the Rosebud.

They give three different pictures of the events that led up to the battle. Each account was written shortly after the battle, and each man formed his own conclusions as to the causes of the disaster.

In each there is at least the implied question of whether or not Custer disobeyed Terry's written instructions, given to him shortly before he started the march that ended with his death.

The first of the documents we shall now peruse, is the formal report of Lieutenant General Sheridan, submitted to General Sherman, Commanding General of the Army, and through him to the Secretary of War. It outlines Sheridan's pincer movement campaign, and in the end gives his conclusions regarding the tragedy. It is printed in the report of the Secretary of War in 1876.

"Headquarters Military Division of the Missouri
New Orleans, La., Nov. 25, 1876
"General: I have the honor to submit for the information of the General of the Army, a brief report of the

events occurring in the Military Division of the Missouri since my last annual report. . . . On February 7, 1876, authority was received, by indorsement of the General of the Army on letter of the honorable Secretary of the Interior, to commence operations against the hostile Sioux. They were, at that time, Sitting Bull's band, of 30 or 40 lodges, and not exceeding 70 warriors, and Crazy Horse's band, not exceeding 120 lodges and numbering probably 200 warriors. Meantime General Terry had learned that Sitting Bull's band was on the Dry Fork of the Missouri, some 200 miles farther west, instead of the Little Missouri, as first supposed.

"On the 8th of February, the letter of the honorable Secretary of the Interior was referred to General Terry, with directions to take such steps with the forces under his command as would carry out the wishes of the Interior Department and the orders of the General of the Army. No specific directions could be given, as no one knew exactly, and no one could have known where these Indians were, as they might be here today and somewhere else tomorrow.

"General Terry was also informed that General Crook would operate from the south in the direction of the headwaters of Powder River, Pumpkin Buttes, Tongue River, Rosebud and Big Horn Rivers, where Crazy Horse and his allies frequented, and that departmental lines would be disregarded by the troops until the object requested by the Secretary of the Interior was attained. General Terry further was informed that the operations of himself and General Crook would be made without concert, as the Indian villages are movable and no objective point could be fixed upon, but that, if they should come to any understanding about concerted movements there would be no objection at division headquarters. . . .

"About the same time that General Crook was making his preparations to move, as just described, General Terry also projected an expedition against Sitting Bull's band, which was then believed, from information he had received, located on the Little Missouri River, but afterward found to be on the Dry Fork of the Missouri, some two hundred miles farther west. Before, however, the Seventh Cavalry could be concentrated at Fort Abraham Lincoln the season became so inclement—a great number of men being badly frost-bitten in reaching the fort—and the snow so deep that it was thought advisable to abandon the expedition until later in the season. . . .

"Early in the spring, as no change had then been made in the orders, Generals Terry and Crook made preparations to resume the operations, General Crook concentrating at Fort Fetterman fifteen companies of cavalry and five companies of infantry; and on May 29 he marched from that point for Goose Creek, and established his supply-camp there on the 8th of June. . . .

"General Terry concentrated at Fort Lincoln the 7th Cavalry, three Gatling guns, and six companies of infantry and on the 17th of May marched from that post for the mouth of the Powder River, where he arrived and established his supply-camp on the 7th of June. From this point, Major Marcus A. Reno, Seventh Cavalry, with six companies of that regiment, scouted up the Powder River to its forks, across the country to the Rosebud and down the Rosebud to its mouth. In the meantime, General Terry moved with his main forces up the south bank of the Yellowstone and formed a junction with Colonel John Gibbon's command, consisting of four companies Second Cavalry and six companies of the Seventh Infantry, that had marched eastward along the north bank of the Yellowstone from Fort Ellis, in Montana, to the mouth of the Rosebud.

"During Major Reno's scout a large Indian trail was discovered leading up the Rosebud, but as his orders did not contemplate an attack with his small force, it was only followed a sufficient distance to enable him to definitely locate the Indians in the vicinity of the Little Big Horn River. He then returned to the mouth of the Rosebud.

"*General Terry, now pretty well informed of the locality of the Indians, directed Lieutenant Colonel George A. Custer to move with the Seventh Cavalry up the Rosebud until he struck the trail discovered by Major Reno, with instructions that he should not follow it directly to the Little Big Horn but that he should send scouts over it and keep his main force farther south, to prevent the Indians from slipping in between himself and the mountains. He was also to examine the headwaters of Tulloch's Creek as he passed it, and send word to General Terry of what he found there.*

"Custer moved on the 22nd of June, following the trail as soon as he struck it, and after marching about 125 miles from the place of starting, attacked the Indians in their village on the west bank of the Little Big Horn and about thirty miles above its mouth, between 10 and 12 o'clock on the morning of the 25th of June. In the meantime General Terry moved up the Yellowstone River with Colonel Gibbon's column, arriving at the mouth of the Little Big Horn on June 26.

"The attack of General Custer proved disastrous, resulting in the destruction of himself, twelve officers and five companies of the Seventh Cavalry, and in a heavy loss in killed and wounded to the detachment commanded by Major Reno, whose command of three companies was saved from annihilation by the timely arrival of Major Benteen with four companies, and by intrenching its position on an eminence on the east bank of the river. His position at this point was soon completely enveloped by the Indians who kept up a constant fire until the approach of General Terry with Gibbon's column, on the evening of June 26.

"As much has been said in regard to the misfortune that occurred to General Custer and the portion of his regiment under his immediate command in this action, I wish to express the conviction I have arrived at concerning it. From all the information that has reached me, I am led to believe that the Indians were not aware of the proximity of Custer until he had arrived within about eight or nine miles of their village, and that then their scouts who carried the intelligence back to the valley were so closely followed up by Custer that he arrived on the summit of the divide overlooking the upper portion of the village almost as soon as the scouts reached it. As soon as the news was given, the Indians began to strike their lodges and get their women and children out of the way, a movement they always make under such circumstances. Custer, seeing this, believed the village would escape him if he awaited the arrival of the four companies of his regiment still some miles in his rear. Only about 75 or 100 tepees could be seen from the summit or divide, and this probably deceived him as to the extent of the village. He therefore directed Major Reno with three companies to cross the river and charge the village while he with the remaining five companies would gallop down the east bank of the river, behind the bluff, and cut off the retreat of the Indians. Reno crossed and attacked gallantly with his three companies, about 110 men, but the warriors, leaving the women to strike the lodges, fell on Reno's handful of men and drove them back to and over the river with severe loss. About this time Custer reached a point about three and one-half or four miles down the river, but instead of finding a village of 75 or 100 lodges, he found one of perhaps from 1,500 to 2,000, and swarming with warriors, who brought him to a halt. This, I think, was the first intimation the Indians had of Custer's approach to cut them off, for they at once left Reno and concentrated to meet the new danger. The point where Custer reached the river, on the opposite side of which was the village, was broken into choppy ravines, and the Indians crossing from Reno got between the two commands, and as Custer could not return, he fell back over the broken ground with his tired men and tired horses (they had ridden about seventy miles with but few halts) and became, I am afraid, an easy prey to the enemy. Their wild savage yells, overwhelming numbers and frightening war paraphernalia made it as much as each trooper could do to take care of his horse, thus endangering his own safety and efficiency. If Custer could have reached any position susceptible of defense, he could have defended himself, but none offered itself in the choppy and broken ravines over which he had to pass, and he and his command were lost without leaving any one to tell the tale. As soon as Custer and his gallant officers and men were exterminated, and the scenes of mutilation by the squaws commenced, the warriors returned to renew the attack upon Reno, but he had been joined by Benteen and the four companies of the regiment that were behind when the original attack took place, and the best use had been made of the respite given by the attack on Custer to entrench their position. Reno's command was thus enabled to repulse every attack made by the Indians, until relieved by General Terry on the morning of the 27th, as before mentioned.

"*Had the Seventh Cavalry been kept together, it is my belief it would have been able to handle the Indians on the Little Big Horn, and under any circumstances it could have at least defended itself; but, separated as it was into three distinct detachments, the Indians had largely the advantage, in addition to their overwhelming numbers. If Custer had not come upon the village so suddenly, the warriors would have gone to meet him, in order to give time to the women and children to get out of the way, as they did with Crook only a few days before, and there would have been, as with Crook, what might be designated a rear-guard fight, a fight to get their valuables out of the way, or, in other words, to cover the escape of their women, children and lodges.*"

It is interesting to note that in this report General Sherman several times refers to Benteen's four companies—when there were actually only three companies under him.

—2—

In charge of the actual campaign in the field was General Terry. We have seen how this kindly and judicious commander was able to break the Grant jinx on Custer, and restore his regiment to him at the last moment.

Let us now look at Terry's official report made to his superior, Lieutenant General Sheridan, which says in part:

"On the 10th of February last I received from the Lieutenant-General commanding orders to commence operations against the hostile Sioux. At the same time I was informed that similar instructions had been given to Brigadier-General Crook, then as now commanding the Department of the Platte, who would operate from Fort Laramie in the direction of the headwaters of Powder River, Pumpkin Butte and the Big Horn. Preparations for the movement were immediately commenced, and it was supposed that the troops could be made ready to march early in April. The collection of troops and supplies for the expedition, however, was dependent on the opening of the Northern Pacific Railroad.

"That road was opened earlier than is usual in the spring, but severe snowstorms again closed it. Owing to this fact, and to the necessity of waiting for the arrival of troops ordered from the Department of the Gulf to this Department, it was not until the middle of May that all preparations were completed.

"The force originally intended for the field consisted of the nine companies of the Seventh Cavalry then in this Department, Companies C and G of the Seventeenth Infantry, Company B of the Sixth Infantry, a battery of Gatling guns manned by detachments from the Twentieth Infantry, and forty Indian scouts. Subsequently, it was increased by the three remaining companies of the Seventh Cavalry, which, on my application, were ordered from the

Picnic shortly before Custer left on his fatal campaign. Eight of the men in this picture were killed on the Little Big Horn. *Left to right:* Lieut. James Calhoun (killed); Mr. Sweet; Capt. Stephen Baker; Boston Custer (killed); Lieut. W. S. Edgerly; Miss Matson (with fan); Capt. Myles Keogh (killed); Mrs. James Calhoun; Mrs. Custer (in black hat); General Custer (killed); Dr. H. O. Paulding (on ground); Mrs. A. E. Smith; Dr. G. E. Lord (killed); Capt. T. B. Weir (seated); Lieut. W. W. Cooke (killed); Lieut. R. E. Thompson; the two Misses Wadsworth; Capt. Tom Custer (killed); Lieut. A. E. Smith (killed).

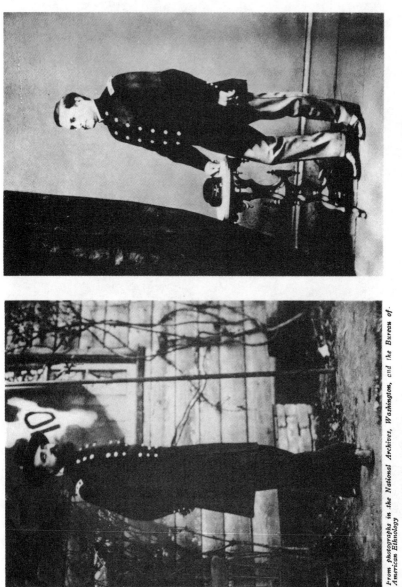

Left: Brig. Gen. Alfred H. Terry, taken in front of his Division headquarters, shortly before the end of the Civil War. *Right:* Major Reno, second in command at the Battle of the Little Big Horn, and the target of much bitter criticism.

Department of the Gulf, to their regiment, in order that they might accompany it into the field.

"Lieutenant Colonel G. A. Custer, of the Seventh Cavalry, was at first assigned to the command of this force; but under subsequent instructions I assumed the command in person, Lieutenant Colonel Custer being assigned to the command of his regiment.

"On the 27th of February I directed Colonel John Gibbon, of the Seventh Infantry, commanding the district of Montana, to prepare for the field all the troops which could be spared from the garrisons in his district, and to be ready to march from Fort Ellis down the valley of the Yellowstone.

"These orders were crossed on their way to Montana by a dispatch from Colonel Gibbon, in which he suggested the same movement. . . .

"I arrived personally at Fort Lincoln on the 10th of May. Soon after my arrival I received information from more than one independent source which led me to believe that the main body of the hostile Sioux was on the Little Missouri River, and between that stream and the Yellowstone. I therefore sent to Fort Ellis a telegraphic dispatch, to be forwarded to Colonel Gibbon, directing him to move down the Yellowstone to 'Stanley's Stockade,' to cross the river and move out on 'Stanley's trail' to meet the column from Lincoln. This column marched on the morning of May 17. For some days its progress was slow, for the wagons were heavily laden and recent rains had made the ground extremely soft.

"The Little Missouri was reached on May 29. Here a halt was made for a day in order that the valley of the river might be reconnoitered. This was done by Lieutenant Colonel Custer with a portion of his regiment, but no indications of the recent presence of Indians were discovered. The march was resumed on the 31st; but on the 1st and

2nd of June a heavy snowstorm detained the column on the edge of the bad lands which border the left banks of the Little Missouri. . . . On the 8th, leaving the column in camp, I went with an escort to the mouth of the Powder, and there found the steamer *Far West* with supplies.

"The next day I went on the steamer up the Yellowstone to meet Colonel Gibbon. . . .

"The next day Major M. A. Reno, Seventh Cavalry, with six companies of his regiment, and one Gatling gun, was directed to reconnoiter the valley of the Powder as far as the forks of the river, then to cross to Mizpah Creek, to descend that creek to near its mouth, thence to cross to Tongue River and descend to its mouth. . . .

"On the morning of the 15th, Lieutenant Colonel Custer, with six companies of his regiment, one Gatling gun, and a train of pack mules, marched for Tongue River, all the wagons with their infantry-guard having been left at the depot. He reached the Tongue on the 16th. Here we waited for news from Major Reno until the evening of the 19th, when a dispatch was received from him, by which it appeared that he had crossed to the Rosebud and found a heavy Indian trail; and that after following it for some distance he had retraced his steps, had descended the stream to its mouth, and was then on his way to the Tongue. Orders were at once sent to him to halt and await the arrival of Lieutenant Colonel Custer; and the latter was instructed to march the next morning for the mouth of the Rosebud. He arrived at this last-named point on the 21st. On the same day Colonel Gibbon's column was put in motion for a point on the north bank of the Yellowstone, opposite the mouth of the Big Horn; with it were sent the Gatling guns which had until this time accompanied the Seventh Cavalry.

"*At a conference which took place on the 21st between Colonel Gibbon, Lieutenant Colonel Custer, and myself, I communicated to them the plan of operations which I had decided to adopt. It was that Colonel Gibbon's column should cross the Yellowstone near the mouth of the Little Big Horn, and thence up that stream, with the expectation that it would arrive at the last-named point by the 26th; that Lieutenant Colonel Custer with the whole of the Seventh Cavalry should proceed up the Rosebud until he should ascertain the direction in which the trail discovered by Major Reno led; that if it led to the Little Big Horn it should not be followed; but that Lieutenant Colonel Custer should keep still farther to the south before turning toward that river, in order to intercept the Indians should they attempt to pass around his left, and in order, by a longer march, to give time for Colonel Gibbon's column to come up.*

"This plan was founded on the belief that at some point on the Little Big Horn a body of hostile Sioux would be found; and that although it was impossible to make movements in perfect concert, as might have been done had there been a known fixed objective to be reached, yet, by the judicious use of excellent guides and scouts which we possessed, the two columns might be brought within co-operating distance of each other, so that either of them which should be first engaged might be a 'waiting fight'—give time for the other to come up. At the same time it was thought that a double attack would very much diminish the chances of a successful retreat by the Sioux, should they be disinclined to fight. It was believed to be impracticable to join Colonel Gibbon's column to Lieutenant Colonel Custer's force; for more than one-half of Colonel Gibbon's troops were infantry, who would be unable to keep up with cavalry in a rapid movement; while to detach Gibbon's mounted men and add them to the Seventh Cavalry would leave his force too small to act as an independent body. . . ."

—3—

To complete the testimony of the three ranking officers involved in the campaign, we must now turn to General Gibbon, and his report to Lieutenant General Sheridan:

"Headquarters District of Montana
Fort Shaw, Montana, Oct. 17, 1876

"Sir: I have the honor to submit the following report of the military operations of the troops under my command during the past spring and summer.

"In accordance with telegraphic instruction from the brigadier general commanding the department, five companies of the Seventh Infantry left Fort Shaw on the 17th of March, and proceeded toward Fort Ellis. . . .

"That night, June 8, I received by scouts the department commander's dispatch of that day from Powder River and the next morning met him on the steamboat *Far West* a few miles below our camp. In accordance with his instructions the command was at once prepared to move up the river again, but a furious rainstorm that afternoon delayed the movement by converting the alkali flats surrounding us into impassable ground. The cavalry, however, got off on the afternoon of the 10th and the infantry the next day, and after a march of fifty miles was again concentrated in camp below the mouth of the Rosebud on the 14th. On the 18th Major Reno, with a force of cavalry, arrived opposite our camp after a scout on Powder, Tongue, and Rosebud Rivers, during which he reported he had seen no Indians, and the next day he proceeded down the river.

"A cavalry scout up the river having reported the side streams almost impassable, by reason of floods from recent rains, I started Captain Freeman with three companies of infantry on the 21st, up the road to build bridges. General Terry reaching the camp by steamer shortly afterwards, the whole command was started up the river. I, at his request, accompanied him on the *Far West*, for the purpose of conferring with Lieutenant Colonel Custer, who reached a point on the opposite side of the river with the whole of the Seventh Cavalry that afternoon.

"*That evening the plan of operations was agreed upon. Lieutenant Colonel Custer, with the Seventh Cavalry, was to proceed up the Rosebud till he struck an Indian trail, discovered during Major Reno's scout. As my scouts had recently reported smoke on the Little Big Horn, the presence of an Indian camp some distance up that stream was inferred.*

"Lieutenant Colonel Custer was instructed to keep constantly feeling toward his left, well up toward the mountains, so as to prevent the Indians escaping in that direction, and to strike the Little Big Horn, if possible above (south) of the supposed location of the camp, while my command was to march up the Yellowstone to the mouth of the Big Horn to the mouth of the Little Big Horn and up that stream, with the hope of getting the camp between the two forces. As it would take my command three days to reach the mouth of the Big Horn, and probably a day to cross it over the Yellowstone, besides two more to reach the mouth of the Little Big Horn, and Lieutenant Colonel Custer had the shorter line over which to operate, the department commander strongly impressed upon him the propriety of not pressing his march too rapidly. He got off with his regiment at 12 o'clock the next day (22nd): three Gatling guns, under Lieutenant Low, Twentieth Infantry, being detached from his regiment and sent to join my command. The steamer got away at 4 o'clock that day, and reached Fort Pease early on the morning of the 24th. My command, except the train and Captain Kirtland's company (B, Seventh Infantry) being at once ferried across, was that evening moved out to the crossing of Tullock's Fork. I did not accompany it, and General Terry took command of the troops in person. The next day the steamer entered the mouth of the Big Horn and proceeded up that stream.

"The next morning early (25th) I left the *Far West* and overtook the infantry portion of the command, General Terry having made a night march with the cavalry and Gatling guns and later in the day that portion of the command was overtaken on a high ridge overlooking the valley

of the Little Big Horn near its mouth, where, by direction
of General Terry, I resumed command of my troops. Shortly
afterward our scouts brought in news that they had encountered some Indians and, giving chase, had run them
across the Big Horn. They had dropped articles in their
flight which proved them to be Crows, assigned to duty
with Lieutenant Colonel Custer's command. *They, having
discovered that their pursuers belonged to their own tribe,
refused to come back, and called across the river that Custer's command had been entirely destroyed by the Sioux,
who were chasing the soldiers all over the country and
killing them.* We now pushed up the valley of the Little
Big Horn as rapidly as the men could march, large fire being
seen in the distance. Efforts were made to communicate with
Lieutenant Colonel Custer by scouts, but our Crow interpreter deserted and took the Crows with him, and two
attempts made by white men to precede the command with
dispatches failed, the scouts in both cases running into Indians. As we proceeded up the valley the fires increased in
number and volume, giving rise to the impression that Custer
had captured the camp and destroyed it. The Indians, who
late in the afternoon remained in sight on the hills in front
of us, rather militated against the supposition, however, and
after marching until dark we halted and bivouacked on the
prairie.

"The next morning the march was resumed and after
proceeding about three miles we came in sight of a large
deserted Indian camp, in which two tepees were still standing and these were found to contain the dead bodies of Indians. Many lodge-poles were still standing, and the quantity
of property scattered about testified to the hasty departure
of the Indians. Our scouts reported only a few scattering
horsemen in sight on the distant hills. We continued to move
rapidly forward, still uncertain as to the fate of Custer's
command, Captain Ball's company about a mile in advance.
While passing through the Indian camp a report reached me

from our scouts in the hills to the north of the river that a large number of bodies of white men had been discovered, and shortly afterward Lieutenant Bradley came in with the information that he had counted 194 bodies of dead soldiers. All doubt that a serious disaster had happened to Lieutenant Colonel Custer's command now vanished, and the march was continued under the uncertainty as to whether we were going to rescue the survivors or to battle with the enemy who had annihilated him. At length we caught sight of a number of animals congregated upon the slope of a distant hill, and on a point nearer to us three horsemen were evidently watching us. After Captain Ball's company had passed them these cautiously approached us, our troops being in plain sight and marching in two columns abreast of each other. At length, being convinced we were friends, they came forward more rapidly and announced that the Seventh Cavalry had been cut to pieces and the remnant, under Major Reno, were intrenched in the bluffs close by. Communication was now soon opened with Major Reno. His command was found intrenched upon the tops of several small ridges, their dead and living horses lying about them, with some fifty wounded men lying on the hot, dusty hilltops, where, until about 6 o'clock on the evening before, they had been unable to obtain any water except at the imminent risk of life. We were informed that in this spot they had been surrounded by overwhelming numbers of Indians from the close of Major Reno's charge on the 25th (about 2:30 P.M.) until about 6 P.M. the next day, the Indians pouring upon them all that time a very close and almost continuous fire from the neighboring ridges, some of which commanded the position in reverse. The first inquiry made was if General Custer was with us, and the command appeared to know nothing of the fate of himself and that portion of his command immediately with him until we informed them of it. As described to us, the whole movement of the Indians when they abandoned their camp, was visible from Major

Reno's position, and the last portion disappeared in the hills to the south just at dusk on the 26th, when my command was eight and three-quarters miles from Major Reno's position. . . ."

—4—

The evidence is in. Each reader must act as his own judge and juror: "Did Custer disobey Terry's last orders?"

In the entire regiment only one man had the complete and unquestioned confidence of Custer—his brother Tom. How much he discussed his plans even with Tom is a matter of pure conjecture. So no one can ever know the whys and wherefores of his actions.

These Montana hills were a vast and forbidding land in Custer's days. Motor roads and radios make them small and safe today. And Time and hindsight now make difficult decisions seem simple and easy.

Chapter 4

Did Custer Refuse
Advice from His Scouts?

*H*OW many Indian warriors were camped on the west bank of the Little Big Horn that Sunday morning of June 25?

Against the real figure how many did Custer *think* he would have to fight?

Did Custer refuse to believe the estimated number of warriors his scouts told him he would have to fight?

Did he fail to follow the advice of his experienced guides and interpreters?

There seems little question but that when Terry and Custer left Fort Lincoln it was supposed there were not more than some 800 hostile warriors who might be considered on the war path. The Indian Department gave out no alarming figure. It was not until the expedition was hundreds of miles removed from all telegraph facilities that word came to Lieutenant General Sheridan that there were great numbers of hostiles away from the reservations. He sent this important information to Terry but it arrived *after* the tragedy.

One of the best accounts of what the guides thought about the number of Indians and the chances of Custer closing with them, is contained in that excellent book *William Jackson, Indian Scout,* by James Willard Schultz. It is worth careful reading.

I Fought with Custer

"General Custer, with his Seventh Cavalry, a pack train carrying fifteen days' rations and extra cartridges, his own scouts, and six Crow scouts under John Bruyer, from Gibbon's command, left the mouth of the Rosebud about noon, June 22. My brother and I rode with an old friend of ours, Frank Girard, a man who had once been captured by Crazy Horse's band of Sioux, and had lived with them so long that he had acquired no little of their ways, and their religion.

"On the third day, we struck the trail of the hostiles, the one that Reno had found several days before. And what a trail it was; a trail all of three hundred yards wide, and deeply worn by travois and lodge-pole ends. We went into camp close to the trail, and, cooking our supper, we scouts counciled together about the outlook. All agreed that at least fifteen hundred lodges of the enemy had made that broad trail. Said Bloody Knife: 'My friends, this big trail proves what we heard, that the Ogallala, Minneconjou, Sansarc, and Teton Sioux have left their agencies to join Sitting Bull and Crazy Horse; but I am sure that even this trail does not account for all that have left their agencies. There surely are other trails of them; and trails, too, of Cheyennes and Arapahoes.'

" 'Many Yanktonnais and Assiniboin have answered Sitting Bull's call for help, and joined him,' said Frank Girard.

" 'Yes. They too,' Bloody Knife continued. 'It is as I have told Long Hair: this gathering of the enemy tribes is too many for us. But he will not believe me. He is bound to lead us against them. They are not far away; just over this ridge, they are all encamped and waiting for us. Crazy Horse and Sitting Bull are not men-without-sense; they have their scouts out, and some of them surely have their eyes upon us. Well, tomorrow we are going to have a big fight, a losing fight. Myself, I know what is to happen to me; my sacred helper has given me warning that I am not to see the set of tomorrow's sun.'

"Sad words, those. They chilled us. I saw Charlie Reynolds nod agreement to them, and was chilled again when he said in a low voice: 'I feel as he does: tomorrow will be the end for me, too. Anyone who wants my little outfit of stuff' —pointing to his war sack—'can have it right now.' He opened it, began passing out tobacco, a sewing-kit, several shirts and so on. Many refused the presents; those who accepted them did so with evident reluctance.

"We had little appetite for our coffee and hardtack, and the meat that we were broiling. While we were eating, word was passed from mess to mess to put out the fires. That was quickly done, and soon afterward, Lieutenant Varnum, who was in charge of the scouts, came over and said that it was General Custer's plan to attempt a surprise attack upon the camp of the enemy. The command was to rest until about midnight, and then again take the trail; some of us scouts, meantime, were to push on ahead and try to locate the camp.

"Said Bloody Knife: 'We cannot surprise the enemy! They are not crazy; without doubt their scouts have watched every move that we have made.'

" 'Well, Bloody Knife, that is probably true, but we must try to surprise them, must we not?'

" 'Yes, o'course. We *try!*' he replied.

" 'Very well. We will go out in three parties: Bruyer, you take two of your Crows and go forward on the right of the trail. Bloody Knife, you take the left of the trail, with two of your Rees. You Jackson boys, and you, Reynolds, come with me on the trail,' ordered Varnum.

"We saddled our horses, mounted and struck out all together. We kept together for all of a mile, and then Bruyer and the Crows and Bloody Knife and the Rees branched off and left us to follow the trail. We moved on cautiously, often stopping to listen to the howling of the wolves, and to look for the red gleam of sparks from some sick one's lodge-fire. So we went on and on through the night, getting no sight or sound of the enemy. At dawn, the command overtook us, and Lieutenant Varnum reported to General Custer. There we rested and had some breakfast.

"While we were eating, several of the packers rode swiftly up through the command to General Custer and we soon learned that they had lost a box of hardtack off one of the mules, and, on going back, had found some Indians around it, stuffing the contents into their clothing. None could now doubt that the enemy had all along kept watch of our advance. With a grim laugh, Charlie Reynolds said to me: 'I knew well enough that they had scouts ahead of us, but I didn't think that others would be trailing along to pick up stuff dropped by our careless packers.'

"Convinced at last that we could not possibly surprise the enemy, General Custer ordered a quick advance, with the scouts and himself in the lead. We had not gone far when Bloody Knife and his two Rees joined us, and reported that on the other side of the ridge they had found the day-old trail of many more of the enemy going toward the valley of the Little Big Horn.

"On we went over the divide. We soon met John Bruyer and his two Crows. They were excited, and Bruyer said to Custer: 'General, we have discovered the camp, down there on the Little Horn. It is a big one! Too big for you to tackle! Why, there are thousands and thousands of Sioux and Cheyennes down there.'

"For a moment the general stared at him, angrily, I thought, and then sternly said: 'I shall attack them! If you are afraid, Bruyer——'

" 'I guess I can go wherever you do,' Bruyer quickly answered; and at that, the general turned back to the command, we following him. He had the bugler sound the officers' call and the command rested while they got together, and Custer gave his orders for the attack upon the camp.

"None of the scouts had been far in the lead, and they all came in. Rees and Crows and whites and Robert and I, we were a gathering of solemn faces. Speaking in English, and the sign language, too, so that all would understand, Bruyer described the enemy camp. It was, he said, all of three miles long, and made up of hundreds and hundreds of lodges. Above it and below and west of it were thousands and thousands of horses that were being close-herded. With his few riders, Long Hair had decided to attack the camp, and we were going to have a terrible fight: we should all take courage, fight hard, make our every shot a killer. He finished and none spoke. But after a minute or two, Bloody Knife looked up and signed to Sun: 'I shall not see you go down behind the mountains tonight.' And at that I almost choked. I felt that he knew that his end was near, that there was no escaping it. I turned and looked the other way. I thought that my own end was near. I felt very sad.

"The officers' council did not last long, and, when it ended, Lieutenant Varnum came hurrying to us scouts and said that the command was going to split up to make the attack on the camp, and that we were to go with Major Reno's column, down the trail of the hostiles that we had been following from the Rosebud. We were soon in the saddle and headed down a narrow valley toward the river."

—2—

One of the most straightforward accounts of the battle was told by Scout Herendon the day after the *Far West* arrived at Bismarck with the reports of the fight. It was printed in the July 8 issue of the *New York Tribune*—thirteen days after the tragedy.

Herendon estimated that the number of Indian warriors in the battle was between 2,500 and 3,000. His story is as follows:

"Bismarck, D. T., July 7, 1876

"George Herendon, a scout sent by General Terry with General Custer's column, relates the following as his experience in the recent battle. He was sent by General

Custer's command, to carry despatches from Custer to Terry:

"We left the Rosebud on the 22nd of June at twelve o'clock; marched up the Rosebud about twelve miles and encamped for the night. On the morning of the 23rd we broke camp at five o'clock when we struck a large lodge pole trail about ten days old and followed it along the Rosebud until toward evening, when we went into camp on the trail. On the morning of the 24th we pulled out at five o'clock and followed the trail five or six miles, when we met six Crow Indian scouts, who had been sent out the night previous by General Custer to look for the Indian village. They said they had found fresh pony tracks and that ten miles ahead the trail was fresher. General Custer had the officers' call blown and they assembled around him, but I did not hear what he said to them. The scouts were again sent ahead and moved along at a fast walk. We moved at one o'clock, and, while the officers were eating their lunch, the scouts came back and reported that they had found where the village had been quite recently. They moved again, with flankers well out to watch the trail and see that it did not divide. About four o'clock we came to the place where the village had been apparently only a few days before, and went into camp two miles below the forks of the Rosebud. The scouts again all pushed out to look for the village, and at eleven o'clock at night Custer had everything packed up and followed the scouts up the right-hand fork of the Rosebud.

"About daylight we went into camp, made coffee, and soon after it was light the scouts brought Custer word that they had seen the village from the top of the divide that separates the Rosebud from Little Horn River. We moved up the creek until near its head, and concealed ourselves in a ravine. It was about three miles from the head of the creek where we then were to the top of the divide where the Indian scouts said the village could be seen, and after hiding his command General Custer, with a few orderlies, galloped forward to look at the Indian camp. In about an hour, Custer returned and said he could not see the Indian village, but the scouts and a halfbreed guide, Mich Boyer, said they could distinctly see it some fifteen miles off. While General Custer was looking for the Indian village the scouts came in and reported that he had been discovered, and that news was then on its way to the village that he was coming. Another scout said two Sioux war parties had stolen up and seen the command; and on looking in a ravine nearby, sure enough fresh pony tracks were found. Custer had 'officers call' blown, gave his orders and the command was put in fighting order. The scouts were ordered forward and the regiment moved at a walk. After going about three miles the scouts reported Indians ahead, and the command then took the trail. Our way lay down a little creek, a branch of the Little Horn, and after going some six miles we discovered an Indian lodge ahead, and Custer bore down on it at a stiff trot. In coming to it we found ourselves in a freshly abandoned Indian camp, all the lodges of which were gone except the one we saw, and on entering it we found it contained a dead Indian. From this point we could see into the Little Horn Valley and observed heavy clouds of dust rising about five miles distant. Many thought the Indians were moving away and I think General Custer believed so, for he sent word to Colonel Reno, who was ahead with three companies of the Seventh Regiment, to push on the scouts rapidly and head for the dust. Reno took a steady gallop down the creek bottom three miles to where it emptied into the Little Horn, and found a natural ford across Little Horn River. He started to cross, when the scouts came back and called out to him to hold on, that the Sioux were coming in large numbers to meet him. He crossed over, however, formed his companies on the prairie in line of battle, and moved forward at a trot but soon took a gallop. The valley was about three-fourths of a mile wide. On the left a line of low, round hills, and on the right the river bottom, covered with a growth of cottonwood trees and bushes. After scattering shots were fired from the hills and a few from the river bottom and Reno's skirmishers returned the shots, he advanced about a mile from the ford to a line of timber on the right and dismounted his men to fight on foot. The horses were sent into the timber, and the men formed on the prairies and advanced toward the Indians. The Indians, mounted on ponies, came across the prairies and opened a heavy fire on the soldiers.

"After skirmishing for a few minutes, Reno fell back to his horses in the timber. The Indians moved to his left and rear, evidently with the intention of cutting him off from the ford. Reno ordered his men to mount and move through the timber. Just as the men got into the saddle the Sioux, who had advanced in the timber, fired at close range and killed one soldier. Colonel Reno then commanded the men to dismount, and they did so, but he soon ordered them to mount again and moved out onto the open prairie. The command headed for the ford, pressed closely by Indians in large numbers, and at every moment the rate of speed was increased, until it became a dead run for the ford. The Sioux, mounted on their swift ponies, dashed up by the side of the soldiers and fired at them, killing both men and horses. Little resistance was offered and it was a complete rout to the ford. I did not see the men at the ford, and do not know what took place further than that a good many were killed when the command left the timber. Just as I got out my horse stumbled and fell and I was dismounted, the horse running after Reno's command. I saw several soldiers who were dismounted, their horses having been killed or having run away.

"*I think the Indian village must have contained about 6,000 people, fully 3,000 of whom were warriors. The Indians fought Reno first and then went to fight Custer, after which they came back to finish Reno. The same Indians were in all the attacks. I think the Indians were commanded by Sitting Bull in person. There were eight or nine other chiefs in the field.*

"I saw five chiefs, and each one carried a flag for their men to rally around. Some of the flags were red, others yellow, white and blue and one a black flag. All the chiefs handled their warriors splendidly. I think Crazy Horse and his band were in the fight. The Indians must have lost as many men in killed and wounded as the whites did. Custer's men made a good fight, and no doubt killed a great many Indians. I don't think a single man escaped from Custer's part of the field. They were completely surrounded on every side by at least 2,500 warriors.

"A Crow Indian scout named 'Curley' came in the day after the battle and stated he was in the fight with Custer. He says the fight lasted over one hour, Custer contending against ten times his number. The men fought splendidly until the Big Chief (Custer) fell, and then they became somewhat demoralized. Most of the officers and men had been killed before Custer. 'Curley' says the Indians fought Custer on foot, and charged his men again and again. He thinks a great many more Indians were killed in the fight than were in Custer's command. 'Curley' is a truthful Indian, and his statement may be relied on."

—3—

Sixteen years after the battle, James McLaughlin, famous Indian agent, who knew Sitting Bull and many of the Sioux chiefs as well as any white man, wrote a long letter to Olin D. Wheeler, in answer to certain inquiries. It was probably first published in Wheeler's "Six Thousand Miles Through Wonderland." The part referring to Sitting Bull and the important bearing Reno's retreat had on the outcome of the battle, is especially important:

"Sitting Bull was dull in intellect, and not near as able a man as Gall, Hump, Crow and many others who were regarded as subordinate to him; but he was an adept schemer and very cunning, and could work upon the credulity of the Indians to a wonderful degree, and this, together with great obstinacy and tenacity, gained for him his world-wide reputation.

"Sitting Bull claimed in his statement to me, that he directed and led in the Custer fight; but all the other Indians with whom I have talked contradict it, and say that Sitting Bull fled with his family as soon as the village was attacked by Major Reno's command, and that he was making his way to a place of safety and was several miles out in the hills when overtaken by some of his friends with news of victory over the soldiers, whereupon he returned, and, in his usual style, took all the credit of victory to himself as having planned for the outcome, and as having been on a bluff overlooking the battlefield, appeasing the evil spirits and invoking the Great Spirit for the result of the fight. And when considering the ignorance and inherent superstition of the average Sioux Indian at that time, it is not to be wondered at that the majority, if not all, were willing to accept it, especially when united in common cause and what they considered as their only safety from annihilation. As a matter of fact, there was no man who led or directed that fight; it was a 'pell-mell' rush under a number of recognized warriors as leaders, with Gall of the Hunkpapas, and Crazy Horse of the Cheyennes, the more prominent.

"Sitting Bull had a pair of twin boys born about that time; one of them died about a year ago, and the other is yet living. He—Sitting Bull—denied having left one of these boys behind in his camp, but admitted that his family had gotten separated; and that the story of his being in the hills during the fight was accounted for by his absence, for a time, in searching for the missing members of his family.

"The Indians with whom I have talked, deny having

mutilated any of the killed, but admit that many dead bodies were mutilated by women of the camp; and they also claim that the fight with Custer was of short duration. They have no knowledge as to minutes and hours, but have explained by the distance that could be walked while the fight lasted, and they vary from twenty minutes to three-quarters of an hour, none placing it longer than forty-five minutes. This does not include the fight with Reno before his retreat, but from the time the second command—Custer's—advanced, and the fight with his command commenced.

"The opinion of the Indians regarding Reno's first attack and short stand at that point, all agree that it was his retreat that gave them the victory over Custer's command. The 'helter skelter' retreat of Reno's command enthused the Indians to such an extent that, flushed with excitement and this early success, they were reckless in their charge upon Custer's command, and with the large number of Indians thus fully enthused that small command was but a slight check to their sweeping impetuosity. The Indians also state that the separate detachments made their victory over the troops more certain."

Chapter 5

Was Reno's Retreat Responsible for Custer's Defeat?

SECOND only to the criticism leveled at General Custer himself, Major Reno and his reputation have had to bear the brunt of the most vicious attacks and slanderous statements.

Did Major Reno completely lose his head when the Indians attacked him in the valley of the Little Big Horn?

Was his retirement across the river a rout or an orderly retreat?

Did Reno show cool bravery once he reached the hilltop, or was he still a victim of fright?

Should he have tried to go to Custer's rescue when Benteen showed him the controversial last message from Custer: "Come on. Big Village. Be quick, bring packs. W. W. Cooke. P. S. Bring pack."

Can Reno be held partially responsible for the complete annihilation of Custer and the five troops who rode under his immediate command?

—2—

First, let us look into the military record of the man. The following is taken from the New York *Herald*, of July 7, 1876:

"Major Marcus A. Reno, commanding the right wing of the regiment, was born in Carrolltown, Illinois. He was a cadet at West Point from September 1, 1851, to July 1, 1857, when he graduated, ranking twenty in his class. On July 1, 1857, he was made Brevet Second Lieutenant of dragoons, and served on frontier duty at Fort Walla Walla, Washington Territory, in 1858 and 1859, scouting. June 14, 1858, he was commissioned Second Lieutenant of dragoons, and served until 1861 at Fort Dalles, Oregon, and at Fort Walla Walla. At the opening of the Civil War he was ordered to the East, and on November 12, 1861, received a commission as Captain of the First cavalry. . . . In the action at Kelly's Ford, Va., March 17, 1863, he was disabled by injuries, and brevetted Major for gallant and meritorious services on the field. . . . June 1, 1864; battle of Trevillian station, June 11, 1864; the action at Darbytown, July 28, 1864, and various skirmishes during June and July. . . . At the battle of Cedar Creek, October 19, 1864, he was brevetted Lieutenant Colonel for gallant and meritorious services. On July 20, 1865, he was commissioned Colonel of the Twelfth Pennsylvania cavalry volunteers. . . . On March 13, 1865, he was commissioned Brevet Colonel and Brevet Brigadier General of United States volunteers for gallant and meritorious services during the rebellion."

Further notes on Major Reno are contained in the following paragraphs:

"Major M. A. Reno was a native of Illinois and a great-grandnephew of Philippe François Renault who came to this country with Lafayette. Renault was rewarded for services to the United States Government with large tracts of lands, for possession of which the Reno heirs have been fighting for a quarter of a century, for their valuation now amounts to $400,000,000.

"Major Reno was graduated from West Point and while

there, was closely associated with General Custer and also with General Jackson of Nashville. During Major Reno's visit to Nashville in 1888, he was a guest of General Jackson, at Belle Meade, for several days of his stay. It was their second meeting, since their parting at West Point, their first being in action during the Civil War, when each called to the other and waved salutes from the firing line.

"Major Reno was married to Miss Mary Hannah Ross, whose father, Mr. Robert Ross, a Pennsylvania capitalist, founded one of the largest banks and the first glass works in Harrisburg, the State capital. Major Reno's wife was a niece of the late Senator Don Cameron's wife, who was a Miss Haldeman, of Harrisburg, and a kinswoman of the founder of the Louisville *Courier Journal*. Major Reno had only one child—Robert Ross Reno, who married Miss Ittie Kinney, daughter of Colonel George S. Kinney, of Nashville."

Among Major Reno's effects after his death there was found the following account of the battle. It is supposed to have been his last testament of the whole affair:

". . . The last time I ever saw General Custer alive, was on the morning of June 25, the day upon which he saw the sun shine for the last time. The two columns, commanded by himself and myself respectively, were moving parallel to each other and he waved his hat for me to come to him.

"I did so. He was riding a fine thoroughbred horse that he had gotten in Kentucky, when the regiment was after the Ku Klux Klan of the South. He was dressed in a full suit of buckskin, with Indian fringes along the seams of his pants and of his coat sleeves. I had known Custer for a long time; as cadet at West Point and during the Civil and Indian wars, and on this particular morning, he did not wear his usual confident and cheerful air, but seemed rather depressed, as with some premonition of coming horror. What that was is now a matter of history.

"*I remember, as I rode back to my command, the last remark I ever made to him was—'Let us keep together.' In his jaunty way he lifted his broad brimmed hat as much as to say, 'I hear you.' But alas! he did not heed me, and that afternoon he was cold in death's embrace. . . .*"

"I assumed command of the companies assigned to me at once and proceeded to march in the direction of the Indians, without any definite instructions or orders. I saw the battalion under Benteen move off far to the left and I did not see him again until about 2:30 P.M. of that same day. At half past 12 P.M. the Adjutant gave me an order from Custer in the following words:

" 'Go in at as rapid a gait as you think prudent, for the village is only two and a half miles off and *running away* and you will be supported by the whole outfit.'

"I proceeded at a fast trot until I crossed the Little Big Horn, and as soon as the battalion was in hand, I charged, supposing myself followed by Custer, with the companies under his command. For as I led the advance and was the first to be engaged and draw fire, my command was, in consequence, the one to be supported and not the one from which support could be expected.

"With the Ree scouts on my left, I charged down the valley, driving the Indians, who came out from a belt of cottonwoods to meet us, with ease before me for about three miles. It was too easy, in fact, for I soon saw that I was being drawn into some kind of a trap; I knew that these Indians could fight harder, especially as we were nearing their village, the entrance to which they certainly would not leave unopposed.

"Neither Custer nor Benteen was in sight, a fact I attributed to the great clouds of dust, and as I drew nearer to the villages, the ground seemed suddenly to grow Indians;

they came running towards me in swarms and from all directions. . . .

"I was soon convinced that I had, at least ten to one against me and I was forced on the defensive. This I did, taking possession of a point of woods which furnished, near its edge, a shelter for the horses. Under cover of the timber, I dismounted my battalion, detailing number four of each group of 'fours' to hold the horses, thus reducing our fighting force to about seventy-five men. I then deployed the companies as skirmishers, the right resting on the timber, the left extending across the valley, and our front facing the village. The Sioux now made their first attack and the firing was heavy and rapid for one hour and a half. *The enemy increased so greatly in numbers that we were forced into the timber for protection, but I firmly believe that if, at that moment, all our companies had been together the Indians would have been driven from their village.*

"Almost immediately after entering the wood, I found that we were being surrounded, and I knew my only hope was to get out of the timber and reach some high ground. The wood was about twenty feet lower than the plain where the Indians were, and the advantage of position was theirs. I mounted my command and charged through the Reds in a solid body. As we cut our way through them, the fighting was hand to hand and it was instant death to him who fell from his saddle, or was wounded. As we dashed through them, my men were so close to the Indians that they would discharge their pistols right into the breasts of the savages, then throw them away and seize their carbines, not having time to replace their revolvers in the holsters.

"The scene that ensued was such as can be seen only once in a lifetime. Our horses were on the dead run with, in many instances, two and three men on one animal. We plunged into the Little Big Horn and began the climb of the opposite bluffs. This incline was the steepest that I have ever seen either horse or mule ascend and our only way was through a buffalo trail, worn in the banks, and only sufficiently wide to permit one man to pass at a time. In this narrow place there were necessarily much crowding and confusion and many of the men were compelled to cling to the horses' necks and tails for support, to prevent their being trampled to death or falling back into the river. Into this mass of men and horses, the Indians poured a continuous and deadly fire and under its leaden hail, the loss of life was frightful and the Little Big Horn was transferred into a seeming river of human blood. . . .

"As soon as my men reached the top of the bluffs, they dismounted and opened fire upon the Indians, in order to cover the ascent of their comrades, and when the remnant of my command was about me again, I quickly threw them into a line of defense, while below us, in the plain, we could see the Indians stripping, scalping and mutilating the bodies of our dead. Fortunately, at this juncture, I saw Benteen with his three companies and Captain McDougall with Company B, and the pack train, coming to us over the bluffs. Benteen informed me that he had hunted all morning for the Indians, and seeing no sign of them anywhere, he thought it best to return to the Little Big Horn valley and join the main command. He had seen nothing of Custer, but he had received from a trumpeter this order from Cooke.

" 'Benteen come on; big village. Be quick. Bring packs.'

"He therefore hastened to the Little Big Horn, expecting to find Custer there. He now became seriously uneasy over Custer's non-appearance and as senior officer of our united command, I sent Captain Weir, with his company from Benteen's column to open communication with Custer; while, in the meantime, I was dismounting my men, putting my wounded under protection, had driven the horses and mules of the pack train in a depression in the hills and had placed my men along the crests of the bluffs. In a very short time Captain Weir sent back word by Lieutenant Hare, that he was having a heavy fight with the Indians who surrounded him in overwhelming numbers and that he could go no farther. He was ordered to return, which he did with difficulty and he had scarcely reached our lines, when we were most furiously attacked on all sides by the Sioux. . . .

"From one of the hills that overlooked our corral, the enemy poured a deadly fire, killing scores of horses and mules, while many of the packers in the train were shot dead and wounded. But my men stood firm, although the fight continued with unabated fury till nine P.M. when it had grown very dark and the Sioux ceased firing, for the Indians will not fight after nightfall. Thus ended the 25th day of June. . . . All during the night, the Indians remained in hearing distance of my position and kept up a most fearful scalp-dance and the darkness was made lurid by their blazing fires, in which many prisoners were burned at the stake.

"Finally our work was completed. We had done all we could, to fortify our position and I felt confident now that I could hold my own during the coming attack. The morning of June 26 dawned about half past two A.M. and exactly at that moment, we heard the crack of two rifles, which warned us that the assault would soon be made. This was the signal for the beginning of a fire that I have never seen equalled. . . .

"About two P.M., the grass in the bottom was set on fire and was followed up by the Indians who encouraged its burning. Evidently it was being fired for a purpose, which I discovered later to be the creation of a dense smoke, behind which they were packing and preparing to move their village tepees. Between six and seven P.M. the Indians came out from behind the clouds of smoke and dust and we had a good view of them as they filed away in the direction of the Big Horn mountains, moving in almost perfect military order. The length of their column was fully equal to that of a large division of the Cavalry Corps of the Army of the Potomac, as I have seen it on its march.

"We now thought again of Custer, of whom nothing

Famous picture of "Custer's Last Battle" that hung in thousands of taverns over America for two generations. It was presented to the Seventh Cavalry by Mr. Adolphus Busch, and was destroyed by fire at Fort Bliss, Texas, on June 13, 1946.

Last moments of Custer's Stand, painted by the distinguished artist and Marine officer, Col. John W. Thomason, Jr.

had been heard or seen since the morning previous, when he separated his command, and we concluded that the Indians had gotten between him and us and had driven him towards the boat at the mouth of the Little Big Horn river. That he and his entire command lay dead, only a short distance from us, down the valley, did not once occur to us as being within the realms of the possible. Afterwards we found that his massacre had been accomplished before Benteen joined me on the bluffs, at about the time of my fight with the Indians in the timber, where, had I remained five moments later, I am convinced—as I was then—that my column would have shared the same awful fate as Custer's. . . .

"Custer's disaster was not the defeat of the Seventh Cavalry, who held their ground for two days, after his massacre, against a savage force outnumbering ours ten to one; and had he not separated his regiment, he and his five companies would not only have escaped their awful fate, but our united force could have whipped Sitting Bull and his entire village.

"I think it was about ten A.M. that General Terry rode into my lines. He knew nothing definitely of Custer, but said that he heard from Crow scouts that the Indians had whipped Custer; but this he did not believe. He assumed command and immediately sent Benteen with his company to search for Custer and very soon our brave leader's unfortunate fate was known to us all. I had, in this last fight, lost forty men and had sixty wounded and all day of the 27th I was employed in caring for my sufferers, getting them doctors, medicine and canvas to protect them from the scorching sun and by evening I had them moved down to General Terry's camp. It was then too late to move my own camp, so we were compelled to remain another night on the bluffs, but fortunately during the cool night, the odor from the dead men and animals that surrounded us on all sides, was not so terrible as it had been under the heat of the sun. On the morning of the 28th at five A.M. I proceeded with my command to Custer's battleground, where we buried the mutilated remains of all our dead comrades. The scene was beyond description. It filled us with horror and anguish. For the dead had been mutilated in the most savage manner and they lay as they had fallen, scattered in wildest confusion over the ground, in groups of two and three, or piled in an indiscriminate mass of men and horses. They had lain thus for nearly three days under the fierce heat of the sun, exposed to swarms of flies and carrion-crows and the scene was rendered even more desolate by the deep silence which seemed to hang like a weird mystery over our dead friends. By force of contrast, this very quietness spoke more plainly than words, of the fierce hand to hand conflict, the din and crash of battle, the demoniac war-cry of the Sioux and of how our brave and daring men fell before the overpowering strength of a savage foe.

"We found General Custer on the bluffs and near him lay the bodies of eleven of his officers. As a tribute to his bravery the Indians had not mutilated General Custer and he lay as if asleep; but all the other men had been most brutally mangled and had been stripped of their clothing. Many of their skulls had been crushed in, eyes had been torn from their sockets, hands, feet, arms, legs and noses had been wrenched off; many had their flesh cut in strips the entire length of their bodies and there were others whose limbs were closely perforated with bullet-holes, showing that the torture had been inflicted while the wretched victims were yet alive. There were twenty-nine enlisted men missing from this field of blood and they undoubtedly had been taken prisoners and perished at the stake, while the Indians were celebrating their scalp dance on the night of the 25th, in sight of my camp.

"Lying almost at Custer's feet was young Reed, a nephew of the General's, who had been visiting him at Fort Lincoln and who had pleaded to go on the campaign, where this handsome lad of nineteen met such an untimely fate. Within a few feet of the General, lay his two brothers, Boston and Tom. There was in the whole army no more popular man than gallant Tom Custer. He was young, handsome, a prince of good fellows and full of that bravery that ever characterized the Custers. He had served with distinction during the war and had frequently before been engaged in Indian fights. As we approached him we were horrified to see that his body had been opened and his heart torn out. Thus I know that the vengeance of Rain-in-the-Face had been at work. Several years before Rain-in-the-Face had murdered two white men of our Fort and afterwards boasted of it in the Reservation. He was arrested and brought to trial by Tom Custer, but before the time appointed for his case had arrived, the wily Indian had escaped, sending back word to Captain Tom that he would be revenged by cutting out his captor's heart. Rain-in-the-Face kept his word, by literally tearing out the loyal heart of young Tom Custer. Near these three brothers and their boyish nephew, lay their brother-in-law, Lieutenant Calhoun, who had fallen on the skirmish line. . . .

"Custer's command was completely annihilated, not one of his men escaping, except a Crow scout—an Indian named Curley. He says that he remained with General Custer until he saw that everything was lost; then seeing a Sioux jump off his pony to kill a wounded officer, he sprang on the pony and wrapping himself in the Sioux's blanket he effected his escape. He says that Custer's command was entirely surrounded but that the men made a brave resistance and only succumbed to overwhelming numbers.

"He also stated that during the fight, the soldiers had some trouble with their carbines, for from his hiding place he could see the men sitting down under fire, and working with their guns—a story that had confirmation in the fact that I found knives with broken blades, lying near the dead bodies on the battlefield. Curley also tells of one soldier who seeing all was lost, tried to save himself by flight and he had reached a ravine unperceived, when he was suddenly confronted by a dozen young bucks and rather than fall into their hands and be tortured, the soldier placed his revolver to his head and fired. Many Indians, too young to fight, were ordered to stampede the horses and this was effected by the youthful bucks suddenly springing up before the horses and waving their blankets before them. The horses took fright and were driven into the Indian lines and thus they gained not only numbers of fine horses, but also a large amount of ammunition that was packed in the saddles. After the fight, Curley states the squaws, old gray-haired warriors and even children came on the battleground to plunder and mutilate the dead and crush in their skulls with heavy stone mallets.

"After leaving Custer's field I went with my command over my own battleground. Here we found the waistband of Sergeant Hughes' trousers very much stained with blood; he had been Custer's flag bearer, and as his was among the missing bodies we concluded that he had been brought here alive and had been given a death of torture. There lay a dead cavalryman with arrow sticking in his back and his skull crushed in. One ghastly find was near the center of the field where three tepee poles were standing upright in the ground in the form of a triangle, and on top of each were inverted camp kettles while below them, on the grass, were the heads of three men whom I recognized as belonging to my command. These heads had been severed from their trunks by some very sharp instrument, as the flesh was smoothly cut and they were placed within the triangle, facing one another, in a horrible sightless stare. Their bodies were never found.

"The plain was strewn with Indian ponies—some still struggling in their death agony—and horses that were branded 'Seventh Cavalry,' while frequently we came upon great blackened spaces in the grass which showed us where the fires had been built, in which so many of our men had perished, and around which the Indians had celebrated their horrible scalp-dance on the night of the 25th. . . .

"After burying our dead, my next move was to go over Custer's trail and study it. Our great mistake from the first was that we underestimated the strength of the Indians, and it was this alone which led to such disastrous results. I am convinced that, had Custer known the great force of the Sioux, he would never have divided his command. Just before he ordered me to charge the Indians, a scout came in and announced that the village was near and the Indians were 'running away.'

"This seemed true for we could see a great cloud of dust ahead of us with mounted Sioux moving about as if greatly excited. This information must have had weight with Custer and caused him to change his plan of attack; for instead of following me, as I was informed he would, his trail proved that he intended to support me by moving farther down the stream and attacking the village in flank, that thus our two commands might work toward each other.

"But he found the distance to the ford greater than he imagined and it must have taken him fully three-quarters of an hour to reach it, although his trail proves that he rode rapidly. This gave the Sioux an opportunity to see and understand his maneuver and an hour to prepare for his attack, at the lower end of the village. I am convinced that until General Custer actually made his charge upon the village and rode into an ambuscade of fully two thousand Indians, he was not aware of their great strength.

"The point from which he made his charge was cut into deep ravines swarming with hidden foe, who poured upon him a sudden, staggering fire. Could he have gained any position, where defense was possible, he might have saved himself, but that was impossible, for he was entirely surrounded; he could not retreat and even from the very first, I assume he must have known what the result would be.

"Recognizing this, I can well believe how he and his gallant men determined to sell their lives as dearly as possible and fall as only brave men can, fighting to the last. . . .

"After much reflection I have concluded that several great blunders were the direct causes of the Custer Massacre. It is an established fact that Custer disobeyed the orders of the general in command of the expedition; for instead of waiting to meet General Gibbon and General Terry on June 26, at the Rosebud, and then cooperate with them in their concerted plan of action, as he had been directed, as soon as he struck the trail of the Indians he followed it till he came upon the Indian village on June 25.

"Then without attempting to communicate with either Terry or Gibbon and without taking the trouble to ascertain the strength or position of the Indians, he divided his regiment into three separate battalions—an act which nothing can justify—and dashed against the Indians, thus recklessly driving his own and my commands into an ambuscade of five thousand Sioux.

"Nor did Custer take into consideration the unfed and exhausted condition of his men and horses, and he entirely ignored the fact that the Indians were on the *qui vive* and ready for attack, at noon, whereas it would have been an easy matter to surprise them very early in the morning.

"The only explanation for such conduct on the part of so brilliant an officer as Custer undoubtedly was, otherwise, was his great personal ambition.

"He had thought himself partially disgraced because he had been superseded in command of the expedition, by General Terry, and it was well known that he was resolved, if possible, to carry off all the honors of the campaign. For, being in command of the only cavalry regiment attached to the expedition, he knew the brunt of the fighting would necessarily fall on him, and he made no secret of his intention to cut loose from Terry, where there was fighting to do and to carry on the campaign on his own hook.

"Absolutely insensible to fear, he was also reckless and daring in the extreme, and driven by an intense desire to distinguish himself by some brilliant exploit he made his headlong dash to a horrible death, without the most casual regard for the maxims of military prudence.

"Even now, after the lapse of nearly ten years, the horror of Custer's battlefield is still vividly before me, and the harrowing sight of those mutilated and decomposing bodies crowning the heights on which poor Custer fell will linger in my memory till death."

—3—

On the evening of June 27, 1876, a petition was circulated among the surviving men and non-coms of the Seventh Cavalry. Certain it is an important sidelight on the feelings of the troopers, before the fear and excitement of the battle had died out.

"Camp Near Big Horn, On Yellowstone River,
July 4, 1876

"To His Excellency The President and the Honorable Representatives of the United States—Gentlemen: We the enlisted men and survivors of the battle on the heights of the Little Big Horn River on the 25th and 26th of June, 1876, of the Seventh regiment of cavalry, who subscribe our names to this petition, most earnestly solicit the president and the representatives of our country that the vacancies among the commissioned officers of our regiment made by the slaughter of our brave, heroic and lamented lieutenant colonel, George A. Custer, and the other noble dead commissioned officers of our regiment who fell close by him on the bloody field, daring the savage demons to the last, be filled by the officers of the regiment only; that Major M. A. Reno be our lieutenant colonel, vice Custer, killed; that Captain F. W. Benteen be our Major, vice Reno, promoted; the other vacancies to be filled by the officers of the regiment by seniority. Your petitioners know this to be contrary to the established rule of promotion, but prayerfully solicit a deviation from the usual rule in this case, as it will be conferring a bravely-fought-for and justly-merited promotion on officers who, by their bravery, coolness and decision on the 25th and 26th of June, 1876, saved the lives of every man now living of the Seventh Cavalry, who participated in the battle, one that would have ended with the loss of life of every officer and enlisted man on the field only for the position taken by Major Reno, which we held with bitter tenacity against fearful odds to the last. To support the assertion, had our position been taken one hundred yards back from the brink of the heights overlooking the river, we would have been entirely cut off from water, and from behind these heights the Indians would have swarmed in hundreds, picking off our men by detail, and before midday of June 26 not one officer or enlisted man of our regiment would have been left, to tell of our dreadful fate, as we would have been completely surrounded.

"With the prayerful hope that our petition be granted, we have the honor to forward it through our commanding officer."

The strange and touching letter was duly signed by 236 privates and non-commissioned officers of the Seventh Cavalry.

In answer to this petition there arrived one month later the formal reply of the Commanding General of the Army:

"Headquarters of the Army of the United States, Washington, D. C., August 5, 1876. The judicious and skilful conduct of Major Reno and Captain Benteen is appreciated, but the promotions caused by General Custer's death have been made by the President and confirmed by the Senate; therefore this petition cannot be granted.

W. T. Sherman, General."

The first reports of the great disaster had hardly reached the public before a scapegoat was sought on whom the blame might be pinned. For a time there was rather definite criticism of General Terry, but soon this was transferred to Major Reno.

The most strident voice in the attacks on Reno was that of Custer's biographer, Captain Frederick A. Whittaker. In interviews, articles and speeches, Whittaker, who had served under Custer in the Civil War, assailed Reno and his conduct in the battle. So widespread became the criticism that finally Major Reno asked the President for a Court of Inquiry. Finally the following army order was posted:

"By direction of the president, and on the application of Major Marcus A. Reno, Seventh Cavalry, a court of inquiry hereby is appointed to assemble at Chicago, Ill., on Monday, the 13th day of January, 1879, or as soon thereafter as practicable, for the purpose of inquiring into Major Reno's conduct at the battle of the Little Big Horn River on the 25th and 26th of June, 1876. The court will report the facts and its opinion as to whether, from all the circumstances in the case, any further proceedings are necessary."

For several weeks the trial dragged on in Rooms No. 14 and 16 in the old Palmer House. With a few exceptions it is proper to say that, by and large, it became more a whitewash than a serious attempt to get at the bottom of the tragedy. At all costs the honor of the regiment and of the army had to be sustained. Of the officers called only Lieutenant Godfrey permitted himself to be critical of Reno.

Scouts Gerard and Herendon were both somewhat confused in their lengthy testimony, and two civilian packers accused Reno of being intoxicated on the night of June 25. But on the whole, the long and often dreary testimony brought out little, or nothing, that was not previously known.

On February 21, 1879, the findings of the Court, with the opinion of Judge Advocate General W. M. Drum, were submitted to Secretary of War, George W. McCreary. For some unknown reason the official document was dated March 11.

"Findings of the Court

Headquarters of the Army
Adjutant General's Office
Washington, March 11, 1879

"I. The Court of Inquiry of which Colonel John H. King, Ninth Infantry, is President, instituted by direction of the President, in Special Orders No. 255, Headquarters of the Army, Adjutant General's Office, November 25, 1878, on the application of Major Marcus A. Reno, Seventh Cavalry, for the purpose of inquiring into Major Reno's conduct at the battle of the Little Big Horn River, on the 25th and 26th days of June, 1876, has reported the following facts and opinions, viz.:

"First. On the morning of the 25th of June, 1876, the Seventh Cavalry, Lieutenant Colonel G. A. Custer commanding, operating against the hostile Indians in Montana Territory, near the Little Big Horn River, was divided into four battalions, two of which were commanded by Colonel Custer in person, with the exception of one company in charge of the pack train; one by Major Reno and one by Captain Benteen. This division took place from about twelve (12) to fifteen (15) miles from the scene of the battle or battles afterwards fought. The column under Captain Benteen received orders to move to the left for an indefinite distance (to the first and second valleys) hunting Indians, with orders to charge any it might meet with. The battalion under Major Reno received orders to draw out of the column, and doing so marched parallel with and only a short distance from, the column commanded by Colonel Custer.

"Second. About three or four miles from what afterwards

was found to be the Little Big Horn River, where the fighting took place, Major Reno received orders to move forward as rapidly as he thought prudent, until coming up with the Indians, who were reported fleeing, he would charge them and drive everything before him, and would receive the support of the column under Colonel Custer.

"Third. In obedience to the orders given by Colonel Custer, Captain Benteen marched to the left (south) at an angle of about forty-five degrees, but, meeting an impracticable country, was forced by it to march more to his right than the angle above indicated and nearer approaching a parallel route to that trail followed by the rest of the command.

"Fourth. Major Reno, in obedience to the orders given him, moved on at a fast trot on the main Indian trail until reaching the Little Big Horn River, which he forded, and halted for a few minutes to re-form his battalion. After re-forming, he marched the battalion forward towards the Indian village, down stream or in a northerly direction, two companies in line of battle and one in support, until about halfway to the point where he finally halted, when he brought the company in reserve forward to the line of battle, continuing the movement at a fast trot or gallop until after passing over a distance of about two miles, when he halted and dismounted to fight on foot at a point of timber upon which the right flank of his battalion rested. After fighting in this formation for less than half an hour, the Indians passing to his left rear and appearing in his front, the skirmish line was withdrawn to the timber, and the fight continued for a short time—half an hour or forty-five minutes in all—when the command, or nearly all of it, was mounted, formed, and at a rapid gait, was withdrawn to a hill on the opposite side of the river. In this movement one officer and about sixteen soldiers and citizens were left in the woods, besides one wounded man or more, two citizens and thirteen soldiers rejoining the command afterwards. In this retreat Major

Reno's battalion lost some twenty-nine men in killed and wounded, and three officers, including Doctor De Wolf, killed.

"Fifth. In the meantime Captain Benteen, having carried out, as far as was practicable, the spirit of his orders, turned in the direction of the route taken by the remainder of the regiment, and reaching the trail, followed it to near the crossing of the Little Big Horn, reaching there about the same time Reno's command was crossing the river in retreat lower down, and finally joined his battalion with that of Reno, on the hill. Forty minutes or one hour later the pack train, which had been left behind on the trail by the rapid movement of the command and the delays incident to its march, joined the united command, which then consisted of seven companies, together with about thirty or thirty-five men belonging to the companies under Colonel Custer.

"Sixth. After detaching Benteen's columns Colonel Custer moved with his immediate command, on the trail followed by Reno, to a point within about one mile of the river, where he diverged to the right (or northward), following the general direction of the river to a point about four miles below that [afterward taken by Major Reno] where he and his command were destroyed by the hostiles. The last living witness of this march, Trumpeter Martini, left Colonel Custer's command when it was about two miles distant from the field where it afterwards met its fate. There is nothing more in evidence as to this command, save that firing was heard proceeding from its direction from about the time Reno retreated from the bottom up to the time the pack train was approaching the position on the hill. All firing which indicated fighting was concluded before the final preparations were made in Major Reno's command for the movement which was afterwards attempted.

"Seventh. After the distribution of ammunition and a proper provision for the wounded men, Major Reno's entire command moved down the river in the direction it was thought Custer's column had taken, and in which it was known General Terry's command was to be found. This movement was carried sufficiently far to discover that its continuance would imperil the entire command, upon which it returned to the position formerly occupied, and made a successful resistance till succor reached it. The defense of the position on the hill was a heroic one against fearful odds.

"The conduct of the officers throughout was excellent, and while subordinates, in some instances, did more for the safety of the command by brilliant displays of courage than did Major Reno, there was nothing in his conduct which requires animadversion from this Court.

Opinion

"It is the conclusion of this Court, in view of all the facts in evidence, that no further proceedings are necessary in this case, and it expresses this opinion in compliance with the concluding clause of the order convening the court.

"II. The proceedings and opinion of the Court of Inquiry in the foregoing case of Major Marcus A. Reno, Seventh Cavalry, are approved by order of the President.

"III. By direction of the Secretary of War, the Court of Inquiry of which Colonel John H. King, Ninth Infantry, is President is hereby dissolved.

"By command of General Sherman:

E. D. Townsend

Official Adjutant General"

And thus one of the most famous Courts of Inquiry in the history of the U. S. Army came to its dreary close.

—4—

Reno's end, in keeping with the latter years of his life, was a tragic one. Within a year or two of the battle he was tried by Court Martial for indecent proposals to a brother officer's wife. He was convicted and sentenced to be dishonorably discharged from the service. Reno's family had sufficient influence in Washington to have the sentence commuted to two years' temporary dismissal from the army without pay.

Back in the service again, Reno found the publicity and innuendoes of his enemies too devastating for his temperament. He was tried for "Conduct unbecoming an officer and a gentleman." The case revolved around a drunken brawl in a billiard hall. This time Reno was summarily dismissed.

His last years were bitter and unfortunate. There is a legend that he was found dead in the streets of the national capital, but there seems little question that he actually died in a Washington hospital.

Two or three western writers and Indian authorities, notably Fred Dustin and E. A. Brininstool, have valiantly tried to vindicate Reno and his battle actions. But the cloud that has for so long been hanging over his head has been hard to dissipate.

Chapter 6

Did Benteen Disregard Custer's Order "Come On! Bring Packs"?

*I*N Part One of this book the personal story of Sergeant Windolph has largely covered the actions of "H" Troop, and the two other troops under Captain Benteen's immediate command. The Sergeant's undying affection for his old company commander is evident even to the casual reader.

But to many students of the battle the colorful, white-haired captain has been a somewhat less complete hero than he has been to his old Top Sergeant. Some critics are rather severe in their handling of Captain Benteen and his reactions to the two messages for help sent by General Custer, when the General realized what a hard fight he had on his hands.

These critics claim that Benteen should have gone to the support of Custer, regardless of the cost. They argue that the last message from Custer, carried by the little Italian trumpeter-orderly, Martini, left no room for doubt. Custer was in desperate shape. He needed help. He needed his reserves of ammunition.

Custer and Benteen had been distinctly cool to each other since the episode of the critical letter regarding the alleged "abandonment" of Major Elliott and his seventeen troopers at the Battle of the Washita, in December, 1868.

There are some who have insisted that Benteen kept alive his bitterness and resentment against his commanding officer: that his resentment had become such an all-encompassing hate that it colored many of Benteen's reactions.

Three documents written by Benteen remain as evidence. The first consists of the official report he wrote out for Reno nine days after the death of Custer:

"Camp Seventh Cavalry, July 4, 1876

"Sir: In obedience to verbal instructions received from you, I have the honor to report the operations of my battalion, consisting of Companies D, H and K, on the 25th ultimo.

"The directions I received from Lieutenant Colonel Custer were, to move with my command to the left, to send well-mounted officers with about six men who should ride rapidly to a line of bluffs about five miles to our left and front, with instructions to report at once to me if anything of Indians could be seen from that point. I was to follow the movement of this detachment as rapidly as possible. Lieutenant Gibson was the officer selected, and I followed closely with the battalion, at times getting in advance of the detachment. The bluffs designated were gained, but nothing seen but other bluffs quite as large and precipitous as were before me. I kept on to those and the country was the same, there being no valley of any kind that I could see on any side. I had then gone about fully ten miles; the ground was terribly hard on horses, so I determined to carry out the other instructions which were, that if in my judgment there was nothing to be seen of Indians, valleys, &c., in the direction I was going, to return with the battalion to the trail the command was following. I accordingly did so, reaching the trail just in advance of the pack train. I pushed rapidly on, soon getting out of sight of the advance of the train, until reaching a morass, I halted to water the animals, who had been without water since about 8 P.M.

of the day before. . . . This watering did not occasion the loss of fifteen minutes, and when I was moving out the advance of the train commenced watering from that morass. I went at a slow trot until I came to a burning lodge with the dead body of an Indian in it on a scaffold. We did not halt. About a mile farther on I met a sergeant of the regiment with orders from Lieutenant Colonel Custer to the officer in charge of the rear guard and train to bring it to the front with as great rapidity as was possible. Another mile on I met Trumpeter Morton [Martini] of my own company, with a written order from First Lieutenant W. W. Cooke to me, which read:

"'Benteen, come on. Big village. Bring packs.
W. W. Cooke'

"'P. Bring pac's.'

"I could then see no movement of any kind in any direction; a horse on the hill, riderless, being the only living thing I could see in my front. I inquired of the trumpeter what had been done, and he informed [me] that the Indians had 'skedaddled' abandoning the village. Another mile and a half brought me in sight of the stream and plain in which were some of our dismounted men fighting, and Indians charging and recharging them in great numbers. The plain seemed to be alive with them. I then noticed our men in large numbers running for the bluffs on right bank of stream. I concluded at once that those had been repulsed, and was of the opinion that if I crossed the ford with my battalion, that I should have had it treated in like manner; for, from long experience with cavalry, I judge there were 900 veteran Indians right there at that time against which the large element of recruits in my battalion would stand no earthly chance as mounted men. I then moved up to the bluffs and reported my command to Major M. A. Reno. I did not return for the pack train because I deemed it perfectly safe where it was, and we could defend it, had it been threatened, from our position on the bluff; and another thing, it savored too much of coffee-cooling to return when I was sure a fight was progressing in the front, and deeming the train as safe without me.

Very respectfully,
F. W. Benteen
Captain, Seventh Cavalry

Lieutenant Geo. D. Wallace,
  Adjutant Seventh Cavalry"

—2—

The second of Benteen's observations of the battle consists of a very long letter that he wrote his wife, then at Fort Abraham Lincoln. It is reprinted exactly as it was written. Its real interest lies in the fact that it was written in the first flush of the tragic encounter:

"July 4, 1876, Montana
Camp Seventh Cavalry, Yellowstone River
Opposite mouth of Big Horn River
"My darling wife:
  "I wrote you hastily yesterday, to get it off on steamer *Far West*, which boat steamed off at 11 o'clock as intended by her. I acknowledged the receipt of your four letters, the fifth one hasn't come as yet, but, perhaps you meant that five had been written in all. I had just commenced this one to have it in readiness for an opportunity to send, when a courier or orderly comes around with a Circular, announcing that a mail leaves at 6 P.M. today, so I shall be in readiness this time, and have an opportunity of collecting my thoughts. I will commence this letter by sending a copy of the last lines Cooke ever wrote, which was an order to me to this effect.

  " 'Benteen. Come on. Big Village.
      Be quick, bring packs. W. W. Cooke.
      (P.S. Bring pac's)' He left out the *k* in last packs.

"I have the original but it is badly torn and it should be preserved. So keep this letter, as the matter may be of interest hereafter, likewise of use. This note was brought back to me by Trumpeter Martini of my company (which fact saved his life). When I received it I was five or six miles from the village, perhaps more, and the packs at least that distance in my rear. I did not go back for the packs but kept on a stiff trot for the village. When getting at top of hill so that the valley could be seen—I saw an immense number of Indians on the plain, mounted, of course, and charging down on some dismounted men of Reno's command; the balance of Reno's command were mounted, and flying for dear life to the bluffs on the same side of river that I was. I then marched my three companies to them and a more delighted lot of folks you never saw. To commence— On the 22nd of June—Custer, with the Seventh Cavalry left the Steamer *Far West*. General Terry and General Gibbon's command (which latter was then in on the side of river and in same camp in which we now are) and moved up the Rosebud, marching 12 miles—the next day we marched thirty-five miles up the same stream. The next day we marched thirty-five more miles up same stream and went into bivouac, remaining until 12 o'clock P.M. We then marched until about daylight, making about ten miles; about half past five we started again—and after going six or seven miles we halted and officers' call was sounded. We were asked how many men of the companies were with the Company Packs, and instructed that only six could remain with them—and the discourse wound up with—that we should see that the men were supplied with the quantity of ammunition as had been specified in order and that the first company that reported itself in readiness should be the advance company. I knew that my Company was in the desired condition and it being near the point of Assembly I went to it, assured myself of same, then announced to General Custer that 'H' Company was ready; he replied the Advance

is yours, Colonel Benteen. We then moved four or five
miles and halted between the slopes of two hills and the
Regiment was divided into Battalions—Reno getting Companies 'A. G. and M.' I getting 'D. H. K.' From that point
I was ordered with —— to go over the immense hills to
the left, in search of the valley, which was supposed to be
very near by and to pitch in anything I came across—and
to inform Custer at once if I found anything worthy of
same. Well, I suppose I went up and down those hills for
ten miles—and still no valley anywhere in sight, the horses
were fast giving out from steady climbing—and as my orders
had been fulfilled I struck diagonally for the trail the command had marched on, getting to it just before the pack
train got there—or on the trail just ahead of it. I then marched
rapidly and after about six or seven miles came upon a burning tepee—in which was the body of an Indian on a scaffold,
arrayed gorgeously— None of the command was in sight at
this time, the ground from this to the valley was descending
but very rough. I kept up my trot and when I reached a
point very near the ford which was crossed by Reno's
Battalion I got my first sight of the Valley and river—and
Reno's command in full flight for the bluffs to the side I
was then on—of course I joined them at once. The ground
where Reno charged on was a plain five or six miles long
and about one mile or more wide; Custer sent him in there
and promised to support him—after Reno started in, Custer
with his five Companies instead of crossing the ford went
to the right—around some high bluffs—with the intention,
as is supposed, of striking the rear of the village; from the
bluff on which he got he had his first glimpse of the whole
of it—and I can tell you 'twas an immense one. From that
point Cooke sent the note to me by Martini, which I have
quoted on first page. I suppose after the five companies had
closed up somewhat Custer started down for the village,
all throats bursting themselves with cheering (so says Mar-

tini). He had three and one-half or four miles to go before he got to a ford—as the village was on the plain on opposite side to Custer's column. So, when he got over those four miles of rough country and reached the ford, the Indians had availed themselves of the timely information given by the cheering—as to the whereabouts and intentions of that column, and had arrangements completed to receive it. Whether the Indians allowed Custer's column to cross at all, is a mooted question, but I am of the opinion that nearly —if not all of the five companies got into the village—but were driven out immediately—flying in great disorder and crossing by two instead of the one ford by which they entered. 'E' Company going by the left and 'F I and L' by the same one they crossed. What became of 'C' Company no one knows—they must have charged them below the village, gotten away—or have been killed in the bluffs on the village side of stream—as very few of 'C' Company horses are found. Jack Sturgis and Porter's clothes were found in the village. After the Indians had driven them across, it was a regular buffalo hunt for them and not a man escaped. We buried 203 of the bodies of Custer's command the second day after fight.

"I must now tell you what we did—when I found Reno's command we halted for the packs to come up—and then moved along the line of bluffs towards the direction Custer was supposed to have gone. Weir's company was sent out to communicate with Custer but it was driven back. We then showed our full force on the hills with Guidons flying, that Custer might see us—but we could see nothing of him, couldn't hear much firing, but could see an immense body of Indians coming to attack us from both sides of the river. We withdrew to a saucer-like hill, putting our horses and packs in the bottom of saucer and threw all of our force dismounted around this corral; the animals could be riddled from only one point—but we had not men enough to extend our line to that—so we could not get it—therefore the Indians amused themselves by shooting at our stock, ditto, men—but could cover themselves. Both of my horses (U. S. horses) were wounded. Well they pounded at us all of what was left of the first day and the whole of the second day—withdrawing their line with the withdrawal of their village, which was at dusk the second day. Corporal Lett, Meadow and Jones were killed; Sergeant Paul, both of the Bishops, Phillips, Windolph, Black, Severs, Cooper, etc. (twenty-one wounded). I got a slight scratch on my right thumb which, as you see, doesn't prevent me from writing you this long scrawl. As this goes via Fort Ellis it will be a long time in reaching you. General Terry with General Gibbon's command—came up the morning of the third day, about 10 o'clock. Indians had all gone the night before. *Had Custer carried out the orders he got from General Terry the commands would have formed a junction exactly at the village, and have captured the whole outfit of tepees, etc., and probably any quantity of squaws, pappooses, etc., but Custer disobeyed orders from the fact of not wanting any other command—or body to have a finger in the pie—and thereby lost his life (3000 warriors were there).*

". . . A Crow Indian, one of our scouts, who got in the village, reported that our men killed a great many of them—quite as many, if not more, than was killed of ours. The Indians during the night got to fighting among themselves and killed each other—so the Crow said—he also said as soon as he got possession of a Sioux blanket, not the slightest attention was paid to him. There was among them Cheyennes, Arapahoes, Kiowa and representatives probably from every Agency on the Missouri River. A host of them there sure!

"Well—Wifey, darling, I think this will do for a letter, so with oceans of love to you and Fred and kisses I am devotedly

Your husband,
Fred Benteen"

The third of the Benteen documents was found among the papers of the late Brigadier General E. S. Godfrey. It is undated, but was probably written about 1891 or 1892.

The manuscript is believed to have been turned over to General Godfrey by the younger Benteen, at Jefferson Barracks, in 1911. The assertion has been made that it was loaned, and that a request had been made to General Godfrey for its return, but no such request was found among General Godfrey's papers.

Only a part of the long, rambling document is quoted here:

"After leaving the watering places a few miles brought us to a beautifully decorated tepee of buffalo hide, just on trail; I dismounted, after riding around the lodge, peeped in, and saw the body of an Indian on a scaffold or cot of rude poles: by this time the battalion was up—and away we went again: a mile or two brought orders through a Sergeant to the officer in charge of pack trains. I told him where I had last seen it: another couple of miles brought an order for me thro' the orderly trumpeter of day; from the adjutant of regiment: to the effect—Benteen, Big village, Be quick; Bring packs;
P. S. Bring Packs,
W. W. Cooke, Adjutant

"Well, the Packs were safe behind; I knew *that, better than anybody;* I couldn't waste time in going back, nor in halting where I was for them: So, we went—V. V. V.

"I resume with the last order received from the Adjutant of the Seventh Cavalry; the last lines penciled by him: viz.: 'Benteen, come on. Big village. Be quick. Bring packs. P. S. Bring Packs.' John Martini, the trumpeter, bringing this dispatch was a thick-headed, dull-witted Italian, just about as much cut out for a cavalryman as he was for a King; he informed me that the Indians were 'skedaddling'; hence, less the necessity for retracing our steps to get the packs, and the same would be gained by awaiting the arrival of them where we then were; we did neither, but took the 'Trot!' and, from the ford where Reno first crossed the beautifully blue Little Big Horn we saw going on what evidently was not Skedaddling on the part of the Indians, as there were twelve or fourteen dismounted men on the river bottom, and they were being ridden down and shot by 800 or 900 Indian warriors.

"We concluded that the lay of the land had better be investigated a bit, as so much of the Italian trumpeter's story hadn't 'Panned out.' So—off to the left I went, seeing a group of three or four Absaraka or Crow Indians; from them I learned this: Otoe Sioux, Otoe Sioux; the 'Otoe' meaning, innumerable or—heaps of them:—and we soon found that there were enough of them.

"From the point I saw the Crows I got the first sight of the men of Reno's battalion who had retreated from the river bottom, recrossed the river a couple of miles below, and were showing up on the bluffs on the side of the river that my battalion had kept and was then on: the battalion being in line, Reno, knowing of course we were soldiers; came riding to meet me as I moved towards him: my first query of Reno was—where is Custer?—showing him the last order received from the Adjutant of Regiment; Reno replied that he did not know, that Custer had ordered him across the river to charge the Indians, informing him that he would support him with the whole 'outfit,' but he had neither seen nor heard from him since:—Well, our battalion got there just in the nick of time to save Reno's——"

Did Benteen disregard Custer's plea "Come on. Big village. Be quick, bring packs!"?

And what would have been the result had he sent a few men back to the pack train from the watering hole, where

Trumpeter Martini found him—brought up a half-dozen of the ammunition mules—and then led his battalion straight through Reno's demoralized men on the hill, and on down the trail Custer had made?

Or suppose after he had joined Reno he had insisted by the sheer superior weight of his character that the mounted men charge northward with him while the men who had lost their horses, along with the armed civilian packers and a guard, remained on the hill with the pack train? What would have been the result?

These are questions that will be debated as long as old soldiers get together.

Chapter 7

**Bitter Controversies That
Lived Long After the Battle**

---

*T*HE attractive young son of the actual Colonel of the Seventh Cavalry rode to his death with Custer on that hot Sunday afternoon of June 25. Second Lieutenant James G. Sturgis had graduated from West Point in the Class of '75 and was the junior "shave tail" of the regiment.

His father at this time was on special recruiting duty in the St. Paul Headquarters. It had long irked the distinguished officer to have the actual command of his regiment held firmly in the hands of his junior, Lieutenant Colonel Custer. Through the favoritism Lieutenant General Sheridan had for the youthful Custer, the "Boy General" had commanded the Seventh in all its Indian campaigns. Sheridan carefully saw to it that General Sturgis was given special duty that kept him away from his outfit and thus permitted Custer to ride at its head. Sturgis fumed and fretted, but he could do nothing about it.

Once the news of the tragedy reached the country, and General Sturgis felt the full shock of grief over the death of his son, he could no longer hold back his long-pent-up resentment of Custer. The following article taken from the *Army and Navy Journal* of July 29, 1876, tells the pathetic story:

"The Chicago *Tribune* prints a telegram from St. Louis dated 18th inst., in which its correspondent gives an account of an interview with General Sturgis concerning the latter's recent criticism on General Custer. The correspondent says:

"General Sturgis said: What I especially deprecate is the manner in which some papers have sought to make a demigod out of Custer, and to erect a monument to Custer, and none to his soldiers. On the field of slaughter the bodies of 300 or more soldiers were found piled up in a little ravine, while behind were found those of Custer and his little band of chosen officers. When the officers of these men fell, who was there to rally them? Why were not some of the other officers sent forward with them? If relief had come to the party between these two points, what a sight it would have been to find 300 soldiers collected on one side, and, in the rear, the commander of the little force surrounded by its officers! Mind I don't want to impugn their bravery. Custer was a brave man, but he was also a very selfish man. He was insanely ambitious for glory, and the phrase 'Custer's luck' affords a good clue to his ruling passion. The public opinion regarding Custer is to a great extent formed from his writings and newspaper reports, and people having read these are very apt to refuse a hearing to the contrary statement, saying, in effect, 'Oh, we know better than that,' and it is on account of this feature in public opinion that I do not desire to put myself in a false position. People say: 'Oh, yes; General Sturgis has had his son killed. He feels it, and, while the feeling lasts, is liable to exaggeration. Then, too, he was the head of this regiment and anxious to be sent out with it, but was not sent. Custer was sent in his stead, and now he feels hurt.' But that isn't it, altogether. What I would criticize is the want of judgment which drew these men into a trap. Before the war there were some of the Army officers who had made reputations as Indian fighters. The record will show them most successful Indian fighters, and, without any undue conceit, I think I may claim a place in that list. I never went after them that I didn't catch them. The report of the Secretary of War in 1860 will show that I followed the Kiowas and Comanches so that their camps were entirely broken up, and they caused no further trouble. Oakes and Hazen were also good Indian fighters. But the war is over; the old authorities that knew us are all gone. A new set of officers has arisen, and a young America has grown up at the same time. Indian warfare is no picnic, as some people regard it. The Sioux can raise 6,000 or 7,000 men in a day's notice, and are quite formidable. Custer, you see, talked with Sheridan from day to day and begged him to give him a chance to go on an expedition. I was sent up to St. Paul against my will. As an illustration of the feeling with which Custer was regarded, let me tell you a short story. Two years ago, I was at St. Paul and Mr. Robinson of the *Times*, came to me at the time Custer was making his expedition to the Black Hills. He spoke of Professor Richeson, who was anxious to accompany Custer's expedition, and asked me what I thought about the propriety of his doing so. I told him frankly just what I felt—that Custer, in organizing and conducting that expedition, was really hunting a fight with the Indians for his own glorification and I didn't believe Custer knew sufficient of Indian character to fight the tribes to advantage, but was liable, in consequence of his underestimation of Indian resources and his overestimation of his own skill, to be led into a trap, in which case, I told the gentleman, there would be no one left alive to tell the tale. As a result of that interview the party contemplating the excursion did not leave St. Paul.

"It is true there was no attack in that campaign but now, at the first important attack, the prophecy was fulfilled. When I knew that my boy had gone out, and that General Terry was in command I considered that we were tolerably fortunate. Terry has a matured judgment, and I looked for the campaign to be conducted on good military principles, instead of which Custer made his attack recklessly, earlier by thirty-six to forty-eight hours than he should have done, and with men tired out by forced marches. Why, if they had caused the Indians to retreat, they could not possibly have followed them. I feel, too, that when the news is received from individuals of the regiment, it will fully sustain the position I take. Custer was not a popular man among his troops, by any means. He was tyrannical, and had no regard for the soldiers under him.

"General Sturgis gave it as his opinion that the Government will have to call for mounted volunteers to quell the Indian war, and that it will take at least 7,000 well-equipped cavalry men to do the work.

"E. A. Sherburne, formerly of the Twenty-fourth Iowa Volunteers, in a letter to the Chicago *Tribune*, in reply to this, says:

" 'Custer's luck,' as General Sturgis sneeringly styles Custer's success, was what naturally resulted to a soldier whose heart was a stranger to fear, who went to battle with an eye gleaming like a blazing star, and whose arm was ever found in the thickest of the fight, dealing blows both well directed and resistless. General Sturgis' object seems to be to get before the mind of his listener a comparison of his 'record' with that of the dead general, which shall be injurious to the latter."

During the late Summer and Fall of 1876 and for most of the following year, the Custer controversy raged fierce and prolonged. Even the President of the United States became involved.

In its issue of September 16, 1876, the *Army and Navy Journal* carried an account that left little doubt as to how General Grant felt about the battle and its leader. It said, in part:

"The New York *Herald* has interviewed the President, at Long Branch, and reports as follows:

"Correspondent—Was not Custer's massacre a disgraceful defeat of our troops?

"The President (with an expression of manifest and keenly felt regret)—I regard Custer's massacre as a sacrifice of troops, brought on by Custer himself, that was wholly unnecessary—wholly unnecessary. He was not to have made the attack before effecting the junction with Terry and Gibbon. He was notified to meet them on the 26th, but instead of marching slowly, as his orders required, in order to effect the junction on the 26th, he enters upon a forced march of eighty-three miles in twenty-four hours and thus has to meet the Indians alone on the 25th.

"Correspondent—Mr. President, do you share the general admiration for Sitting Bull as a tactician—as an Indian Napoleon?

"The President—Oh, no! He is just as wily as most of the Indians, who will never fight our troops unless they have them at a decided disadvantage.

"Correspondent—Then your confidence in the present leaders of the campaign is unshaken, Mr. President?

"The President—Entirely. General Crook is the best, wiliest Indian fighter in this country. He has had vast experience in Indian fighting. His campaign against the Idahos and many other tribes show his brilliant talent as an Indian fighter. He is as wily as Sitting Bull in this respect, that when he finds himself outnumbered and taken at a disadvantage he prudently retreats. In Custer's case Sitting Bull had ten men to every one of Custer's."

—2—

Were some of Custer's men captured, then brought down to the Indian camp and burned to death in the horrible night of orgies immediately after the annihilation?

Several officers who were with Reno or Gibbon have reported on finding a half-dozen tell-tale circles where the grass had been burned and there were evidences of barbarity. The fact that the bodies of some twenty men and two officers were never found, also leads to the belief that wounded men were taken to the valley and tortured. This is further substantiated by the fact that parts of garments, bloodstained and torn, were found in the abandoned Indian camp.

Further evidence is contained in a story given out by an old trapper, obviously a squaw man, whose yarn is so fantastic and incredible, and downright untruthful, that it is published in the September 16 issue of the *Army and Navy Journal* under the suspicious heading of "A Leather Stocking Tale." It is reprinted for whatever it may be worth:

"The Minneapolis *Pioneer Press and Tribune* publishes an interview with an old trapper named Ridgely, who has been for a long time in the Yellowstone country, and who says that he witnessed the Custer massacre, having been a prisoner in Sitting Bull's camp and seen every movement of the troops. He was taken prisoner last March, and kept in the camp of the Indians ever since until the Custer massacre. He was kindly treated while there. He says Sitting Bull organized not to fight the whites, but to drive the miners from the Black Hills.

"Previous to Custer's attack, mounted couriers from Sitting Bull's camp had for eight days watched his forces, its divisions into small detachments being noted with manifestations of extreme delight. Ambuscades were immediately prepared, and while the Indians stood ready for an attack, many of them clambered on the side of the hill overlooking Custer's line of march. The Indian camp was divided by a bluff, a point of which ran toward the Rosebud, and in the direction of one of the fords of the river available to the camp; by this ford Custer followed their trail down to the water's edge. There were but twenty-five tepees visible to Custer, but there were seventy-five double tepees behind the bluff not visible. Custer attacked the smaller village and was immediately met by one thousand five hundred or two thousand Indians in regular order of battle. Every movement was made with military precision. Ridgely says he stood on the side of the hill where he had a complete view of the battle, which was not more than a mile and a half distant. Custer began the fight in the ravine near the ford, and fully half of his command seemed to be unhorsed at the first fire. Then the soldiers retreated before him to the rear, and were shot down with astonishing rapidity, the commanding officer falling from his horse in the middle of the engagement, which began at 11 A.M. and did not last more than fifty-five minutes.

"After the massacre of Custer's forces the Indians returned to camp with six soldiers as prisoners. They were delirious with joy over their success. The six soldiers were tied to stakes at a woodpile in the village and were burned. Sitting Bull was met after the fight and he exultingly remarked that he had 'killed many soldiers and one damned General,' but he did not know who he was. The squaws then armed themselves with knives, visited the battlefield, and robbed and mutilated the bodies of the slain. While the soldiers were burning, the Indians turned their attention to a force, evidently Reno's attacking the lower end of the village. Ridgely says that Custer's command had been slaughtered before a shot was fired by Reno's force, which attacked the lower end of the camp about two o'clock P.M. The Indians returned in the evening and said they had fought desperately but Ridgely says they did not make a statement of their losses. They said the soldiers had been driven back twice, and they piled up stones and the attack was unsuccessful. The prisoners were kept burning for more than an hour, but Ridgely was not permitted to speak with them so he could tell who they were. One was noticeable from his small size and gray hair and whiskers. Reno killed more

Indians than Custer, who fell in the midst of the fight, and two captains, believed to be Yates and Keogh, were the last to die.

"The night after the massacre the Indians were wild with delight, and many were drunk on whiskey stolen from the whites. The squaws performed the duty of guards, for the prisoners, and becoming drowsy, Ridgely and two companions escaped, securing ponies and began their long journey homeward. The party ate game, and lay in the woods four days to avoid the Indians. On the way his horse stumbled, breaking Ridgely's arm, but the party finally reached Fort Abercrombie and thence Ridgely came here. He describes Sitting Bull as a half-breed, of large size, and very intelligent with a peculiar gait."

Reno's conduct in the fight will always remain a highly mooted question. There are further pieces of testimony that are violent in their condemnation of him.

One is a letter from William O. Taylor who was a private in "A" Troop that was part of Reno's battalion. It bears the date of Orange, Mass., February 20, 1910, and was written to Brigadier General Godfrey. It was found among the General's papers. The following is an extract from the lengthy letter:

". . . It so happened that both times the troop 'counted fours' on that 25th of June, 1876, I was a No. 4 man and as such had to care for led horses when the troop was dismounted. Hence I did not see much of the firing line in the first part of the valley fight, being in the woods with the led horses. I do not know as I can add anything to the story of that unexpected and demoralized rout that you do not know. It seemed but a very few moments after we had taken the horses into the timber before the men came rushing back for them. I did not see any officers in there except Lieutenant Varnum, I think, nor did I hear any orders as to what we were to do. After my led horses were taken I followed in the direction the men had taken, mounting and dismounting several times, but for what purpose I did not know. As I came out of the timber into the open I saw the soldiers heading for the bluffs and firing their revolvers at the Indians, who were rushing in the same direction but a few yards away, with a tendency to crowd us. My horse played out just after crossing the river, and things looked rather dark as I trudged up the steep bluff, a comrade with whom I was talking being shot dead at my side; but the top was soon reached, and most unexpectedly, the Indians seemed to draw off and left us alone. Then Benteen came up, and you know the rest. . . .

"Somehow [General Charles] King's idea of the approach of Custer [to Custer field] seems to my mind the most probable, for Custer was not given to lagging or roundabout ways. He wanted to get into the fight as soon as he could, and his actions after the first clash might be judged, I think, from this viewpoint: He believed Reno to be fighting at the other end of the camp and was driving the Indians and would continue to fight; as he had ordered Benteen to join him [Custer] and 'be quick,' he had every reason to expect his appearance any minute. So why was it not good tactics to fall back from the vicinity of the river, drawing the Indians away from their village and Reno, and giving Benteen a chance to strike them on their flank or rear? But Reno proved incompetent, and Benteen showed his indifference—I will not use the uglier words that have often been in my mind—both failed Custer, and he had to fight it out alone. . . .

"Among the several things that impressed me greatly was the general demoralization that seemed to pervade many of the officers and men—due in a great measure, I think, to Major Reno. When an enlisted man sees his commanding officer lose his head entirely, and several other officers showing greater regard for their personal safety than anything else, it would be apt to demoralize any one taught almost to breathe at the word of command. . . ."

In the manuscript room in the New York Public Library, there are two cardboard letter files that contain a considerable amount of hitherto unpublished Custer material. The files were purchased at a public auction and are largely made up of private papers of the late Brigadier General Godfrey, that were secured by the late W. J. Ghent, eminent Indian authority.

Several of those documents have already been used in this volume, but by far the most sensational and damning are three or four papers that together bring a most astounding charge against Reno.

They are printed now in their chronological order, without comment save that there can be no doubt as to the authenticity of the documents. The first is a letter from Captain Benteen to Captain Godfrey and obviously refers to some highly explosive Benteen material that Godfrey wished to include in his famous *Century Magazine* article that he published five years later in 1891. (In the article, incidentally, Godfrey says only: "The question of moving was discussed, but the conditions coupled to the proposition caused it to be indignantly rejected.")

Here is the letter:

"Fort McKinney, Wyo. Ter.
Jan. 3d 1886

"Dear 'God.'

"Your favor just rec'd. To commence, Don't you think that Reno has been sufficiently damned before the country that it can well be afforded to leave out in the article the proposition from him to saddle up and leave the field of the Little Big Horn on the 1st night of fight?

"Don't think that I would do it, but that he did so propose, there is no manner of doubt. 'But the greatest of these is Charity!'

"Happy New Year to you all, love from all the B's to thine,

Yr. friend,
BENTEEN"

The second document regarding the mysterious charge, is found in a letter from Godfrey to John G. Neihardt, who had been in touch with Godfrey regarding material for his (Neihardt's) book "The Song of the Indian Wars." It reads in part as follows:

"Jan. 6, 1924

"My dear doctor:

". . . A while after dark [June 25] Captain Weir came to my place and thanked me for my action in dismounting my troop and holding back the onrush of the hostiles following up the retreat of Troops M and D—and added: 'You saved Troop D.' (Weir and I had had a little tiff when he attempted to encroach on my troop grazing ground.)

"Again during the night Captain Weir came to me and in a low tone and trembling voice, said: 'If there should be a conflict of judgment as to what we should do in an emergency between Reno and Benteen, whose judgment would you follow?' Without hesitation I replied 'Benteen.' Apparently with a sense of relief he said 'All right,' and went away. He gave no explanation and I asked no questions. On the morning of the 28th as we were marching to the Custer battlefield to bury the dead, Benteen was riding beside me with my troop. I said: 'Benteen, it's pretty bad.' 'What do you mean?' he asked. 'Oh,' I said, 'Reno's conduct!' With a grave look on his face he turned to me and said: 'God, you don't know half; I could tell you something that would make your hair stand on end!' ('God' was my nickname.) 'All right,' I said, 'What is it?' Glancing back toward the troop, he said: 'No, I can't do it now.' 'Will

you tell me sometime?' 'Yes.' On two or three occasions
when we were together I asked him to tell me, but each time
somebody would bob up to kill the privacy, until 1881
when we were on a fishing trip, and as we were alone for
sure, I again asked him to tell me. He did so, but I could
see that it was with reluctance. The gist of it was that after
the firing ceased, Reno came to him and proposed to march
away on the back trail; to destroy what property could
not be packed on the remaining mules; mount all men who
could ride, and *abandon the wounded* who were unable to
ride or would delay the march of retreat. Benteen refused
to be bound by any such plan. I never had a good opportunity to ask Captain Weir, but expected he would enlighten
me at sometime, but he was sent on recruiting service soon
after our return from the expedition and died the 9th of
December following. His death promoted me to be captain
of his Troop. I have always thought that Weir knew of
Reno's proposed plan and Benteen's rejection, for he and
Reno were side by side on our line of defense."

The final reference to the "Benteen secret" is contained
in two typewritten pages that include a note of explanation
by W. J. Ghent:

"This brief speech, which I heard when delivered, was
not printed in the Report of the O.I.W. for 1930, nor was
any mention made of the confirmatory statement then given
by General W. J. Nicholson (since deceased) who asserted
that Benteen had told him, under an oath of secrecy, the
same story in 1877, and that he had never repeated it until
that evening."

The speech was made by General Godfrey, at that time
the most distinguished survivor of the battle, at an annual
dinner of the Order of Indian Wars, on January 25, 1930.
Apparently it was taken down verbatim by a stenographer:

"I am not going to tell you anything about the details of the campaign in '76, as far as I was concerned. It has only been three or four years since the country resounded with editorials, etc., on the battle of the Little Big Horn and I suppose you have been fed up on it. So I will just relate one incident connected with it.

"On the night of the 25th of June, after it became dark, Colonel Weir crawled up to me and, after some complimentary remarks about [my] saving his troop, etc., he hesitated a while and said: 'Godfrey, suppose there should be a clash of opinion as to what we should do, as between Major Reno and Captain Benteen, whose judgment would you follow?' I said, 'Benteen's.' He drew a long breath, said 'All right, all right' and went away.

"On the 28th, on our way to bury the dead on the Custer Battlefield, Captain Benteen and I were riding along, looking at the valley where Reno had made his retreat on the 25th; I said to Benteen, after we had scanned the country, 'It's pretty damn bad.' He turned to me and said, 'What do you mean?' I replied, 'Reno.' He said, 'God, I could tell you things that would make your hair stand on end.' Just at that instant an orderly came up and joined the men behind, and Benteen said, 'I cannot tell you now.' I said, 'Will you tell me sometime?' He replied, 'Yes.' Time and time again I asked him to tell me what he meant on that occasion, and always something came up for an excuse to delay him, as somebody came in the vicinity. I waited and made it my point to keep at him.

"In '81, after I had read my paper on the Little Big Horn to the officers and cadets at the Military Academy, Benteen came up and paid me a visit. We were sitting out on the porch of double quarters and I went at him again. Just as I got through, a young lady stepped out on the other side of the house. So that gave him an excuse again.

"Sometime during the summer following we had a fishing excursion on the Jersey coast, and one evening everybody, except Benteen and myself, went down to the beach. I said, 'Now, Benteen, there is no one around for a mile of us and there is no getting out of your promise to tell me; are you going to pay the debt?' He said, 'God, let bygones be bygones.' But I said, 'No, you promised and I want to know it because I am interested in the history.' Well, he hesitated quite a long time. Finally he said, 'On the evening of the 25th, Reno came to me and told me of his plan of getting away. He said, "I propose to mount all my men that can ride on horses and mules, and destroy the property that we cannot take with us, and make a retreat to the wagon train at the mouth of the Powder River." I said, "What are you going to do with the wounded that cannot ride?" He said, "We will have to abandon them." I said, "You can't do that." That was the end of it.' "

Chapter 8

```
They Fought Against Custer:
The Indians' Side
```

ONE of the very earliest accounts of the Indian version of the historic Custer fight was given by Crazy Horse, irreconcilable Indian chief, who was to meet his death when he was placed under arrest by soldiers at Fort Robinson in northwestern Nebraska.

His version of the fight is contained in a dispatch to the old Chicago *Times* sent by its special correspondent only a few days before the brilliant young chief met his death under mysterious and possibly unnecessary circumstances:

"Chicago *Times* Special
Camp Robinson, Neb., May 24, via Cheyenne,
May 25 (1877)

". . . Your correspondent has obtained some very valuable information in regard to the Custer Massacre from Crazy Horse through Horned Horse as his spokesman, which is authentic and confirmed by other principal chiefs. I interviewed these chiefs this afternoon, Lieutenant Clark arranging for the meeting and William Hunter acting as interpreter, a man perfectly reliable and thoroughly conversant with the Indian language. This is the Indian version, and the first published. The attack was made on the village by a strong force at 11 o'clock in the morning, at the upper end of the village. This was the force commanded by Major Reno, and very shortly afterward the lower end of the village was attacked by another strong force, that commanded by Custer.

"The village was divided into seven different bands of Indians, each commanded by a separate chief, and extended in nearly a straight line. The bands were in the order mentioned below, commencing from the lower end, where Custer made his attack: First, the Uncpapas, under Sitting Bull; second, the Ogallalas, under Crazy Horse; third, the Minneconjous, under Fast Bull; fourth, the Sansarcs, under Red Bear; fifth, the Cheyennes, under Ice Bear, their two principal chiefs being absent; sixth, the Santees and Yanktonais, under Red Point, of the Santee; seventh, the Blackfeet, under Scabby Head. The village consisted of eighteen hundred lodges, and at least four hundred wickiups, a lodge made of small poles and willows for temporary shelter. Each of the wickiups contained four young bucks and the estimate made by Crazy Horse is that each lodge had from three to four warriors. Estimating at three made a fighting force of seven thousand Indians. This is the lowest estimate that can be made, for there were a good many Indians without shelter, hangers-on, who fought when called upon, and the usual number was much above seven thousand. The attack was a surprise and totally unlooked for. When Custer made the charge the women, papooses, children, and in fact all that were not fighters, made a stampede in a northerly direction. Custer, seeing so numerous a body, mistook them for the main body of Indians retreating and abandoning their villages, and immediately gave pursuit. The warriors in the village, seeing this, divided their forces into two parts, one intercepting Custer between their noncombatants and him, and the other getting in his rear. Outnumbering him as they did, they had him at their mercy, and the dreadful massacre ensued.

"Horned Horse says the smoke and dust were so great

that foe could not be distinguished from friend. The horses were wild with fright and uncontrollable. The Indians were knocking each other from their steeds, and it is an absolute fact that the young bucks in their excitement and fury killed each other, several dead Indians being found killed by arrows. Horned Horse represented this hell of fire and smoke and death by intertwining his fingers and saying: 'Just like this, Indians and white men.' These chiefs say they suffered a loss of fifty-eight killed and over sixty wounded. From their way of expressing it, I should judge that about 60 per cent of their wounded died.

"While this butchery was going on, Reno was fighting in the upper part of the village, but did not get in so far as to get surrounded, and managed to escape. They say had he got in as far, he would have suffered the same fate as Custer, but he retreated to the bluffs, and was held there until the Indians fighting Custer, comprising over half the village, could join the northern portion in besieging him. These Indians claim that but for the timely arrival of General Terry they would have certainly got Reno. They would have surrounded and stormed him out or would have besieged and eventually captured him. From what I know of Crazy Horse I should say that he no doubt is capable of conducting a siege. In both the Rosebud fight and the Custer massacre the Indians claim he rode unarmed in the thickest of the fight, invoking the blessing of the great spirit on himself that if he was right he might be victorious, and if wrong that he might be killed. Some details were also learned in regard to the Rosebud fight."

The leader of the fighting Cheyennes at the battle was Two Moons. In *McClure's Magazine* for May, 1898, twenty-two years after the battle, Hamlin Garland published Two Moons' comprehensive account. It is well worth reprinting:

"That spring (1876) I was camped on Powder River

with fifty lodges of my people—Cheyennes. The place is near what is now Fort McKenney. One morning soldiers charged my camp. They were in command of Three Fingers (Colonel McKenzie). We were surprised and scattered, leaving our ponies. The soldiers ran all our horses off. That night the soldiers slept, leaving the horses one side; so we crept up and stole them back again, and then we went away.

"We traveled far, and one day we met a big camp of Sioux at Charcoal Butte. We camped with the Sioux, and had a good time, plenty grass, plenty game, good water. Crazy Horse was head chief of the camp. Sitting Bull was camped a little ways below, on the Little Missouri River.

"Crazy Horse said to me, 'I'm glad you are come. We are going to fight the white man again.'

"The camp was already full of wounded men, women and children.

"I said to Crazy Horse, 'All right. I am ready to fight. I have fought already. My people have been killed, my horses stolen; I am satisfied to fight.'

"Here the old man paused a moment, and his face took on a lofty and somber expression.

" 'I believed at that time the Great Spirits had made Sioux, put them there—he drew a circle to the right—and white men and Cheyennes here—indicating two places to the left —expecting them to fight. The Great Spirits I thought liked to see the fight; it was to them all the same like playing. So I thought then about fighting.' As he said this he made me feel for one moment the power of a sardonic god whose drama was the wars of men.

" 'About May, when the grass was tall and the horses strong, we broke camp and started across the country to the mouth of the Tongue River. Then Sitting Bull and Crazy Horse and all went up the Rosebud. There we had a big fight with General Crook, and whipped him. Many soldiers were killed—few Indians. It was a great fight, much smoke and dust.

" 'From there we all went over the divide, and camped in the valley of Little Horn. Everybody thought— Now we are out of the white man's country. He can live there, we will live here. After a few days, one morning when I was in camp north of Sitting Bull, a Sioux messenger rode up and said, "Let everybody paint up, cook, and get ready for a big dance."

" 'Cheyennes then went to work to cook, cut up tobacco, and get ready. We all thought to dance all day. We were very glad to think we were far away from the white man.

" 'I went to water my horses at the creek, and washed them off with cool water, then took a swim myself. I came back to the camp afoot. When I got near my lodge, I looked up the Little Horn towards Sitting Bull's camp. I saw a great dust rising. It looked like a whirlwind. Soon Sioux horseman came rushing into camp shouting, "Soldiers, come! Plenty white soldiers."

" 'I ran into my lodge and said to my brother-in-law, "Get your horses; the white man is coming. Everybody run for horses."

" 'Outside, far up the valley, I heard a battle cry, Hay-ay, hay-ay! I heard shooting, too, this way [clapping his hands very fast]. I couldn't see any Indians. Everybody was getting horses and saddles. After I had caught my horse, a Sioux warrior came again and said, "Many soldiers are coming."

" 'Then he said to the women, "Get out of the way, we are going to have hard fight."

" 'I said, "All right, I am ready."

" 'I got on my horse and rode out into my camp. I called out to the people all running about: "I am Two Moon, your chief. Don't run away. Stay here and fight. You must stay and fight the white soldiers. I shall stay even if I am to be killed."

" 'I rode swiftly toward Sitting Bull's camp. There I saw the white soldiers fighting in a line [Reno's men]. Indians covered the flat. They began to drive the soldiers all mixed up—Sioux, then soldiers, then more Sioux, and all shooting. The air was full of smoke and dust. I saw the soldiers fall back and drop into the river-bed like buffalo fleeing. They had no time to look for a crossing. The Sioux chased them up the hill, where they met more soldiers in wagons, and then messengers came saying more soldiers were going to kill the women, and the Sioux turned back. Chief Gall was there fighting, Crazy Horse also.

" 'I then rode toward my camp, and stopped squaws from carrying off lodges. While I was sitting on my horse I saw flags come up over the hill to the east like that [he raised his fingertips]. Then the soldiers rose all at once, all on horses, like this [he put his fingers behind each other to indicate that Custer appeared marching in columns of fours]. They formed into three bunches [squadrons] with a little ways between. Then a bugle sounded, and they all got off horses, and some soldiers led the horses back over the hill.

" 'Then the Sioux rode up the ridge on all sides, riding very fast. The Cheyennes went up the left way. Then the shooting was quick, quick. Pop-pop-pop very fast. Some of the soldiers were down on their knees, some standing. Officers all in front. The smoke was like a great cloud, and everywhere the Sioux went the dust rose like smoke. We circled all round him—swirling like water round a stone. We shoot, we ride fast, we shoot again. Soldiers drop, and horses fall on them. Soldiers in line drop, but one man rides up and down the line—all the time shouting. He rode a sorrel horse, with white face and white forelegs. I don't know who he was. He was a brave man.

" 'Indians keep swirling round and round, and the soldiers killed only a few. Many soldiers fell. At last all horses killed but five. Once in a while some man would break out and run toward the river, but he would fall. At last about a hundred men and five horsemen stood on the hill all bunched together. All along the bugler kept blowing his commands.

He was very brave too. Then a chief was killed. I hear it was Long Hair [Custer], I don't know; and then the five horsemen and the bunch of men, may be so forty, started toward the river. Then man on the sorrel horse led them, shouting all the time. He wore a buckskin shirt and had long black hair and mustache. He fought hard with a big knife. His men were all covered with white dust. I couldn't tell whether they were officers or not. One man all alone ran down toward the river, then round up over the hill. I thought he was going to escape, but a Sioux fired and hit him in the head. He was the last man. He wore braid on his arms [sergeant].

" 'All the soldiers were now killed, and the bodies were stripped. After that no one could tell which were officers. The bodies were left where they fell. We had no dance that night. We were sorrowful.

" 'Next day four Sioux chiefs and two Cheyennes and I, Two Moon, went upon the battlefield to count the dead. One man carried a little bundle of sticks. When we came to dead men, we took a little stick and gave it to another man, so we counted the dead. There were 388. There were thirty-nine Sioux and seven Cheyennes killed, and about a hundred wounded.

" 'Some white soldiers were cut with knives to make sure they were dead; and the war women had mangled some. Most of them were left just where they fell. We came to the man with big mustache; he lay down the hills towards the river. The Indians did not take his buckskin shirt. The Sioux said, "That is a big chief. That is Long Hair." I don't know. I had never seen him. The man on the white-faced horse was the bravest man.

" 'That day as the sun was getting low our young men came up the Little Horn riding hard. Many white soldiers were coming in a big boat, and when we looked we could see the smoke rising. I called my people together, and we hurried up the Little Horn, into Rotten Grass Valley. We

Frank Weasel Bear, Cheyenne warrior, in front of his cabin on the reservation near Birney, Montana. As a boy of 14 he took part in the battle.

Chief Eagle Bear (on right), last of the Ogallala Sioux who fought in the battle. This picture was taken shortly before he died in December, 1938.

Sitting Bull, chief medicine man of the Sioux, whose actual leadership in the tragic Battle of the Little Big Horn is questioned by many historians.

Sitting Bull's cabin on the Standing Rock Reservation in South Dakota, where he was killed by Indian Police in 1890.

camped there three days, and then rode swiftly back over our old trail to the east. Sitting Bull went back into the Rosebud and down the Yellowstone and away to the north. I did not see him again.' "

—2—

Two of the Indian survivors of the battle were Weasel Bear and Chief Eagle Bear. They are both dead, but it was the good fortune of the authors to talk at length with both of those old warriors, and to get from them their accounts of the fight. Certainly it is at least unique that the same pens that put down the final account of the last surviving soldier who fought *with* Custer should likewise now write out the halting stories of two of the last of the red warriors who fought *against* Custer.

It was in the summer of 1938 that "Uncle Jim" Gatchell of Buffalo, Wyoming, drove us to the Cheyenne Reservation near Birney, Montana. We picked up an Indian interpreter, Willis Rowland, on the way to Weasel Bear's camp. We found the old man sitting in the shade of his one-room log shack. He was close to eighty and he had seen much of life and death, much of hunger and sorrow. He had started fighting the white man way back in 1874.

"I had been taught by my father to hate and fight white man," he said very slowly and softly to the interpreter. "All the elder Indians had told us over and over again about the horror of the Chivington Massacre, when white soldiers had killed 400 unarmed Cheyenne men, women and children. That was in 1864, and from that time on we were told never to trust white men.

"I was twelve years old when I got my first shot at the soldiers. This was the Bates fight of July 4, 1874. When I went into this fight I was a little afraid at the start. But after that I had no fear when I went into battle. . . . After the Bates fight we went to Pumpkin Buttes. (We called them the Gourds.) We stayed there that fall and hunted buffalo for our winter supply of meat and robes. From there we went to the Black Hills. My mother tried to treat me as a little boy, but I was a man. I had been in a fight against the soldiers.

"In the winter of 1874 and 1875 we stayed on in the Black Hills and hunted bear and buffalo. There were no white soldiers we could find. In the next summer we moved back to Wyoming. That fall we hunted buffalo and then moved to Montana, and spent that winter at the mouth of Prairie Dog creek on the Tongue River.

"Late in the spring of 1876 a rumor came to our camp that the white soldiers were coming out to put us on a reservation. This we did not like. And when the grass was high enough to feed our ponies and let them get strong, we moved up Tongue River with the idea of joining Sitting Bull on the Greasy Grass (Little Big Horn). About a week before we moved to join Sitting Bull, we received word that some white soldiers were coming from the south to fight the Sioux. So word was sent to Crazy Horse. We Cheyenne had fifty-seven in our band, and we made a forced ride, and surprised the soldiers at the Big Bend of the Rose-bud. In this fight the Great Spirit was with us, and we whipped the white soldiers and drove them back south and they did not molest us any more.

"After this fight our two villages moved over to the Greasy Grass and joined the Sioux, who were led by their great chief, Sitting Bull. We Cheyennes were led by Two Moons.

"I had been herding horses down the river from our camp when some one came out shouting, 'The soldiers are coming.' I helped drive the pony herd back west, and then galloped to my tepee and got my gun. Reno's men had dismounted by this time, and were lying down in skirmish line. We charged, and soon Reno mounted and led his men on the run from the edge of the woods. He crossed the river and rode up a steep bank to a hill. Some of us started after the soldiers.

"Then Chief Little Wolf rode among us shouting, 'Come back! More soldiers are going to attack us down the river.' My friend Kills-in-the-Night had lost his horse, and I got him up behind me, and we rode as fast as we could. We crossed the river and followed a ridge. We saw a loose horse, and my friend dropped off my horse and caught this one. There was lots of dust, and pretty soon much smoke from the guns.

"We ran into some soldiers and I had my horse killed. At the same time I was shot through the foot and the shoulder. I lay there stunned. Then my friend, Kills-in-the-Night came and picked me up, and we went on into the fight. It was soon over after that. There were Indians all around the white men, and we finally ran over them.

"That night there was a big celebration. We had seven Cheyenne killed. We Cheyenne were the ones who killed Custer. . . . Early that night there were reports that more soldiers were coming up the Greasy Grass. Next morning I joined my band across the river where we fought Reno's men some more. My foot was swollen and pained me, but I kept it pulled up with a rope. A little after noon we broke camp and went up the river towards the Big Horn Mountains. Later we went to the Red Forks on the Powder River. On November 25 we fought Colonel McKenzie and got whipped. After that battle some of us went to Ten Sleep Canyon, and others went to south end of Lake de Smet. Later we went to the mouth of the Powder and there surrendered to the government, and after a while we were sent to the reservation in Oklahoma. All that was a good many years ago."

—3—

In an old cabin three miles north of Porcupine in the Pine Ridge Reservation in South Dakota, we located old

Chief Eagle Bear. He was lying on a cot inside the log hut and he was obviously about to die. Sitting on a box at the head of the cot, fanning his father-in-law with a turkey feather, was Philip Good Shield. Squatting on the floor with his back against the wall at the foot of the cot were Jealous and Standing Bear. On a bench by the door, sat our interpreter, Tom White Cow Killer.

It was a strange interview this September day of 1938. Chief Eagle Bear's father had been a minor Sioux chief of the Ogallala clan. The father had been badly wounded in the Custer fight. Our friend, Eagle Bear, was sixteen years old at the time of the battle. This September day he was almost eighty—the last of the Ogallala Sioux who had actually taken part in the historic fight.

It was a strange and touching story that came so slowly and painfully from the lips of the dying old man. After each question there would be a long silence. The son-in-law, Philip Good Shield, would put our questions to the old Chief. He was lying back on his pallet, his eyes closed. In a thin voice, hardly more than a whisper, would come his words. He was talking out of the long ago.

"I with the other young men were out with the horses when we first heard the firing. I rushed back on my favorite pony and picked up my pistol and bow and arrow. Others had tomahawks and clubs, and bows and arrows. Only a few of the young warriors had guns. I was lucky; I had a pistol, as well as my bow and arrow.

"We started shooting at the soldiers down to the south of our tepees. We fought there for a while, and then the soldiers started to run away on their horses. We went after them. But soon the chiefs rode among us shouting, 'Everybody come this way. There are many soldiers down the river!' So we rode north as fast as we could."

Slowly the words dropped from the dry lips of the old man. Now and again one of the Indians would fill a pipe, and the old man would take a puff or two. Then he would take up his story, answering the questions the best way he could, and trying to remember faithfully the little details. He was a very old man, even if he was only seventy-nine.

"We rode down the river and crossed it, and came up behind the soldiers. It was a big fight . . . I do not know how long it lasted. I think maybe it was one hour and a half. . . . I do not think I saw Custer's body. There were a lot of dead soldiers everywhere . . . One soldier on a white horse almost got away—but we kept shooting at him, and before long we knocked him off his horse.

"After the fight the squaws said, 'Come and get feast.' We had a big victory dance that night. We killed many, many soldiers but it did no good to us. We all had to go to the reservations."

Another old Indian came in. He had ridden up on a flea-bitten pony, and his saddle and bridle were tied up with string. He was Eagle Bear's younger brother, Fool's Crow. He was only seventy-three years old.

"Yes, I was at the Greasy Grass," he answered through the interpreter. "But I was only eleven snows old. I was not in the fight. I was with the women, but I watched the fight. And afterwards we went over the field. There were many dead soldiers. I don't remember about cutting any of them with our knives. I was only eleven snows old when the fight took place."

Fool's Crow slowly filled the red stone pipe, with the long blacked stem. After he had lit it, he passed it on to his brother. The dying old man opened his blood-shot eyes and nodded his thanks.

He died before the snows fell that Fall.

Chapter 9

**The Death of Custer
on the Lonely Ridge**

*W*HO actually killed Custer?

We have a score of versions of the General's final minutes. Probably he was one of the last of the 220 to die. Certainly he died fighting, and the little band of devoted soldiers around him sold their lives dearly.

If there is one man living who can speak with authority about those last tragic minutes there on the knoll, in the heat and dust and smoke and terror of the battle's closing moments, it is James T. Gatchell of Buffalo, Wyoming. For fully fifty years, "Uncle Jim" has been gathering material about the Custer fight. His collection of battle relics, that he keeps in the back end of his remarkable drug store in Buffalo, is priceless. But the collection of unwritten stories and facts he has gathered in this half century, are far more priceless.

Friends have long tried to get Jim Gatchell to write out what he knows of the little Custer War, that apparently will never lose its interest or its mystery. So far he has refused.

But on the field of honor itself he generously gave the authors the following facts that he has sifted from the mass of legends, tales, truths and half-truths that have come to him from a thousand and one sources—both red and white—

from Captain Benteen and Two Moons, from General Edward S. Godfrey and Gall, from Colonel Charles Francis Bates and Medicine Bear.

"Beyond any question of doubt Custer was killed by the Cheyennes," he solemnly explained.

"Immediately after the last soldier was killed, which was probably about the time of Custer's death, the Cheyenne chiefs and head men personally guarded Custer's body against mutilation. They explained to the Sioux chiefs and warriors who crowded about that he was the Cheyennes' great enemy, and they wanted every one to know and to see that they had killed him.

"They were bitter against him on account of what he had done to Black Kettle's band of Southern Cheyenne at the Battle of the Washita, in December, 1868. They hated all white soldiers, partly on account of the horrible massacre of 400 Cheyenne by Colonel Chivington and his Colorado Volunteer cavalry at Sand Creek in 1865.

"According to half a dozen Cheyenne warriors who personally pointed out the exact spot to me, Custer's body was found lying alone on the *east* slope of the hog-back, at perhaps a hundred feet or more from where the battle monument stands. (Weasel Bear, however, claimed the body lay on the *west* slope.)

"Custer's watch, pistols and all his personal belongings were taken, but his clothing was not touched. He wore a beaded buckskin shirt, plain trousers and high cavalry boots.

"He was shot in the temple and left breast, but there were no powder marks—thus refuting the theory that he committed suicide. No one with Custer committed suicide. Nor were there prisoners taken and tortured. All wounded soldiers were killed at once by war clubs, arrows, lances or bullets.

"All the bodies, save only Custer's, were badly mutilated. Mutilation of an enemy was both a war and a religious custom of all Plains Indians. They believed men lived in the spirit world with the same bodies they were buried with, in this world. So it was the custom to inflict as much physical damage on their dead enemies as was possible. Consequently, bodies were ripped open, legs and arms and sometimes heads were hacked off. But we know that Custer's body was not touched. It was a curious reflection of Indian regard for the great chief whom they so hated."

—2—

The above is the word-of-mouth story from Jim Gatchell's own lips. To this is added the following account punched out on his own typewriter by this modest historian:

"My own first meeting of Cheyenne Indians was in the early summer of 1894. In August of that year, in company with Frank Grouard, the celebrated scout, I made my first visit to the Custer Battlefield. At that time there was quite a village of Cheyenne camped at the battle site seeing, as they said, 'the place where eighteen winters ago we had a great battle with the soldiers and the Great Spirit allowed us to win.'

"In that party were a number of warriors who became in later years warm personal friends. Among them were Two Moons, Harshay Wolf, Braided Locks, Medicine Bear, Weasel Bear, Wooden Legs, Turkey Legs, Limpy and Yellow Dog. When going over the battlefield they pointed out many places where different events of the battle took place, and when we came to spot marked, 'Here Custer Fell,' they told me that it was not the spot where Custer was killed. At my request they showed me the exact spot some hundred feet down the ridge.

"I had noticed as we got near the place, that Medicine Bear had assumed quite an air of importance, and when I asked the reason I was told that he had the honor of being the third one to touch *coup* on the dead body of Custer.

However, they would not tell me then who were the first two.

"It was at the Twentieth Anniversary of the battle, June 25, 1896, that I heard the story of Medicine Bear in detail. To this event flocked all the Indians who had a part in the battle, who could possibly come. There I met a great many Sioux whom I had known in the Dakotas, who introduced me officially to their Cheyenne allies, and there my long friendship with that tribe began.

"Again in company with Frank Grouard and several Sioux Indians, I went to the Cheyenne village after the day's celebration, where I heard the story of Medicine Bear in full. Willis Rowland was the Cheyenne interpreter, and he very carefully translated Medicine Bear's story for me.

"Medicine Bear, the Cheyenne, claimed that he was the third man to count *coup* on Custer's body. Two Indians were near the body at the moment when he touched the dead general with his long *coup* stick. They were Two Moons, the great Cheyenne chief, and Harshay Wolf. They were the first two who had counted *coup* on Custer. The great Indian honor was theirs.

"I do not know whether Two Moons and Harshay Wolf were the Indians who actually killed Custer, or whether he went down in a last mad, swirling charge, but I have every reason to believe that they were the first two to touch his body. And I firmly believe Medicine Bear was the third.

"They have all been dead these many years. It is fifty years now this summer, that I have kept their secret."

−3−

The swift twilight of the high country falls over the lonely ridge. A chill closes in with the night.

Long ago, on this tragic evening of June 25, 1876, the last Sioux warrior has mounted his pony and ridden away with his loot—a rifle, a pistol, a bandelero of precious cartridges, a saddle, an army bridle. Some of them were now riding the big, grain-fed cavalry horses with the letters "U S" burned on the left hoof. The animals could not understand the gruff words spoken to them; they would rear back when a warrior tried to mount them from their right sides.

Even the squaws and the children had left the field of battle. The two or three Cheyenne braves who alone remained behind, talked among themselves; they could now leave Custer's body without fear he would be mutilated.

Off to the eastward, on the brow of a hill, a coyote raised his mournful voice. On to the westward in the valley below, there were great fires and the tom-toms were pounding out the victory dances.

Now and again the high-pitched wailing of the women mourning for their own dead, floated up from the long string of camps. They seemed to answer the call of the coyote.

For this day there had been death—death, the final victor of all wars and all life.

THE END

Acknowledgments

There are a number of men and women, living and dead, to whom the authors would like to pay their respects for the help they have given in preparing this volume. First, of course, comes the hero of our narrative, former First Sergeant Charles P. Windolph, who gave us countless days and hours to dig back into his memory.

Then we would mention the late Brigadier General Edward S. Godfrey, veteran of the battle, with whom we spent a thrilling week-end a few years before he died. Our sense of gratitude is even greater, if such a thing is possible, to that very great Custer historian, the late Colonel Charles Francis Bates, of Bronxville, New York. Along with these two "true believers" stands the lovely figure of General Custer's widow, who contributed several memorable afternoons a few years before she died.

Of those still on this good earth we are especially grateful to "Uncle Jim" Gatchell, of Buffalo, Wyoming, to whom we owe so much for accompanying us on various visits to the Custer battlefield and to the Indian agencies.

But in a way we owe more than we can say to the patience, wisdom and shrewd book knowledge of Mr. Sylvester L. Vigilanti, head of the American History room of the great New York Public Library. And in this same sense we should mention our debt of gratitude to Messrs. Wilmer R. Leech and Edward B. Morrison of the Manuscript Division of the same Library.

Bibliography

Army and Navy Journal: Files 1873 to 1877.

Barry, David F., *The Custer Battle,* Baltimore, 1937.

Bates, Col. Charles Francis, *Custer's Indian Battles,* Bronxville, New York, 1936.

——*Fifty Years after the Little Big Horn,* New York, 1926.

Belknap, William W., *Trail of, in the Senate,* 44th Congress, 1st Session, 1876.

Benteen, Captain Frederick W., *Report,* Executive Doument 1, Part 2, House of Representatives, 44th Congress, 2nd Session.

——Private letters on file, N. Y. Public Library.

Beyer, W. F. and Keydal, O. F., *Deeds of Valor,* Detroit, 1903.

Bismarck *Tribune,* July 26, 1908, and August 23, 1908, Bismarck, North Dakota.

Bourke, John G., *On the Border with Crook,* New York, 1891.

Brackett, William S., Montana Historical Society Contributions, 1903.

Braden, Lieut. Charles, Journal of U. S. Cavalry Association, October, 1904.

Bradley, Lieut. James H., Montana Historical Society Contributions, Volume II, 1896.

Brady, Cyrus Townsend, *Indian Fights and Fighters,* New York, 1905.

——*Northwestern Fights and Fighters,* New York, 1907.

Brininstool, E. A., *Captain Benteen's Story of the Battle of Little Big Horn,* Hollywood, California, 1933.

——Hunter-Trader-Trapper, Columbus, Ohio, August, 1932.

——Hunter-Trader-Trapper, Columbus, Ohio, March, 1933.

——*Winners of the West,* March 30, 1936, St. Joseph, Missouri.

——*Major Reno Vindicated,* Hollywood, California, 1935.

——Hunter-Trader-Trapper, Columbus, Ohio, 1925.

Bruce, Robert, *Custer's Last Battle,* New York, 1937.

Burdick, Usher L., *The Last Battle of the Sioux Nations,* Fargo, North Dakota, 1929.

Burt, Struthers, *Powder River,* New York, 1938.

Byrne, P. E., *Red Man's Last Stand,* London, 1927.

Carnahan, John M., Courier-Herald, April 4, 1915, Saginaw, Michigan.

Carrington, Col. Henry B. and Mrs. Henry B., *Absaraka: Land of Massacre,* Philadelphia, 1878.

——Frances C., *My Army Life and the Fort Phil Kearny Massacre,* Philadelphia, 1910.

Bibliography

Carrol, Matthew, Montana Historical Society Contributions, Volume II, 1896.

Cavalry Journal: Files.

Clymer, Heister, Chairman, House Report No. 799, 44th Congress, 1st Session.

———Report, November 1, 1875. House of Representatives, 44th Congress, 2nd Session, Executive Document 1, Part 5.

———October 30, 1876, House of Representatives, 44th Congress, 2nd Session, Executive Document 1, Part 5.

———November 1, 1877, House of Representatives, 45th Congress, 2nd Session, Executive Document 1, Part 5.

———Volume 1, Beginning of 3rd Session, 45th Congress, 1878.

Coughlan, Col. T. M., Cavalry Journal, 1934.

Coutant, C. G., *History of Wyoming,* Laramie, Wyoming, 1899.

Custer, Elizabeth B., *Boots and Saddles,* New York, 1885.

———*Following the Guidon,* New York, 1890.

———*Tenting on the Plains,* New York, 1893.

Custer, General George A., Galaxy Magazine, July, 1876.

———*My Life on the Plains,* New York, 1874.

Cyclorama of Custer's Last Fight, Boston, 1889.

De Barthe, Joe, *Life and Adventures of Frank Grouard,* St. Joseph, Missouri, 1894.

De Land, Charles Edmund, *Arikara Indians,* South Dakota Historical Collections, Volume III, 1906.

———South Dakota Historical Collections, 1931.

———South Dakota Historical Collections, 1934.

De Trobriand, *Army Life in Dakota,* Chicago, 1941.

Dellenbaugh, Frederick S., *George Armstrong Custer,* New York, 1936.

Dixon, Dr. Joseph K., *The Vanishing Race,* New York, 1914.

Dodge, Col. Richard I., *Hunting Grounds of the Great West,* London, 1877.

———*Our Wild Indians,* Hartford, Connecticut, 1883.

Downey, Fairfax, *Indian-Fighting Army,* New York, 1944.

Dustin, Fred, *The Custer Tragedy,* Ann Arbor, Michigan, 1939.

Finerty, John F., *War Path and Bivouac,* Chicago, 1890.

Forsyth, George A., *Story of the Soldier,* New York, 1900.

Garland, Hamlin, *General Custer's Last Fight,* McClure's Magazine, Vol. XI, No. 5, 1898.

Gibbon, Col. John, *Last Summer's Expedition Against the Sioux,* American Catholic Quarterly Review, April and October, 1877.

———Official Report, Executive Document 1, Part 2, House of Representatives, 44th Congress, 2nd Session, 1877.

Godfrey, Edward S., *Custer's Last Battle,* Century Magazine, January 1892.

Graham, Lt. Col. W. A., *Story of the Little Big Horn,* New York, 1926.

Bibliography

Grinnell, George B., *The Cheyenne Indians,* New Haven, Connecticut, 1923.
——*The Fighting Cheyennes,* New York, 1915.
Guernsey, Charles A., *Wyoming Cowboy Days,* New York, 1936.
Hanson, Joseph Mills, *Conquest of the Missouri,* Chicago, 1909: reprinted New York, 1946.
Hebard, Grace Raymond, and Brininstool, Earl A., *Bozeman Trail,* Cleveland, Ohio, 1922.
Herald, The New York, June 1 to August 31, 1876.
Hughes, Robert P., Journal of the Military Service Institution, January, 1896.
Hyde, George E., *Red Cloud's Folk,* Norman, Oklahoma, 1937.
Inter-Ocean, Chicago, August, 1874.
Jackson, Helen Hunt, *Century of Dishonor,* Boston, 1886.
Kanipe, Sergeant Daniel A., Montana Historical Society Contributions, 1903.
Keim, De B. Randolph, *Sheridan's Troopers on the Border,* Philadelphia, 1885.
King, Captain Charles, *Campaigning with Crook,* New York, 1890.
Libby, O. G., *Arikara Narrative,* North Dakota Historical Collections, 1920.
Luce, Edward S., *Keogh, Comanche and Custer,* privately printed, 1939.
Ludlow, Captain William, *Black Hills of Dakota,* Washington, 1875.
McBlain, John F., *With Gibbon on the Sioux Campaign of 1876,* Cavalry Journal, June, 1896.
McClernand, Lieut. Edward J., Report of Chief of Engineers, for Fiscal Year ending June 30, 1877.
McCormack, George R., National Republic, March, 1934.
McLaughlin, James, *My Friend the Indian,* Boston, 1910.
MacLeod, W. C., *The American Indian Frontier,* New York, 1928.
Manuscript Room, New York Public Library, New York, *Custer Files.*
Maquire, Lieut. Edward, Report of Chief of Engineers for Fiscal Year ending June 30, 1876. Appendix.
Marquis, Thomas B., *Custer Battle,* privately printed, Hardin, Montana, 1933.
——*Custer Soldiers Not Buried,* privately printed, Hardin, Montana, 1933.
——*Memoirs of a White Crow Indian,* New York, 1928.
——*Two Days after the Custer Battle,* privately printed, Hardin, Montana, 1935.
Martin, John, *Custer's Last Battle,* Cavalry Journal, July, 1923.
Miles, General Nelson A., *Personal Recollections,* Chicago, 1897.
Milner, Joe E., and Forrest, Earle R., *California Joe,* Caldwell, Idaho, 1935.

Bibliography

Nye, Lt. Col. W. S., *Carbine and Lance,* Norman, Oklahoma, 1943.

Paxson, Frederick L., *History of the American Frontier,* New York, 1924.

Perkins, J. R., *Trails, Rails and War. Life of General G. M. Dodge,* Indianapolis, 1929.

Reno Court of Inquiry, Chicago, 1879.

Reno, Major M. A., American Magazine, March and April, 1912.

Schmit, Martin F., *General George Crook: His Autobiography,* Norman, Oklahoma, 1946.

Schultz, James Willard, *William Jackson, Indian Scout,* Boston, 1926.

——*My Life as an Indian,* New York, 1906.

Scott, General Hugh L., *Some Memoirs of a Soldier,* New York, 1928.

Seymour, Flora Warren, *The Story of the Red Man,* New York, 1929.

Sheridan, Lt. Gen. P. H., U. S. War Department, Annual Report, 1876.

Sherman, Gen. W. T., U. S. War Department, Annual Report, 1876.

Spotts, David L., *Campaigning with Custer,* Los Angeles, 1928.

Standing Bear, Chief, *My People, the Sioux,* New York, 1928.

Tallent, Annie D., *The Black Hills,* St. Louis, 1899.

Terry, General Alfred H., Official Report, November 21, 1876.

Tribune, New York, 1872, '73, '74, '76.

Van de Water, Frederic F., *Glory Hunter,* Indianapolis and New York, 1934.

Vestal, Stanley, *Warpath,* Boston, 1934.

——*Sitting Bull,* Boston, 1932.

Wagner, Glendolin D., *Old Neutriment,* Boston, 1934.

Walker, Judson Elliott, *Campaigns of Gen. Custer in the Northwest and the Final Surrender of Sitting Bull,* New York, 1881.

Wheeler, Col. Homer W., *Buffalo Days,* Indianapolis.

Whittaker, Frederick A., *Life of Major Gen. George A. Custer,* New York, 1876.

Index

Absaraka Indians, the, 192
American Horse, Indian Chief, 9
Antelopes, 19, 38
Aparejos, 64, 66
Appomattox, 52, 134
Arapahoe Indians, 91, 152, 190
Arikara Indians, 19
Arizona, 47
Army and Navy Journal, the, 45–6, 131–2, 194–7, 199–201
Assiniboin Indians, 152

Bad Lands, the, 26–7, 144
Baker, Captain Stephen, 61
Balinan, 27–8, 29
Ball, Captain, 148, 149
Baltimore, Md., 127
Barrett, 121
Barry, David F., 31
Bates, Colonel Charles Francis, 221, 225
Bates Fight, the, 215
Battle of the Washita, the, 7, 11, 12–14, 117, 183, 221
Bayer, Nuch, 157
Bear Butte, Dakota, 118
Beaver Creek, 61
Belknap, General W. W., 47, 51, 121–3, 131, 132
Belle Fourche River, the, 39
Benteen, Colonel F. W., 5, 15–16, 220–1; accused of disobedience, 183, 191–3, 202; at odds with Custer, 11, 183–4; in Battle of Little Big Horn, 2–3, 89–90, 97–9, 104–6, 109–10, 139, 141, 165, 167, 180, 185, 187, 189–90; before the battle, 78, 79–81, 82–3, 85, 178–4, 187–9, 191; in the Black Hills, 45; commands a battalion, 56–7; in march up the Rosebud, 66, 69, 75–7; model officer, 2, 4, 16–17, 114; promotion asked, 175–6; summoned by Custer, 82, 83, 87, 88–9, 162, 183; sustains charges against Reno, 203–6
Bergen, Germany, 3
Big Horn Mountains, the, 8, 32, 168, 217
Big Horn River, the, 35, 46, 58, 71, 75, 102, 109, 112, 137, 142, 144, 146, 147, 148, 186, 188
Billings, Montana, 55
Birney, Montana, 215

Bishops, the, 190
Bismarck, N. D., 32, 39, 49, 53, 58, 70, 112, 118, 124, 125, 155
Black, 190
Black Hills, the, 8, 9, 19, 32–47, 114, 116–20, 196, 199, 216
Black Kettle, Indian Chief, 7, 221
Blackfeet Indians, the, 91, 209
Blizzards, 10
Bloody Knife, Indian scout, 19, 20, 24, 36, 39, 84, 94, 152–5
Bonnafon, 124, 128
Boyer, Mitch, 64, 65, 157
Bozeman, Montana, 58
"Bozeman Trail," the, 8
Bradley, Lt. J. H., 62, 64, 108–9, 149
Braided Locks, Indian, 222
Brewer, 16
Bridges, James, 36
Brininstool, E. A., 182
Brisbin, Major, 61
Brownsville, Pa., 59
Brush, Captain, 26
Bruyer, John, 152–5
Buffalo, 7, 8–9, 18–19, 30, 38, 43, 46, 216
Buffalo Bill, 10
Buffalo, Wyoming, 215, 220, 225
Burkman, John, 54–5

Cairo, Illinois, 5, 9
Calhoun, Lt. James, 21, 22, 54, 68, 171
California, 42
Cameron, Don, 164
Canada, 35, 54
Carlin, Lt. John A., 61
Castle Creek Valley, 40
Century Magazine, the, 203
Chandler, Z., 47
Charcoal Butte, 211
Cheyenne Indians, 7, 9, 12, 65, 91, 116, 152, 154, 160, 190, 209, 210–14, 215, 216–17, 221–4
Cheyenne River, the, 39, 118
Cheyenne, Wyoming, 35, 208
Chicago, 89, 132, 133, 134, 177
Chicago Times, the, 208–10
Chicago Tribune, the, 195, 197
Chief Hunk, Indian chief, 9
Chisholm Trail, the, 8, 40
Chivington, Colonel, 7, 215, 221

Index

Chivington Massacre, the, 7, 215, 221
Civil War, the, 4, 5, 15–16, 42, 43, 50, 55, 70, 163, 164, 177
Clark, Lt., 208
Clifford, Captain, 61, 62
Clymer, Heister, 51, 123, 130
Collins, Charles, 35
Colorado Volunteer Cavalry, the, 7, 221
Comanche, a horse, 112
Comanche Indians, 196
Congressional Medal of Honor, the, 105
Conquest of the Missouri, The, 58–62, 66–9
Cooke, Lt. W. W., 76, 78, 82, 91, 162, 185, 186, 188, 191
Cooper, 190
Coulsons, the, 58
Coup stick, 101, 222–3
Court of Inquiry, 177–81
Crazy Horse, Indian chief, 9, 46, 65, 137, 152, 159, 160, 208, 209, 210, 211, 212, 216
Crook, General George, 47–8, 65, 91, 137, 138, 141, 142, 198, 211
Crow, Indian chief, 160
Crow Indians, 2, 19, 62, 64, 73, 89, 90, 93, 108, 112, 148, 152, 153, 154, 156, 159, 171, 190, 192
Crow, J. R., 25
Crowell, Captain, 68
"Crow's Nest," 74, 84
Curley, Crow scout, 2, 108–9, 159, 171–2
Curtis, Charles E., 36
Custer Battlefield, the, 222–4, 225
Custer, Boston, 87, 171
Custer, Captain Thomas, 1, 20, 22, 29, 30–1, 68, 81, 82, 110, 150, 171
Custer City, 45
Custer, General George A., 17, 29, 30, 55, 114; accused of disobedience, 71–2, 136–40, 144–8, 150, 174; age, 3; in Battle of Little Big Horn, 2, 97, 102, 107, 108–12, 113, 115, 158–9, 161, 169–71, 180, 198–201, 209–10, 213–14, 215–16, 218–19, 220–4; in Battle of Washita, 7, 11–15, 117; in Belknap trial, 51–2, 123–32; in Black Hills Expedition, 36–48, 114, 116–20, 196; criticized by General Sturgis, 195–7; death of, 1, 65, 108–12, 139, 149, 159, 161, 169–71, 175, 195, 214, 217, 220–4; description of, 10–11, 54, 84, 164; deserted by Benteen, 183–93; favored by Sheridan, 194, 196; his command threatened, 132–5; hunting, 18; Indian fighter, 5–6, 9, 36, 57, 63; in march from Fort Lincoln, 49–62; nearing final battle, 78–86; 90–1, 155–7; rank, 5; reports on gold, 116–

20; underestimates the enemy, 79, 140, 151, 152, 154, 159, 173; unpopular, 11, 50, 197; up the Rosebud River, 63–76; in Yellowstone Expedition, 18–28, 55
Custer Gulch, 44, 120
Custer Hill, 112
Custer Massacre, the, 2, 30–1, 174, 198, 199, 208–11
Custer, Mrs. George A., 4, 54, 56, 60, 225

Dakota, Department of, 51, 71, 117, 120, 130, 133
Dakota Indians, 91
Dakota Territory, 35, 44
Dakotas, the, 5, 10, 34, 39, 117, 223. *See also* North Dakota, South Dakota
Davey, Captain P. B., 34–5
Delano, 124
Democrats, 50, 51, 122
Department of the Gulf, 142–3
De Rudio, Lt., 94, 95
De Wolf, Doctor, 180
Dorman, Negro scout, 94
Drum, General W. M., 178
Dry Fork of the Missouri River, 137, 138
Dustin, Fred, 182

Eagle Bear, Indian Chief, 215, 218–19
Edgerly, Lt., 56, 78, 98, 109
Edward, Everett, 42
Eighteenth Infantry, the, 26, 72
Elliott, Major, 7, 11, 12–14, 183
Evans, John S., 51

Far West, the, 58–62, 64, 66, 68, 70, 109, 112, 144, 146, 147, 155, 186, 187
Fast Bull, Indian Chief, 209
Fehliman, Mrs. George C., 1
Fetterman massacre, the, 8
Finkle, Trooper, 112
First Cavalry, the, 163
Foch, Marshal, 17
Fool's Crow, Indian, 219
Forsyth, General "Sandy," 120
Fort Abercrombie, 201
Fort Abraham Lincoln, 3, 29, 30, 32, 36, 38, 49, 51, 56, 58, 59, 63, 70, 112, 117, 118, 123, 124, 126, 129, 130, 131, 132, 138, 143, 151, 170, 186
Fort Belknap, 124
Fort Berthold, 124
Fort Buford, 61, 70
Fort Dalles, Oregon, 163
Fort Ellis, 48, 58, 62, 64, 138, 143, 146, 190
Fort Fetterman, 138

Index

Fort Laramie, Wyo., 8, 43, 118, 120, 121, 142
Fort McKinney, Wyo., 203, 211
Fort Pease, 147
Fort Peck, 124, 128
Fort Randall, 17, 45, 46
Fort Randolph, 46
Fort Rice, 17, 18, 27, 32
Fort Robinson, Neb., 208
Fort Shaw, Montana, 48, 146
Fort Sill, 51, 122
Fort Snelling, 35
Fort Sully, 17
Fort Walla Walla, Wash., 163
Fox, Sergeant, 70
Franco-Prussian War, the, 4
Freeman, Captain, 146
Frémont, General, 28
French, Captain, 26

Gaffner, Roger, 46
Gall, Indian chief, 9, 46, 160, 212, 221
Gambling, 42, 53, 68
Garfield, James A., 51
Garland, Hamlin, 210
Gatchell, James T., 215, 220–2, 225
Gatling guns, 36, 137, 142, 144, 147
Geiger, trooper, 104
Geogh, Captain, 112
Germans, 3, 4, 50, 104–5, 112, 114
Ghent, W. J., 203, 205
Gibbon, General John, 48, 58, 61, 62, 64–5, 66, 70–1, 72, 73, 75, 102, 108, 138, 145–9, 174, 187, 190, 198; Colonel, 58, 138, 139, 143–5, 152
Gibson, Lt., 80, 184
Girard, Frank, 85, 152, 177
Godfrey, Edward S., Lt., 30, 78, 96, 98, 99, 108, 177; Captain, 203–4; General, 191, 201, 203, 205–7, 221, 225
Gold, 8, 32, 33–4, 40–6, 116–20
Goose Creek, 65, 138
Graham, Lt.-Colonel W. A., 83
Grand Village, the, 12
Grant, Colonel Fred Dent, 38
Grant, Orville, 51, 123–5, 128
Grant, President U. S., 38, 49–50, 50–2, 121–2, 127, 131, 132, 133–5, 142, 175, 181, 197–8
"Greasy Grass," 74, 216, 217, 219
Great Northern Railway, the, 9
Great Sioux Reservation, the, 8, 125, 127–8
Great Spirit, the, 160, 211, 216, 222
Grouard, Frank, 78, 222, 223
Gypsum, 119

Haldeman, Miss, 164

Hale, A. H., 45, 46
Hale, Captain, 20, 26
Hancock, General, 35
Hanson, Joseph Mills, 58
Hare, Lt., 74, 78, 98, 167
Harms, Mrs., 1
Harney's Peak, 33, 40, 44, 117, 120
Harrisburg, Pa., 164
Harshay Wolf, Indian, 222, 223
Hart, Colonel, 26
Hazen, General, 51, 122, 196
Heart River, the, 53–4, 55
Hedrick, 122, 127
Herbertson Engine Works, the, 59
Herendon, George, 78, 94, 155–9, 177
Historical Society of Montana, the, 81–2
Hodgson, Lt. Benny, 94–5
Hodnett, John P., 35
Homesteak Mine, the, 40, 114
Honsinger, Dr., 20, 26, 27–8, 29
Horned Horse, Indian Chief, 208–10
House of Representatives, the, 122–3
Hughes, Sergeant, 172
Hump, Indian Chief, 160
Hunkpapa Indians, 160
Hunt, Frazier, 1
Hunt, Robert, 1–2
Hunter, William, 208
Hunting, 18, 119–20

Ice Bear, Indian chief, 209
Idaho, 34
Idaho Indians, 198
Illinois, 43, 163
Indian Department, the, 51, 128–9, 151
Indian Messiah, the, 113
Inter Ocean, the, 41
Iron, 119

Jackson boys, scouts, 153
Jackson, General, 164
Jealous, Indian, 218
Jefferson Barracks, 191
Jones, Corporal, 103–4, 190
Joseph, Indian Chief, 113
Josephine, the, 60

Kanipe, Sergeant Daniel A., 81, 83, 109
Kansas, 6, 7, 11, 43, 56
Kelly's Ford, Va., 163
Kentucky, 55, 164
Keogh, Captain, 83, 201
Kills-in-the-Night, Indian, 217
King, Colonel John H., 178, 181
King, General Charles, 202
Kinney, Colonel George S., 164
Kinney, Miss Ittie, 164

Index

Kiowa Indians, 190, 196
Kirtland, Captain, 147
Ku Klux Klan, the, 5, 164

Lafayette, General, 163
Lake de Smet, 217
Laramie Mountains, the, 32
Lead, S. D., 1, 40, 114
Lee, General Robert E., 121, 134
Leech, Wilmer R., 225
Leighton, Brothers, 128
Lett, Corporal, 190
Limpy, Indian, 222
Lincoln, Nebraska, 53
Little Big Horn River, the, 1, 30, 53, 58, 65, 74, 75, 78, 80, 81–2, 84, 85, 89, 90, 91, 97, 109, 134, 139, 141, 145, 147, 148, 151, 154, 178–80, 192; Battle of the, 2, 3, 10, 19, 30, 55, 68, 83, 113, 115, 136, 165–9, 175, 177, 178, 203, 206
Little Horn River, the, 71–2, 79, 102, 106, 108, 112, 156, 157
Little Horn Valley, the, 74, 102, 157, 162, 212, 214
Little Missouri River, the, 39, 57, 61, 137, 138, 143–4
Little Wolf, Indian Chief, 217
Long, W. B., 46
Loper, George, 45, 46
Loper, J. A., 46
Louisiana, 49
Louisville Courier Journal, the, 164
Louisville, Ky., 5, 164
Low, Lt., 147
Ludlow, Colonel Williams, 36

McClure's Magazine, 210–14
McCreary, George W., 178
McCurry, 75
McDougall, Captain, 78, 81–3, 89, 109, 167
McIntosh, General, 94
McIntosh, Lt., 94
McKay, 44
McKenzie, Colonel, 211, 217
McLaughlin, James, 159
Maguire, Lt., 57
Marsh, Caleb P., 51, 122
Marsh, Captain Grant, 58, 59–62, 68, 69, 70
Martini, John, trumpeter, 76, 83, 97, 109, 180, 183, 185, 187, 188–9, 191–2, 193
Mathey, Lt., 79, 89
Meadow, Corporal, 190
Meckling, trooper, 105
Medicine Bear, Indian, 221, 222–3

Meyer, G. H., 93
Miller, A. R., 45, 46
Milwaukee, 103
Minneapolis Pioneer Press and Tribune, the, 199–201
Minneconjou Indians, the, 152, 209
Minnesota, 7, 35
Missouri River, the, 3, 5, 16, 18, 32, 33, 35, 49, 52, 59, 112, 117, 125, 135, 190
Mizpah Creek, 144
Monroe, Michigan, 55
Montana, 1, 8, 9, 19, 34, 48, 55, 58, 81–2, 96, 102, 109, 138, 150, 186, 215; District of, 143, 146, 178
Moore, Major, 58, 61, 62
Morrison, Edward B., 225
Moylan, Captain, 20, 22–3, 25
Mud Creek, 81
Musselshell River, the, 19
Mutilation of the dead, 31, 53, 110, 160–1, 175, 221–2, 224

Nashville, Tenn., 4, 6, 164
Nebraska, 8, 47, 53, 208
Neihardt, John G., 204
New Orleans, 49, 136
New York City, 34, 54, 121, 122, 132
New York Herald, the, 121, 162–4, 197–8
New York Public Library, the, 203, 225
New York Tribune, the, 19, 34, 43–5, 51, 155–9
New York World, the, 131–2
Newell, Dan, 105
Newspapers, 11, 19, 30, 34, 35, 41, 42, 43, 51, 120, 121, 135, 155, 162, 195, 197, 208
Nez Percés Indians, the, 113
Nicholson, General W. J., 105–7
Ninth Cavalry, the, 16
Ninth Infantry, the, 178, 181
Ninth Missouri Cavalry, 4
North Dakota, 30
North Platte River, the, 8, 33, 47
Northern Pacific Railroad, the, 32, 49, 142
Northern Plains Indians, 7

Oakes, 196
Ogallala Indians, 152, 209, 218
O'Hara, Sergeant, 93
Oklahoma, 122, 217
One Stab, Indian Chief, 39–40
O'Neill, Private, 95
Order of Indian Wars, the, 205

Paul, Sergeant, 105, 190
Pennsylvania, 163, 164
Philip Good Shield, Indian, 218

Index

Phillips, 190
Pierce, Captain, 46
Pine Ridge Reservation, S. D., 217
Pittsburgh, 58–9
Plains Indians, the, 6
Platte, Department of the, 142
Platte River, the, 117, 120
Plumbago, 119
Porcupine, S. D., 217
Porter, Dr., 69, 189
Powder River, the, 30, 46, 47, 48, 58, 61–2, 63, 137, 138, 142, 144, 207, 210, 217
Prairie Dog Creek, 216
Prospect Valley, Dakota, 117
Pumpkin Buttes, 137, 142, 215–16

Quigley, James, 46

Rain-in-the-Face, Indian Chief, 29–30, 171
Raymond, Captain, 124–5
Red Bear, Indian Chief, 209
Red Cloud, Indian Chief, 8, 39
Red Forks, Powder River, 217
Red Point, Indian Chief, 209
Ree Indians, 73, 89, 90, 93, 153, 154, 165
Reed, 170–1
Renault, Philippe François, 163
Reno Hill, 95, 97, 99, 112
Reno, Major Marcus A., 2, 56, 57; in Battle of Little Big Horn, 88–103, 105–7, 108–10, 140–1, 149–50, 155, 157–61, 165–8, 172, 178–81, 188–90, 192–3, 210, 212–13, 216–17; Court of Inquiry on, 178–81; criticism of, 162, 177, 201–207; early years and marriage, 163–4; in march up the Rosebud, 63–6, 71, 138–9; military record of, 50, 162–4; not popular, 50; prepares for battle, 78, 80, 81–2, 85, 86, 144–7; suggested to succeed Custer, 175–6; suspended from army, 182; tried by Court Martial, 181–2
Reno, Robert Ross, 164
Reynolds, Charles, 28–9, 36, 42–3, 69, 74, 76, 78, 94, 120, 153–4
Rice, E. W., 122, 127, 131–2
Richeson, Professor, 196
Ridgely, trapper, 199–201
Robinson, 196
Rosebud River, the, 64, 65, 66, 69, 71, 72, 78, 79, 84, 136, 137, 138, 139, 144, 145, 146, 147, 152, 155, 156, 187, 199, 210, 211, 215, 216
Ross, Horatio Nelson, 40, 44–5
Ross, Mary Hannah, 164
Ross, Robert, 164
Rotten Grass Valley, 214–15

Rowland, Willis, 215, 223
Rutten, Roman, 93

St. Louis Democrat, the, 11–14
St. Louis, Mo., 129, 195
St. Paul, Minn., 35, 49, 52, 117, 120, 123, 124, 130, 132, 133, 194, 196
Sand Creek, 221
Sansarc Indians, 152, 209
Santee Indians, the, 209
Scabby Head, Indian Chief, 209
Schultz, James Willard, 151
Scott, General Hugh L., 16–17
Second Cavalry, the, 138
Seip, 127, 129
Senate, the, 123, 176
Seventeenth Infantry, the, 19, 36, 142
Seventh Cavalry, the, 3, 60, 138, 175; band of, 15, 38, 53, 56, 66; in battle at Little Big Horn, 139–41, 142–5, 156–60, 162–74, 178–81, 184–93, 195, 197–203, 208–10, 212–14, 216–17, 218–19; in battle of Washita, 12–15; in the Black Hills, 33–48, 116–19; description of, 53, 66; Major Reno's part of, 95–106, 162–74; march from Fort Lincoln, 49–62, 117; march up the Rosebud, 63–76, 136, 146, 151, 156–7; nearing final battle, 78–94, 152–4; organized, 5, 56; reputation of, 2, 5, 7, 9, 17, 53, 56; Troops of: A, 55, 56, 78, 188, 201; B, 56, 78, 167; C, 56, 78, 81, 188–9; D, 56, 78, 98, 99, 183–5, 188, 204; E, 56, 78, 188–9; F, 29, 78, 188–9; G, 56, 78, 188; H, 2, 4, 19, 32, 42, 45, 49, 56, 63, 76, 78, 80, 83, 101, 104, 105–6, 109, 114, 183, 187–8; I, 56, 78, 83, 188–9; K, 56, 78, 96, 99, 183–5, 188; L, 56, 78, 188–9; M, 56, 78, 93, 105, 188, 204; in Yellowstone Expedition, 18–31. See also Benteen, Custer, Reno
Seventh Infantry, the, 138, 142, 146, 147
Severs, "Crazy Jim," 105, 190
Sherburne, E. A., 197
Sheridan, General Philip, 12, 33, 47, 116, 117, 120, 130, 132, 134, 135, 136, 142, 151, 194, 196
Sheridan, Wyoming, 65
Sherman, General William T., 8, 47, 51, 121, 130, 132, 133–5, 136, 141, 176
Sibley, General, 7
Sioux City Times, the, Iowa, 35
Sioux Indians, 2, 5, 8, 9, 19, 22–3, 29, 31, 34, 53, 65, 84–5, 91–2, 113, 116, 137, 142, 143, 145, 148, 152, 154, 157–60, 166, 168, 173, 190, 192, 196, 211–14, 218, 221–3

Index

Sitting Bull, Indian Chief, 9, 46, 47, 54, 65, 137–8, 152, 159–60, 198, 199, 200, 201, 209, 211, 212, 215, 216
Six Thousand Miles Through Wonderland, 159–61
Sixth Infantry, the, 58, 61, 68, 142
Slaper, trooper, 105
Smith, Byron M., 34
Smith, Captain Edward W., 72
Smith, Edward P., 47
Smith, G. E., 93
Smith, Mrs. Algernon E., 60
Some Memoirs of a Soldier, 16–17
Song of the Indian Wars, The, 204
South Dakota, 8, 9, 30–1, 32, 217
Spotted Eagle, Indian Chief, 9
Spotted Tail Indians, the, 34
Springfield carbines, 13, 53, 66, 92, 103–4, 171–2
Standing Bear, Indian, 218
Standing Rock Reservation, 28–9, 31, 124
Stanley, Major-General, 18, 21, 25–7, 64
Stanley Trail, the, 61, 143
Stanley's Stockade, 19, 61, 62, 143
Sturgis, General Samuel Davis, 194–7
Sturgis, Lt. James G., 189, 194

Taft, Alonzo, 132
Taylor, William O., 201
Ten Sleep Canyon, 217
Terry, General Alfred Howe, 48, 50, 51–3, 57, 58, 61–2, 63, 65, 66, 70–1, 75, 79, 102, 109, 123, 130, 132–5, 136–9, 141, 142–5, 146, 147, 151, 156, 169, 174, 177, 181, 190, 196, 198, 210
Teton Indians, the, 152
Texas, 8
Third Cavalry Division, the, 70
Thomas, Sam, 46
Thum, Tom, 128
Tillson, William, 46
Tom White Cow Killer, Indian, 218
Tongue River, the, 19, 48, 58, 62, 63, 64, 65, 66, 71, 137, 144, 146, 211, 216
Townsend, General E. D., 134, 181
Treaties with Indians, 6, 8, 33, 42
Tullock's Creek, 72, 139
Tullock's Fork, 147
Turkey Legs, Indian, 222
Tuttle, 22
Twelfth Pennsylvania Cavalry, the, 163
Twentieth Infantry, the, 36, 142, 147
Twenty-fourth Iowa Volunteers, the, 197
Twenty-second Infantry, the, 18

Two Moons, Indian Chief, 9, 46, 210–14, 215, 221, 222–3

Uncapapa Indians, 65, 209
Union Pacific Railroad, the, 8
U. S. Cavalry Journal, The, 83–8

Varnum, Lt. Charles A., 20, 24, 78, 96, 109, 153–5, 202
Vigilanti, Sylvester L., 225
Virginia, 4
Voit, trooper, 105

Wallace, Lt. George D., 186
Ward, 121
Washington, D. C., 8, 50, 51, 123, 129, 131–2, 134–5, 176, 178, 182
Washita River. *See* Battle of the Washita
Weasel Bear, Indian Chief, 215, 221, 222
Weir, Captain, 78, 81, 88–9, 98, 99, 109, 167–8, 189, 204, 205; Colonel, 206
West Point, 10, 17, 50, 163–4, 194, 206
Wheeler, Olin D., 159
White Bull, Indian Chief, 9
White River, the, 35
Whittaker, Captain Frederick A., 177
William Jackson, Indian Scout, 151–4
Windolph, Adolphina, 3
Windolph, Joseph, 3
Windolph, Sergeant, account of Battle of Little Big Horn and events preceding, 1–114, 115, 183, 225; admired Captain Benteen, 16–17, 114, 183; awarded Congressional Medal of Honor, 105; birth and early years, 3–4; describes General Custer, 11; helped bury Custer, 1, 112; joins Seventh Cavalry, 4; last survivor, 2, 115; marriage and later years, 114; promoted on battlefield, 105, 114; wounded, 190
Wolf Mountains, the, 91
Wooden Legs, Indian, 222
Wyoming, 8, 47, 65, 121, 203, 215, 216, 220, 225

Yankton Indians, 152, 209
Yankton, S. D., 5, 9, 10, 17, 20, 34, 45, 59
Yates, Captain, 26, 29, 75, 97 201
Yellow Dog Indian, 222
Yellowstone Expedition, the, 18–31, 36, 43, 49, 55, 59, 64, 117
Yellowstone River, the, 9, 19, 20, 48, 58, 60–1, 63, 64, 65, 70, 72, 112, 138, 139, 143, 144–5, 147, 175, 186, 199, 215